Anti-Americanism in Russia

Anti-Americanism in Russia

From Stalin to Putin

Eric Shiraev and Vladislav Zubok

palgrave

ANTI-AMERICANISM IN RUSSIA
Copyright ©Eric Shiraev and Vladislav Zubok, 2000.
All rights reserved. Printed in the United States of America. No part of
this book may be used or reproduced in any manner whatsoever without
written permission except in the case of brief quotations embodied in
critical articles or reviews.

First published 2000 by
PALGRAVE™
175 Fifth Avenue, New York, N.Y. 10010 and
Houndmills, Basingstoke, Hampshire, England RG21 6XS
Companies and representatives throughout the world.

PALGRAVE™ is the new global publishing imprint of St. Martin's
Press LLC Scholarly and Reference Division and Palgrave Publishers
Ltd (formerly Macmillan Press Ltd).

ISBN 0–312–22979–8

Library of Congress Cataloging-in-Publication Data
Shiraev, Eric, 1960–
   Anti-Americanism in Russia : from Stalin to Putin / Eric Shiraev and
Vladislav Zubok.
      p.   cm.
   Included bibliographical references and index.
   ISBN 0–312–22979–8 (cloth)
   1. Soviet Union—Relations—United States.   2. United States—
Relations—Soviet Union.   3. Russia (Federation)—Relations—United
States.   4. United States—Relations—Russia (Federation)   5. United
States—Foreign public opinion, Russian.   6. Public opinion—Soviet
Union.   7. Public opinion—Russia (Federation)   8. Propaganda, Anti-
American—Soviet Union.   9. Propaganda, Anti-American—Russia
(Federation)   I. Zubok, V.M. (Vladislav Martinovich)   II. Title.
E183.8.S65 S544   2000
327.47073—dc21
                                                                                00–040–463
                                                                                CIP

Design by Letre Libre, Inc.

First Edition: November 2000
10 9 8 7 6 5 4 3 2 1

To Dennis Snook,
Martin and Lyudmila Zubok—
who encouraged our facination with
the United States in our youth.

Table of Contents

Acknowledgments

Working on this book, we received assistance and guidance from many great individuals of both academic and non-academic worlds. We gratefully acknowledge the helpful advice of Mikhail Gorbachev, Anatoly Chernyaev, and Georgy Shakhnazarov of the Gorbachev Foundation; Oleg Skvortsov of the Institute of General History; Arseny Roginsky and Nikita Petrov of "Memorial Society;" Natalia Kozlova of the Russian State Humanitarian University (Moscow); Igor Malashenko of the Media-Most Group; Deputy of the Duma Yegor Ligachev, veterans of diplomacy Georgy Kornienko, Anatoly Dobrynin and Sergei Tarasenko, Director of the Russian State Archive of Contemporary History Natalia Tomilina. We acknowledge our indebtedness to our relatives and numerous friends in Moscow, St. Petersburg, and other Russian cities who helped us with their ideas, empirical data, insights, and observations of Russia's volatile mentality.

In the United States, a discussion with Alexander George challenged us to refine some of our initial assumptions. Dimitri Simes, from The Nixon Center, Peter Reddaway, from George Washington University, Vladimir Shlapentokh, from Michigan State University, and Mel Goodman, from the National Defense University provided valuable ideas and gave critical suggestions during different stages of our work on this book. We express our appreciation to Betty Glad from the University of South Carolina, Richard Dobson from USIA, Joan Urban, and Deone Terrio for reading the initial drafts of various chapters of this book. Our special thanks to the Institute for European, Russian, and Eurasian Studies at George Washington University, Washington D.C., and personally its acting director, James Goldgeier, for organizing a seminar on the topic of our book.

We are also grateful for the support of the National Security Archive at George Washington University, Department of Political Science at George Washington University, and to the Carnegie Corporation of New York. Without their backing, we would not have been able to conduct "field research" in Russia as often as we did.

For all this, any deficiencies, weakness, errors of facts, and judgments in this book are entirely our own.

Introduction

This book is an attempt to find an answer to the question of why so many Russians dislike America today. Amazingly, Russian anti-Americanism emerged very late—several years after the Cold War was over, after Russia itself embraced democracy and freedom. This was also surprising for us. We grew up in Russian society and came to the United States for the first time at the end of the 1980s–early 1990s, when we were already scholars—a historian and a political scientist. At that time, we could not even imagine that several years later we would undertake a project under this title. Talking to our country-fellows back in Russia, we rarely encountered anti-Americanism. It existed, almost always, among disgruntled nationalists or gullible and ignorant subjects of Soviet propaganda. Most people thought otherwise. We grew tired of explaining to some of our incredulous friends that America was not necessarily the land of honey with the rivers of milk.

Not many years ago, we were concerned with how many educated and sophisticated people idolized and excessively romanticized the United States. Yet we hoped against hope, that this acceptance would not lead to a backlash. Decades of Soviet anti-American and xenophobic propaganda, as we could sense ourselves, had such an enormous inverse effect on Russian intellectuals and the educated public that even a negativist lexicon of this kind ("American hegemony," "U.S. imperialist encroachments," "we will give rebuff," "people's patriotic unity," to name a few) evoked nothing but frustration. We suspected that considerable parts of Russian society were poor, psychologically unstable, and cognitively deprived—unlikely company for prosperous and civilized American and Western European societies. However, when the ultra-nationalist clown, Vladimir Zhirinovsky, shocked the world in December 1993 by winning a large chunk of the Russian electorate—almost one in every four Russians—we believed that those who voted for him were disgruntled nationalists and misfits. Soon, developments proved we were also too romantic and optimistic. By the end of the 1990s, our friends no longer wondered with admiration and envy if they in Russia would ever live like Americans. Instead, they angrily asked what was wrong with Americans and their leadership, why they poke their noses everywhere and impose their will on every country.

Learning about Russian anti-Americanism, we took into account the studies of this worldwide phenomenon at other times and in other countries. We realized that anti-Americanism could exist in at least three forms or phases. First, it could be violent and consist of aggressive actions, including terrorism, against the United States, its citizens, and representatives. Second, it could be non-violent, but could still translate into policies, such as parliamentary rejection of agreements signed by government executives, public boycotting of American products, services, and cultural events, diplomatic demarches, and the refusal to accept help or assistance from the United States. Third, it could be societal and cultural, expressing itself in all kinds of public criticism, rejection, hatred, and denunciation of the United States, its government, specific policies, culture, or people.

In our journey from the period of the Cold War through Gorbachev's and Yeltsin's years, until the elections of Vladimir Putin in March of 2000, we searched for all three forms of anti-Americanism on Russian soil. What was unusual, however, were the dynamics and trajectory of these forms of anti-Americanism. There was "old" Soviet anti-Americanism, the product of the official ideology of class struggle and reinforced by the concept of imperialist encirclement, nourished by the decades of Cold War confrontation between the U.S.S.R. and the United States all over the world. However, anti-Americanism in the Soviet Union developed in a unique way. While the government exerted all its strength to compete with the United States, the society was largely neutral and even friendly toward Americans. We were not surprised when the "old" anti-Americanism collapsed along with Communist ideology; it seemed the end of an unnatural state of mind. What emerged toward the end of the 1990s was a "new" anti-Americanism, when an official course was set to reach partnership with the United States. However, the majority of political factions and public opinion became critical of American influence, policies, lifestyle, and the treatment of Russia and Russians.

This book is not the first to approach this subject. An analysis of the ideology-driven anti-American policies of Soviet Communist rulers was already done in numerous publications during the Cold War. In 1988, sociologist and political psychologist, Vladimir Shlapentokh, published a ground-breaking article on this subject. He paid special attention to the sociological dimensions of anti-American attitudes and behavior in the Soviet Union. After 1991, the rise of negative attitudes in the new democratic Russia caught the eye and was commented upon by Vera Tolz, Peter Reddaway, Judith Devlin, Anatol Lieven, Jonathan A. Becker, Dimitri K.

Simes, and some other keen observers. We discuss the ideas of these scholars and refer to their findings elsewhere in the book.

At the same time, the book is based primarily on our own careful analysis of the Russian media and opinion polls, a comparison of the current
trends with the Soviet past, and with anti-American manifestations in
other countries. Also, we frequently traveled to Russia throughout the
1990s, and spent considerable time in Moscow and St. Petersburg, as well
as in other places in Russia, watching, reading, and conversing with Russians of many walks of life. These personal observations and episodes from
our lives are not alien to the issue of the research: after all, we sought to
take not only a broad sociological and psychological picture, but also our
own personal snapshots of Russian society. All in all, we are the "products"
and witnesses of "old" and "new" anti-Americanism.

Political scientists and psychologists often analyze their research samples
by seeking justification or falsification of hypotheses and theories. This
leads to the principle of parsimony, when plurality of factors and explanations is sacrificed to the dominant theory or concept. Because we are only
approaching with a theoretical framework for the study of anti-Americanism, we could not be parsimonious. Rather our approach is phenomeno-
logical. We began with the assumption that there could be more than one
cause for anti-Americanism. Therefore, we attempted to analyze and discuss it from a cross-disciplinary perspective, using a broad historical perspective, approaches from sociology, political science, and political
psychology. In our initial search for empirical data, we interviewed many
experts and read through numerous sources in order to identify several
empirical subject areas.

We were particularly interested in the effect of the pendulum—as public attitudes toward the United States changed from mistrust and fear to
admiration and hope, then back to suspiciousness and alienation. In struc-
turing the book, we devoted two chapters to the two phases of the shift
that preceded new Russian anti-Americanism. The latter, however, was the
main object of our study and curiosity; we devoted four chapters to it—
the bulk of the book. We hope this will be our original contribution. There
were three major phenomena that we analyzed as the forming factors of
the new anti-Americanism. The first (Chapter 3), was the extraordinarily
long and deep economic depression of the 1990s and, as a result, the
demise of public belief in macroeconomic solutions, private property and,
to an extent, in liberal Democracy. The second (Chapter 4), was the search
for a new national Russian identity that brought to the fore some well-
articulated strands of nationalism, isolationism, and anti-Western sentiment
that had previously been on the margins of Russian public knowledge. The
third (Chapter 5), was Russia's new democratic politics that, along with the

pluralism of opinion and the growth of mutual tolerance, led to the emergence of the anti-American "card" in factional and electoral strategies.

As we progressed toward the completion of the project, we could see that the period of 1998–1999 marked the peak of Russia's anti-Americanism, and we devoted Chapter 6 to the impact of the August 1998 "default" financial crisis. We also paid attention to the 1999 war in Kosovo and Russian public perceptions of the United States during that period. We realize that, in the future, the impact of anti-American sentiments on Russian foreign politics will largely depend on changing domestic politics and the personalities in power. For that reason, Chapter 7 deals with the transition from the Yeltsin presidency to the presidency of Vladimir Putin, the first peaceful and legitimate transition of this kind in the brief history of the new Russia. In our opinion, the personality of Putin, his choices, and policies may have a lasting impact on the relations between Russia and the United States.

Our focus in the book was always on the newest, most dynamic, and most typical trends in Russian political and sub-political attitudes that influenced the image of the United States and, as a consequence, Russian domestic debates and foreign policy decision-making. However, there are many things that are not covered in this book. We did not intend it to be a scrupulous account of Russo-American relations. We did not aim to analyze systematically American policies in Russia, toward Russia, and around Russia—although, again, some trends and policies were mentioned as part of the analysis. Also, the book does not go into the complex issue of the linkages between elite opinion-making and public attitudes about America. We discuss this in our other publications. Sometimes the reader might find we treat Russians in a less differentiated and complex way than he or she might wish.

We critically assess a view that implies—in the tradition of the classical clash-of-civilizations scenario—that Russia and America would remain adversaries forever due to the irreconcilable nature of their national interests and fundamental differences in their cultures. The evidence available to us suggests that this view is too simplistic. The Kremlin was able to demonstrate patterns of clear pragmatic reactions to U.S. foreign policy. We also disagree with those who treat Russian nationalism as an atavistic phenomenon of the past. Russia's unique reintroduction into history on the shoulders its predecessor—the Soviet Union—made inevitable the appearance of some kind of national self-identity search in lieu of the anti-national (although not adverse to playing on nationalist themes) ideology of "international Communism." Finally, we critically assess the assumption that anti-Western, anti-American sentiments in Russia could be ascribed primarily to anti-democratic and authoritarian trends. On the contrary, we believe that, rather than the incomplete nature of Russian Democracy, its rapid progress in the face of economic, institutional, and psychological duress better explains some of the new anti-American manifestations.

Finally, we hope that this book will not be just another academic study. The search for the reasons and nature of the extraordinary inversion in Russian attitudes toward the United States is of great importance in at least two ways. First, it sheds more light on anti-Americanism as a global phenomenon and, specifically, may help fathom similar future "swings of the pendulum" in other countries, including other ex-Soviet republics—now independent states—where in 2000, public opinion still lionized the United States in the hope that Americans would come and resolve their problems. Second, it has practical relevance. Any administration continuously reassesses its course toward Russia in view of the recurring and intense criticism of present-day developments. There are as many opportunities in this reassessment as there are pitfalls. Prudence, balance, and understanding of the broad picture of trends will be needed in abundance, because Russia is still the largest country with the second-largest nuclear capacity and has many opportunities to hurt U.S. interests.

The last point is particularly sensitive for us. We did not write this book as an appeal for vigilance against Russians and Russia, but, on the contrary, a plea for understanding and patience. Tension and conflicts between Russia and the United States are the last thing we want to witness. Although the Iron Curtain is not going to fall again, we want to be sure that our relatives and friends, living on both sides of the Atlantic Ocean, are not separated by emerging barriers of misunderstanding, suspicion, and alienation.

Chapter One

Anti-Americanism in a Cold-War Perspective

Whether you like it or not, history is on our side. We will bury you.

Khrushchev, November 18, 1956.

The program of Willis Conover "Music USA" was a window into America. I began learning English, in order to understand Conover's comments to the music he aired.

A Russian jazzman on VOA programs in the 1950s

April in Moscow is usually cold and breezy. On one of those chilly mornings in April of 1986, a crowd of Muscovites gathered on the Insurrection Square, right in front of the towering slab of a Stalinist skyscraper, and in close vicinity of the American Embassy. It was common to observe such crowds only during official celebrations on November 7 and May 1. State employers were responsible for providing a particular number of "volunteers" for the official street rallies. However, that day in April was not a holiday. The participants were established scientists, professors, and graduate students from several research institutes of the Academy of Science—in particular, the Institute for African Studies and the Institute for the United States and Canada. The purpose of the gathering was, as the officials explained to the people, an organized demonstration against the bombing of Libya by the United States Air Force.

Practically everyone in the crowd regularly listened to the Voice of America and the BBC in their homes. Moreover, because of their work affiliations, these men and women had the privilege of regular access to the semi-classified digest of foreign media produced by the TASS—one of the official Soviet broadcasting agencies. Based on what these people read from the digest, the bombing took place in retaliation to the terrorist attack on a West Berlin disco allegedly sponsored by the Libyan leader, Colonel Muhammar Quaddafi. But this knowledge had little impact in the purpose of the rally. At 10 A.M., the organizers of the meeting—local party officials—commanded the crowd to line up in columns and head in the direction of the U.S. Embassy on Tchaikovsky Street. The small crowd of sociologists and economists, political scientists and historians obeyed without enthusiasm. Soon, other small and large groups from factories, plants, schools, and institutes joined the rally. As the crowd passed by the draped windows of the Embassy, someone—from the middle of the horde—screamed loudly, "Down with American aggressors! Defend the freedom-loving people of Libya!" Nobody in the group of scientists responded. They kept walking sullenly. Most of them performed a ritual they were accustomed to: they pretended to act as loyal Soviet citizens so that the officials would pretend not to notice what they—as experts—read, listened to, and talked about privately.

As soon as the rally was over, we, the authors of this book—who were members of the "protesting" crowd—turned to the right and walked in the direction of the nearest subway metro station. We did not feel great about this fake anti-American demonstration. At that time, most of our colleagues, especially the younger ones, were fascinated with the United States and did not accept the official mantra of Soviet propaganda about the "aggressive nature" of American imperialism. Spontaneously, while we were walking, a discussion sparked between us. Is it possible to end the Cold War? Could two governments, after years of stalemate, finally build sustained and friendly relations between our countries? After all, Russians liked American music, read its literary authors, and followed American style of fashion. One of us decided to play the role of skeptic: "There is a geopolitical law," he said, appealing to the Realist doctrine of international relations and suggesting that "there is no room for friendship in a world set for bipolar confrontation."

"There is a solution," jokingly replied the other. "What if Russia surrenders to the Americans? Remember an anecdote about Estonia appealing to the Kremlin for permission to receive just one hour of national independence? Remember why they requested just one hour? Because Estonians, after such a short-term independence is granted, would declare war on the United States, and then immediately surrender. It will be matter of a few hours for the U.S. marines to land in Tallinn. To surrender in the hands of the Americans is an act of liberation from oppression! Look at what Germany and Japan achieved after surrendering to the United States in 1945." Nevertheless, the more skeptical of the two of us remained undaunted: "Even though the Cold War as we know is over one day, our countries will not become friends with each other. Russians know next to nothing about the United States. Imagine, what will happen when our people will finally get to know America better and realize how profoundly different they are from what our people expected to see! Never mind state-sponsored anti-American propaganda. Even without it, the Russians will feel more estranged from the Americans and their lifestyle than they do right now. After all, the French are legitimate American allies, but do not adore Uncle Sam. . . ." This brief discussion ended naturally when we reached the metro and parted.

Many years later, recalling what had been said during this and many other discussions about the future of Russian-American relations, we realized how contradictory, intricate, naïve, and ambiguous the perceptions of, and attitudes about, the United States were among educated young Russians. Opinion polls on foreign relations were not conducted in the Soviet Union. However, by the end of the Cold War, Russian perceptions of America consisted of an entire gamut of beliefs (Shlapentokh 1988). How were such diverse perceptions formed? Why did such ambiguity exist, despite overwhelming and deliberate anti-American propaganda organized by the government and carried out by educational institutions, the media, and other major socialization agents? In order to answer this question, it is essential to step back in history and analyze the roots of anti-Americanism in Russia.

Soviet Anti-Americanism and its Weakness

All modern Russian rulers balanced on the fault line of history, between two tectonic plates: one representing the traditionalist and backward peasant country profoundly isolated from the outside world, and the other symbolizing the dynamic and ever-superior Western capitalism. Typically, Russian leaders and scores of thinkers confronted the dilemma of overcoming the country's backwardness without losing its cultural heritage. This frustrating predicament led to painful splits and continuous heated debates between so-called Westernizers and Slavophiles. Nevertheless, it was noted long ago that both pushers of the Westernization of Russia and its bitter critics were not as far from each other as they seemed: The most articulate and sophisticated representatives in both camps shared the commonly ambiguous feeling of "love/hate" for Western societies. In fact, this chronically ambivalent attitude toward Western countries—more "civilized" than Russia—is one of the oldest and most persistent of the observed features of the Russian elite's opinion throughout many years of Soviet and pre-Soviet history (Neumann 1996; Carr 1958, 10). For many years, Russian intellectuals debated the question: Are we Europe or not?

A sense of belonging to Europe has long been part of traditional Russian identity after Peter the Great. In classical literary prose, as well as in early Soviet writings, and later in the publications of Soviet dissidents, this was a constantly present theme.[1] Yesterday, as well as 100 years ago, resistance to everything Western was miraculously combined with the attraction to and acceptance of its customs, attitudes, and symbols (Kliamkin and Lapkin 1996). As Richard Dobson (1996) noticed, competing pro- and anti-Western attitudes may coexist on the individual level of the average Russian person.

Vladimir Shlapentokh (1988), in his ground-breaking article on Russian anti-Americanism, pointed out that Russians have always been keen to measure themselves against the West. Part of this mindset is the tradition of singling out one Western country to be either a paragon for acceptance and imitation or a model for blatant rejection. During different periods of history, these countries provided various institutional examples and behavioral patterns for influential Russian elites to pay attention to and imitate. Any thorough student of Russian pre-twentieth-century history should notice that such samples for comparisons included the Western European countries—to name a few—the Netherlands, England, Germany, and France in particular. The upper classes of Russia—emulated by other social strata—constantly attempted to implement many elements of "Western life" into their daily lives, from political and government establishment, to clothes and artistic fashion, from military concepts and strategies, to spoken and written language, and even food. Despite its ambiguous geographic location, Russians considered nations located westward, as somewhat closer to them culturally than the country's southern and eastern neighbors, even though the Russian Orthodox Church was continuously at odds with the Vatican and Protestant denominations.

Since World War II, the role of the "measuring stick" for Soviet perceptions has been played by the United States (Shlapentokh 1988, 158). Throughout the Cold War, the dynamics and underlying mentality of confrontation, of course, affected Russian views about America. The inner balance among various trends shifted under the impact of diverse factors, including state policies and directions of propaganda, living standards, ideological campaigns, security perceptions, cultural influences, and individual experiences. For example, state policies and the subsequent contents of anti-American propaganda switched their emphasis several times. At times, for example, the focus changed from mutual acceptance to polarization, unrelenting confrontation, and even faith in a victory in a future nuclear war. Security perceptions of the elite and general public shifted along with the dynamics of the U.S.-Soviet confrontation: These stages included not only dangerous tension and crises, but also years of anti-fascist alliance and *détente.* On an official level, the anti-American ideological prejudices of the majority of Soviet nomenclature were effectively neutralized by the attitudes of foreign-policy practitioners and the top leadership who respected their fellow superpower and hoped to secretly negotiate and agree with some "sensible" American politicians on a world condominium (Kissinger 1994; Dobrynin 1995; Israelyan 1996; Arbatov 1992).

Stalin was perhaps the only Soviet leader who attempted—with all the power at his disposal—to forge a strong anti-American consensus in the Soviet Union. The "man of steel" had his own inflexible, geopolitical calculations, as well as personal attitudes toward the United States: During the Second World War, he hoped to use cooperation with Franklin D. Roosevelt and his circle of "New Dealers" to promote Soviet interests and spheres of influence. Stalin largely succeeded in this endeavor, particularly in central Europe and the Far East (see Communications 1957). However, in the second half of the 1940s, Stalin realized that the United States—not Great Britain—had become the main adversary of the Soviet Union in the international arena. As a result, he restructured Soviet propaganda to fire at Uncle Sam. After he unleashed the Korean War in June of 1950, and once the United States responded to this challenge with its own intervention under U.N. banners, Stalin began to propagate a twofold image of America. It was an image of a great and powerful nation that was ruled by short sighted billionaires from Wall Street; it was the power that could not match its economic might by its valor on the battlefield.

In the last years of his life, the Soviet dictator undertook maximum preparations for a possible future war with the United States. The anti-American propaganda rose to its highest peak by early 1953, when TASS announced the arrest of a group of Jewish and non-Jewish "Kremlin doctors" who allegedly planned to assassinate the Soviet leadership. The Jewish doctors were then reported to be agents of the Joint, a Zionist organization based in New York. As it turned out, Stalin had far-reaching plans in this ordeal: He intended to implicate the U.S. Embassy in Moscow in the terrorist conspiracy. A huge wave of anti-Semitism, disseminated personally by Stalin, was designed to culminate in the deportation of Soviet Jews to Siberia. Mixing anti-Americanism with anti-Semitism was a powerful brew—previously tested by the Nazis—that Stalin probably meant to use as psychological preparation for a war with the United States (Naumov 1999; Zubok and Pleshakov 1996; Kostyrchenko 1995).

Stalin disdained America because of his ideological concerns: He was—above all—the fire-keeper of the Communist experiment. He also faced the United States as a major geopolitical and military rival, the only superpower that could destroy the Soviets along with their regime. Nevertheless, for all the ups and downs in the Soviet-American confrontation, permanent ambivalence toward the United States remained a stable and persistent phenomenon that re-emerged immediately after Stalin's death. Like other "designated" countries, the United States was both feared and mistrusted as a potential foe, and admired and envied as a role model.

During the years of Nikita Khrushchev (late 1950s–early 1960s), the Kremlin leadership and Soviet propaganda began to categorize their counterparts in Washington into two large groups. The first one was the "bad guys," who were typically located at the Pentagon, the CIA, and various right-wing conservative think-tanks. The second group was comprised of "sober-minded elements," i.e., those who were ready to communicate and negotiate with the Soviets. The Kremlin's old men never abandoned their dream to return to a modicum of the Grand Alliance, where the United States would respect Soviet security interests and its equal place in the pantheon of world powers. Not surprisingly, the most popular political figures among the Soviet political elite were John F. Kennedy and, ten years later, Richard M. Nixon, who spoke to Kremlin rulers in the language familiar to them of spheres of influence and geo-strategic balances (Dobrynin 1995; Volkogonov Collection at the National Security Archive, Washington D.C.).

America's technological and industrial achievements were always the subject of high opinion among Kremlin leaders. They wanted to emulate some of the technological and scientific achievements of the United States on Soviet soil and did it on a large scale. A leading member of the Politburo and veteran Bolshevik, Anastas Mikoyan, recalled in his memoirs that in 1936, Stalin had sent him to America to learn from American businesses. "Beginning from the 1930s we shifted all our attention [from Germany] to America. We sent to the United States several commissions to study their experience in the meat and dairy industries, as well as in others." Mikoyan stayed in America for two months, traveled more than 12,000 miles, and visited dozens of plants and businesses. Upon his return home, he introduced into Soviet life—among many things—American items such as the refrigerator, ice cream, canned fruit juice, white bread (these loaves are called "French" both in Russia and in the United States today) and . . . hamburgers. Moreover, Mikoyan wanted to introduce Coca Cola to the Soviet consumer market, "but the shortage of means prevented us from setting up this business at home." All in all, just one trip of one Soviet official came to change the life of the Soviet consumer. For him, "the stay in the U.S.A. turned out to be my university classes in the area of food industry and American economy. . . . I came back with considerable knowledge and a plan to transfer to our land the experience of the developed capitalist country" (Mikoyan 1999, 300–315).

A positive attitude about America was further enhanced in 1941–1945, when the United States played a crucial role in a conflict by being a Soviet ally during their Patriotic War against the Nazis. This memory left deep imprints on the opinions of Soviet elites and the general public. During the Second World War, the lend-lease program allowed the continuous flood of American goods, machinery, aircraft, food, and know-how into the Soviet Union, contributing to the widespread image of America as a strong, reliable, and wealthy country. It is remarkable that during the Cold War years that followed the end of the "hot" war, the Kremlin leadership continued to be aware that the Soviet Union was far behind the United States in many economic areas. Therefore, by the early 1970s, Kremlin leaders were satisfied to find that Richard M. Nixon and then Gerald Ford both behaved like "sober-minded" and responsible leaders who allowed the Soviet Union—as Franklin D. Roosevelt had done in the 1940s—to benefit from the United States' wealth. Like F.D.R. was associated with the lend-lease program, Nixon and Ford were behind the transfer of technologies and the grain shipments. The Kremlin and the entire Soviet nation became partly dependent—perhaps without wanting to admit it—on Western food and technologies the way a substance-addicted person depends on certain narcotics and denies that this is his or her situation (Volkogonov Collection in the Library of Congress).

The Ambivalence Continues

Among all other Soviet rulers of the second half of the twentieth century, Nikita Khrushchev was the only leader who genuinely believed that the Soviet Union could actually catch up with and surpass the United States in the fields of science, technology, consumer goods, and overall living standards. He began to expound this thesis publicly—making himself an easy target of the covert criticism of more cautious leaders. By the end of the 1950s, he coined the slogan "Catch up and surpass America" the cornerstone of his program of construction of Communism over the next 20 years. At that time, millions of Soviet people shared Khrushchev's optimism. When the first American national exhibition opened at Moscow Sokolniki Park in July 1959, huge crowds of Muscovites stormed in, eager to look at American achievements. At the same time, many of them were confident that they were not just looking at the impossible dream of a foreign country's life. They were actually taking a glimpse of their own forthcoming and prosperous future (Zubok 1998).

The longer-term effects of Khrushchev's slogan—still remembered by millions of Russians—were immense. Zdenek Mlynar, a Czech Communist who lived in Moscow in the 1950s and later participated in the Prague Spring, rightly observed: "Stalin never allowed comparison of socialism with capitalist realities because he insisted that here we build an absolutely

new world, comparable to nothing." This attitude led to autarchy and isolation. Nonetheless, it also ensured that Communist ideology could be
judged only on the basis of the criteria of the righteousness of Communist ideology itself. Khrushchev came with his new motivational slogan
and fundamentally changed the perception of the world for the average
Soviet person. As a result, over the course of many years, people continued
to compare their lives to American living standards. One generation after
another recognized that, in reality, American living standards were infi-
nitely higher than theirs in the Soviet Union. "And those who looked for
explanation, could easily come to the conclusion that the main obstacle"
that prevented them from achieving an American-style life was "the existing economic and political system." In the end, concludes Mlynar,
Khrushchev stimulated a remarkable development in Soviet society. He
undermined the Soviet people's faith in their political and social system,
thus creating a framework of constant comparison between the Soviet
Union and the United States (Gorbachev and Mlynar 1994, 24–25).

Certainly, the Soviet propaganda machine kept working against this
generally positive image of America. There were severe handicaps inside
the system, however, that became liabilities in the process of development
of a full-fledged image of the American enemy during the Cold War. One
hurdle originated within Communist ideology that provided both the
concept and language for the Cold War's anti-American propaganda. This
ideology originated with the proletariat transcending national boundaries
and treating nationalism as a bourgeois disease and rival ideology. Despite
all Stalin's attempts to graft the elements of great imperial chauvinism to
this ideology, it preserved its constituent elements: the division of societies
into classes, the view of social development as caused by the class struggle,
the image of international relations as a clash between "imperialist forces"
nurtured by state capitalism on one hand and "progressive people" on the
other. For this reason, Soviet Cold War propaganda had difficulties presenting the American people as enemies. In fact, they were supposed to be
victims, exploited by omnipotent and greedy American capitalists.

The enemy, as a result, became fragmented, understood, and less intimidating. The enemies were right-wing extremists, the hawks, Pentagon militarists, Wall Street fat cats, and oil magnates from Texas. Thus, a palpable
imbalance in the mutual stereotyping between the Soviets and the Americans was set. For most Americans, the enemies were "*russkies*," the civilization's outcasts: strong and vicious, yet obedient to a diabolic regime
(Ebenstein 1963). For the Russian individuals, the enemies were not all
"Americans" but specific groups and types of people. Conversely, "real"
Americans were fine people; they were merely misled and manipulated by
"bad" Americans. Overall, the Soviet propaganda machine had never been

able to apply its old ideological mold of persuasion and develop effective America-bashing techniques similar to the Russia-bashing practiced rather successfully by their Cold War enemies.

As a result of this mismatch in enemy images between the Soviet Union and the United States, a remarkable development of the Iron Curtain era occurred. Throughout the Cold War, especially after Stalin's death, the Soviet people were able to have access to translated books of American writers and to watch some American movies. Those books and movies were not just for a tiny group of connoisseurs, but also for an audience of millions, in big and small cities and towns. This American cultural expansion into Russia did not result in a similar development in America: The American public (perhaps with the exception of Brooklyn, N.Y.) did not read Russian books and did not watch Russian movies at all.

The relative ineffectiveness of Soviet anti-American propaganda in creating an evil image of the United States was caused, in part, by other obstacles, hurdles somewhat related to ideology. Thus, when Soviet teachers spoke about America in class, when reporters typed their essays for publishing in state-controlled newspapers and magazines, they could rarely move beyond a preordained list of themes, such as American imperialism, militarism, the workers' movement, racial problems, crime in American cities, and a few others. Other features of American society and life—including many obvious advantages and achievements of American society that were already known to a growing amount of the Soviet people—were simply ignored. In combination with alternative sources of information and the popularity of American literature and movies, this cognitive dogmatism and narrowness completely undermined people's trust in anti-American propaganda in the Soviet Union.

All together, a combination of ideological, psychological, and bureaucratic reasons largely explains why most Soviet children and teenagers had an ambivalent image of their "official" foreign adversary (Shiraev and Bastrykin 1988). In addition, Soviet propaganda displayed its inability to use some obvious advantages of a rapidly developing means of mass communication. While in the 1920s and 1940s Soviet ideological propaganda machine was extremely effective, by the 1970s and 1980s it began to skid off the road of effectiveness. For decades, this machine peddled almost identical images of either a skeletal and belligerent Uncle Sam or a fat-bellied tycoon. A record-breaking example of longevity in the art of propaganda was established by a brigade of three cartoonists, who used the first syllables of their names to create the pseudonym "Kukryniksy." Their anti-American posters were remarkably unchanging in terms of genre and topic. However, they appeared with spectacular regularity in many leading Soviet media outlets. [2]

Before the 1980s, the average Soviet person knew very little about America and did not have opportunities to learn from personal experience. Television and newspapers remained the major sources of knowledge about the United States. Curiosity toward this far-away land was satisfied, in part, by infrequent trip travelogues. Newspaper articles and book pages also promoted an ambiguous image of America and its people. On one hand, New York, for example, was called "the city of the yellow devil," according to renowned poet V. Mayakovsky, and a giant "squid" with tentacles, according to journalist N.Vasiliev (1955). On the other, a positive impression of America was further enhanced by such remarkable observers as Ilya Ilf and Evgeny Petrov, especially in their famous book called, *One-storey America,* a best-selling Soviet analogue of John Steinbeck's *Travels with Charlie across America.*

As we mentioned earlier, since Khrushchev, the official propaganda did not mind importing into the Soviet Union some elements of "progressive" American culture, i.e., books of American writers who did not commit any sins against the Soviets or were known as sympathizers with revolutionary developments. Thus, Hemingway's books were promoted in the U.S.S.R. because of his sympathies to the Cuban revolution, John Steinbeck's works—for his description of the miseries of capitalist crisis in *The Grapes of Wrath.* Salinger was promoted for presenting the duplicity of American society through the eyes of a teenager in *The Catcher in the Rye.* Kurt Vonnegut was advanced for his anti-militarist stance in his *Slaughterhouse-Five,* to name a few. Soviet publishers and literary critics quickly learned how to find "progressive" features in American writers, poets, and dramatists, and translate them for a Soviet audience. A trickle of American-translated literature turned into a flood by the 1970s, a cultural development that significantly eroded many official propaganda-sponsored images of the United States.

Of course, the publisher's supply was only a shy response to enormous public demand. People's curiosity about America and the West in general had been part of the cultural landscape of the Soviet Union since the 1950s. After Stalin's death in 1953, the cultural life of Russian elites became less isolated and significantly more exposed to the outside world. The so-called Thaw stimulated the growth of liberal-democratic ideas among Soviet elites. A series of disclosures about the crimes of Stalinism produced a post-traumatic shock that shaped the consciousness of many younger Russian individuals (Alexeyeva 1990). Official Communist ideology, based on Marxist assumptions, began to rapidly erode in people's minds and came to be replaced by either Westernizing liberal ideas or by the values of Russophile ideology (English 2000).

During the late 1950s and early 1960s, the growth of liberalism was strongly connected, not surprisingly, to the rapid growth of a new middle class: scientists, engineers and technology professionals, educators, and a skilled workforce in the Soviet military-industrial complex. The spirit of scientific exploration, both on earth and in space, and enthusiasm about the potential of a scientific-technical revolution boosted expectations of a bright future among many Russians. This techno-scientific spirit of competition in the 1960s, conditioned by the U.S.-Soviet race, continued in part in the 1970s. Then, however, the focus of attention shifted. Never mind huge river-dams and rocket launches. Now attention was primarily directed at American achievements in aircraft design, computers, biotechnology, and agriculture.[3] Optimists believed—in the privacy of their homes, of course—that the American West and Soviet East would eventually converge in an attempt to develop a better, rationally justified model of governance and production. In this new system, the technocratic elites would replace party ideologues and uncultured bureaucrats. On a mass level, these expectations found expression in a booming new cult of science-fiction literature: Soon novels and stories in which Soviet order triumphed over the universe were replaced by books in which Soviet bureaucracy was the object of covert and sometimes open criticism (Vail and Genis 1989). Books by American sci-fi authors, in particular Ray Bradbury and Isaac Asimov, became extremely popular.

Meanwhile, some critics promoted the evolution of official ideology into a kind of Russian National-Socialist ideology, a version of "Stalinism without Stalin" (Shlapentokh 1988, 162). A small minority followed the bold example of Alexander Solzhenitsyn, who chose two paths to follow. First, there was to be a total opposition to the Soviet regime. The second path was his rejection of Western and particularly American civilization on historical, philosophical, and moral grounds (Solzhenitsyn 1998). During the 1980s, the thinkers who followed this path formed the ranks of Russia's New Right (Sergei Kurginian, Alexander Dugin, Mikhail Antonov, to name a few). Their ideas would play an increasingly important role during the last years of Gorbachev's perestroika and in the new Russia (Laqueur 1994).

In the struggle among the advocates of the emerging post-Communist ideologies, the United States was becoming an important cultural symbol: having either a negative or a positive attitude about America was an essential part of ideological orientation and cultural identity. For most representatives of Russia's new middle class, America became the natural antipode of the inefficient, bureaucratic, and backward Soviet Union. By the end of the 1960s, as Soviet patriotism quickly waned, the logic of simple cognitive balancing ("the enemy of my enemy is my friend") permeated people's perceptions of America. The more physicists and professors clashed with party ideologists and poorly educated state bureaucrats, the more they tended mentally (for lack of behavioral possibility) to defect to the "Far West"—the United States. In the 1960s, the famous "Race for the Moon" that captivated the attention of many technocratic-minded intellectuals in the Soviet Union and millions of knowledgeable individuals, ended, in the minds of many people, in an undisputable U.S. victory. Sarcastic gloating about Soviet inefficiency and undeniable admiration about American ingenuity became the two basic behavioral pillars that provided support for the elites' and masses' perception of America.

On the contrary, the Russophiles on the right advocated suspicion and antipathy toward the United States, depicting it in highly abstract terms as the antipode to Russia: America is materialistic whereas Russia is spiritual; America is an artificial nation without culture; Russia is an old civilization (Laqueur 1994, 209–210). In 1957, there was even a public debate in Moscow's weekly, *Literaturnaya Gazeta*. Alexander Kazem-Bek, the organizer of neo-fascist Young Russians movement among European émigrés in the 1930s, who later lived in the United States and then (through KGB channels) returned to the U.S.S.R. in 1956, denounced the United States as a "land without culture." Ilya Ehrenburg, a Jew and famous Russian writer with a strong European liberal background, published a withering rejoinder, claiming that America was a country of great culture and many "progressive" and "fine" writers and musicians.

Most of the educated Russian public tended to follow Ehrenburg's arguments. Liberal trends and positive assessments of the United States prevailed. At the same time, many Russians shared romantic and mystical themes advocated by the Russophiles that resulted in their rejection of the American way of life. They preferred to "defect" not to New York, but to Russian Siberia and the Far East; they found refuge from the stench of the Communist experiment in the freshness of the taiga, at the gulches and ice caps of grandiose mountains, on the clean and clear stretches of great Siberian rivers. The Slavophiles produced a profound mass culture of bards and poets, most of whom—well-known among millions of Russians— continued to appeal to American image with a great degree of caution and resentment. One such popular bard, Yuri Visbor, sang not only about a world of personal emotions, but also glorified Soviet atomic subs cruising in dark ocean depths because "the tired lads in America keep working to make us dead." The slogan of the Slavophiles was simple: We do not want a New World—whatever it may be—because we want to get back the Old World of Russia.

The Kremlin tried to pound and squash both of these growing trends of popular consciousness but, in a pinch, turned against the Slavophiles. The campaign against them was committed with more vigor than the one against their rival Westernizers. Formidable Solzhenitsyn was apparently a more annoying and unacceptable figure for the Soviet rulers than was Andrei Sakharov—the icon of the dissidents and liberals. He was tolerated by the officials at least until his open opposition to the Soviet invasion of Afghanistan in 1980. In the mid-1970s, when the policy of *détente* with the United States and Western Europe flourished, Soviet leadership and the ideological loyalists to the regime were, after all, less critical of the United States than the exiled Russian writer. Solzhenitsyn and other Slavophiles— mostly thinkers-in-exile by that time—believed that Americans had al- lowed themselves to be corrupted and weakened by the virus of cosmopolitanism, and therefore were incapable of withstanding the immi- nent, treacherous onslaught of the Communist juggernaut (Solzhenitsyn 1998; Panin 1998). The Kremlin rulers, in contrast, as they perceived an historic trend toward cooperation and coexistence between capitalism and Socialism, wanted peace, stability, and an agreement with official Washing- ton to end the Cold War on mutually beneficial terms (see Volkogonov Collection).

Mass Culture and America's "Soft Power" over Russians

Even in the late years of Stalin, one could already discern the outlines of a new "social covenant" between the regime and the emerging middle class. This development was completed in the years of Nikita Khrushchev and Leonid Brezhnev. The process meant, along with other changes, the end of an aggressive eradication of middle-class values in Soviet society and, on the contrary, the sharing of these values by most bureaucrats and their dependents (Dunham 1976). In particular, one of the results of this development was the birth of a homegrown mass culture and the enter- tainment industries. As we mentioned earlier, certain respectable elements of American culture—mostly books—became essential elements of this phenomenon.

There was an already new, rising, and unanticipated wave of youth counter culture in the late 1950s, in part as a reaction against the new So- viet "bourgeoisie." The movement's new symbols and idols, however, were not domestic. They mostly came from a repertoire of American mass cul- ture and the European culture of "protest." It was, in a sense, the Soviet version of an already-worldwide phenomenon. The spread of American material and cultural symbols—like blue jeans, cigarettes, and jazz and rock music—was a healthy reaction to the monotony, uniformity, poverty, and duplicity of Soviet life. Music and clothing styles, idolization of cult stars, and beatnik-like behavior became the core elements of this counter cul- ture that, for some reason, took root first among the children of the Soviet nomenklatura (Zubok 1998; Kozlov 1998; Aksyonov 1987). The revolution in mass communications also favored pro-American attitudes. Since the 1950s, American radio broadcasting and cultural exhibitions became extremely effective tools in fighting Soviet anti-Americanism. In the mindsets of many young, trendy, and educated Soviets, John F. Kennedy, Ernest Hemingway, and Marilyn Monroe replaced the hackneyed icons of traditional Soviet heroes (Vail and Genis 1989).

America became "a cool place to be." Incidentally, this image contrasted with the attitudes of Western European youth. For many Europeans, pro-American views were associated with the official materialistic order established by adults and, of course, the highly unpopular Vietnam War. For the young Soviet elite, the new American image replaced the old Cold War perceptions of the United States as the land of Wall Street "sharks," militant racists, bomb-toting generals, and hackneyed politicians. Often learning about America from newspaper cartoons, unlike their parents, young Russians now looked at those cartoon images with a smirk: For them the entire edifice of Soviet anti-American propaganda was a more suitable object of criticism than distant American capitalists and bureaucrats.

Western rock music also had an enormous impact on the socialization of millions of young people in the Soviet Union (Shiraev 1999; Kozlov 1998; Stites 1992). Records of Western rock stars were not typically sold in stores, therefore any chance to get a foreign-made vinyl disk was considered a miracle. Tape recorders in the 1960s changed the situation and broadened the exposure of the Soviet youth to Western rock music. First, there was the invasion of the music of Elvis Presley. Then he was followed by Bob Dylan and Jim Morrison. Later, in the 1970s and 1980s, came Stevie Wonder, Michael Jackson, Bruce Springsteen, Billy Joel, Prince, Bon Jovi, and Guns N' Roses. Although British rock—The Beatles, The Rolling Stones, and a full house of world-known superstars—was undoubtedly the most popular brand, most people in the Soviet Union did not care much whether a star was from London or New York. To them, Western musicians represented Anglo-Saxon culture and music. Generally speaking, they all represented America and a free world (Shiraev and Bastrykin 1988).

The "Fifth Column" vs. the Fundamentalists

This swing toward pro-American views is connected to the main feature of the counter-culture fallout in the Soviet Union: It was predominantly contact-free romanticism infused with creative imagination. Most of the Soviet youth elites never met or personally knew many Americans, and never traveled to the United States. Nevertheless, they had a choking hunger for American mass culture's artifacts and information. The information available was largely impersonal, because both apologists of official ideology and its critics focused on the economic, technological, and political dimensions of America's image (Shlapentokh 1988, 162). As a result, Russian pro-American perceptions—grown on the soil of counter culture—became a matter of mythology and imagination to a greater extent than anti-American views. Thinkers and writers of Russian counter culture, as opinion leaders among their circles, invented their own image of America and, in fact, continued to staunchly believe in it even though they had the chance to familiarize themselves with the objects of their dreams. For the time being, those staunch believers represented, as always, just a fraction of the population, a distinct minority. For the masses, the belief in "their America" remained fickle, unstable, and susceptible to rapid and, at times, radical changes (Shlapentokh 1986).

Meanwhile, since the late 1950s, Nikita Khrushchev and a trickle of Soviet visitors, mostly members of the Communist Party and trade union delegations, state commercial negotiators, well-connected journalists, top athletes, and stars of classical or folk art began their personal discovery of America. Travel logs and essays of journalists and other commentators revealed the old-fashioned clash between the ideas of enthusiastic liberals and anti-American Russophiles. From the very beginning, this personal exposure to America produced in many Russian observers a third type of personal covert ideology. In effect, it was a frustrating psychological fusion: a combination of insatiable desires for material goods and services, deep-seated envy, and a sense of humiliation over their country's poverty and backwardness. Along with embracing of youth counter culture, this cognitive fusion perhaps contributed to the erosion of patriotism in the elites and distinct Soviet "self-legitimacy" (Zubok 1998).

In vain, Russophile intellectuals appealed to a compensatory theme, asserting that American material wealth would cause both spiritual and cultural degradation of the individual. This materialistic emptiness was contrasted with the unique spirituality—more accurately translated as "*soulfulness*"—of Russians. The most ardent of Russophiles were not immune to the allures of American materialism. Envy, in particular, noted Shlapentokh, "helped people to preserve psychological comfort in relation to a country that was beyond reach in economic and technological spheres and whose freedoms and democracy were also impossible to imitate (1988, 166–168). This was the theme that survived the collapse of the Soviet Union and re-emerged later in the 1990s.

To what extent did the spread of anti-Soviet dissent in the country correlate with the proliferation of pro-American sympathies? KGB statistics, albeit collected for specific purposes, indicate the spread of anti-Soviet dissent throughout the entire spectrum of Soviet society, with some groups notably over-represented. For instance, among the authors of anonymous and obviously illegal anti-Soviet leaflets during 1975, unskilled workers accounted for more than 26 percent, white-collar workers and engineers constituted 19 percent, college students—only 5 percent and high-school students—7 percent; retirees were represented in high numbers: 15 percent. These figures remained almost the same in 1978. However, by 1984 as the numbers of dissidents among unskilled workers declined, the amount among white-collar workers grew. A vast majority of those who were interrogated for anti-Soviet activities confessed that they committed those acts "under the ideological influence of the enemy and out of political immaturity" (see Volkogonov Collection, KGB reports in Special Files). As the statistics demonstrate, technocratic-minded intellectuals and the rebellious counter-cultural youth constituted the bulk of the grass roots of the dissent movement. Those were the same groups that provided the fertile soil for the spread of pro-Americanism in the late years of the Soviet Union.

Of course, it would be wrong to look at the entirety of anti-Soviet dissent in Russia as the ideology of an exclusively pro-American "fifth column"—as the Soviet Communist leadership and the KGB often regarded it. It was a complex and diverse cultural and psychological phenomenon rooted in specific problems and dilemmas of the Soviet individual living in a totalitarian society. Many dissidents and their sympathizers grappled with ethical, philosophical, and historical issues that could not easily be explained by their pro-Americanism. In fact, the American theme was not a major subject in the dissidents' discussions. However, maybe by inference, one can conclude that the pro-Western trend was by far the most pronounced in the dissident milieu. And there was a crucial link between the tiny group of "out-of-the-closet" dissenters and Western—mostly U.S. government-funded—media, from the Voice of America to Radio Liberty. Through this linkage, the faint voices of dissent and their hand-copied *samizdat* publications reached an audience of millions. Even the words of the Russophile, Solzhenitsyn, and other non-liberal thinkers, reached the Soviet-educated audience through Western European and American means of communications.

Later, a renowned anti-Soviet thinker and non-admirer of the United States, Alexander Zinoviev, admitted with gratitude: "The revolt of the Soviet intelligentsia and the cultural uprising [of the 1960s and 1970s] happened to a great extent because of attention and support on the part of the West. Many Soviet people broke off with their habitual existence, took risks and accepted sacrifices while reckoning on Western attention and Western assistance. . . . It goes without saying that the general situation of mass revolt and its support by the West affected my mentality as well. It opened perspectives undreamed of before—the perspectives of a break-through to Western culture." (Zinoviev 1999, published in 1988, 421–422). The Cold War alliance between the Western media—primarily the dominating American media—and the anti-Soviet dissidents remained a noticeable phenomenon of Russian social life through the 1980s.

Beside the popularity of American music and culture, this alliance explains how, in the 1960s, American and Western broadcasting turned from ineffective tools of Cold War propaganda (similar in their ineffectiveness to the Radio Moscow that broadcast to the West) to a virtual reality familiar to millions of Russians. Some could tune in to listen to their favorite jazz or rock hits; meanwhile increasing amounts of people used Voice of America as the window to an invisible open society, a global town hall. On the radio, there were anchors speaking in pure Russian with nice, slightly Americanized accents. They discussed real issues. VOA employees—American administrators and Russian émigrés—ran these town-hall meetings with smoothness, a daring degree of intellectual liberty, and humor—features that the Soviet audience greatly appreciated.

However, despite the many changes taking place in the world, almost until the late 1980s, Soviet society remained isolated and was therefore virtually closed to any information that would systematically favor the United States and its policies. The Iron Curtain still remained a hard reality of Soviet life, and the vast majority of Soviet citizens continued to live on a strict propagandist and informational diet: information about the outside world was carefully selected, distorted, and refined. Official newspaper cartoons in *Pravda* and *Izvestia* depicting American "militarists" as trigger-happy cowboys and ape-like vandals still shaped public opinion (Keen 1986). In the 1970s and 1980s, state television became a powerful new ally of the Cold War cartoonists and their admirers. A few well-connected television journalists took advantage of certain conditions caused by *détente* and produced a series of reports about the United States. Valentin Zorin, a Jew from a family purged by Stalin (Zorin, as a child, was adopted by a well-known Soviet diplomat), stood head and shoulders above the rest of his colleagues after producing the series "Bosses Without Masks" depicting "the real" elite of America: money-hungry billionaires of New York, California, and Texas. The series, among other features, directly linked the assassination of John F. Kennedy to a conspiracy of Texan plutocrats. The images of America in this program represented a cold, hostile, and impersonal environment, where the dollar, not people, had the only ultimate value.

These graphic anti-American images maintained mind-shaping influence on the members of the so-called old middle class of Russia (bureaucrats and employees of service industries in particular), as well as the bulk of peasantry and blue-collar workers—no less than a third of the Russian population. Most of these people remained largely impervious to the culture of Westernizers and liberals, i.e., indifferent to foreign radio broadcasting, unsympathetic, and even hostile to dissident literature and any information about how great life overseas was. Most of them were influenced by memories of the 1930s and 1940s: social instability, purges and famine, the Second World War, German occupation, and Soviet victory in the war. They chose to associate stability, peace, and cognitive deprivation with a strong Soviet state. They believed the United States was an enemy that wanted to deprive them of their hard-won gains. Therefore, these individuals continued to respond favorably to the themes—promoted unflaggingly by the propaganda—that endorsed xenophobic isolationism and the Soviet way of life and thinking.

There are many examples of such anti-American resiliency. In a diary-like manuscript, sent to the state television network, a semi-literate peasant woman, Evgenia Kiseleva, from Eastern Ukraine, described her feelings as she watched the summit between Gorbachev and Reagan at Geneva in November 1985. She was riveted to the television set, as "Reagan with a smile turns to our Gorbachev and embraces him by the waistline," but "it seemed to me that his smile was faked. Now he smiles, and his mind is calculating. He considers that our Gorbachev would trust him. But we will not trust him anyway." Responding to the Soviet propaganda denouncing Reagan's Star Wars, Kiseleva wrote: "He [Reagan] takes us for fools. But no, Mr. Reagan, we have been fighting all our lives; we will be fighting you back, bastards, as this or any other country attacks our Russia. And we will not sit still when you come to visit us with your missiles of far range and near range" (Olshanskaya 1991, 9–27).

By the end of the 1980s, it seemed that this outburst of anti-Americanism was a fading phenomenon, as the generation of Kiseleva grew older and entered their 70s and 80s. However, this Russian woman's anti-Americanism was an extension of an historic Russian survivalist tradition and rallying around the strong state. As such, it stood aside from the ideological and cultural battles between Westernizers and Slavophiles. It remained an essential component of the isolationist and underclass mentality that survived and outlived both Ms. Kiseleva and the Soviet Union.

Chapter Two

The Collapse and Euphoria

A total dismantling of socialism as a world phenomenon has been taking place. This may be inevitable and good. Since this is the reunification of mankind on the basis of common sense.

Anatoly Chernyaev, top foreign policy assistant to Gorbachev,
in his diary (October 1989).

The wind of change blew timidly through the steamy air of the 1989 Leningrad summer, when two young university professors pulled the heavy oak door of a downtown pub near the Griboedov Canal. The men went there to enjoy a special kind of new entertainment—a forbidden fruit of the old times, just a bite of which five years earlier could have resulted in a chain reaction of punishments, including the loss of jobs and criminal charges. The forbidden fruit was . . . two mugs of German beer and smoked hot dogs. The essence of this entertainment, however, was that the bill for the beer and dogs was paid with American dollars—a daring act in which thousands of Russians began to take pleasure only by the late 1980s. The old system was falling apart and the societal fabric began to unravel. Nevertheless, the future seemed bright. As if after a long hibernation, an increasing number of Russians realized that they could do what "normal" people do; try "normal" products, and be treated as "normal" people should be. The professors in the pub earnestly felt that the whole world, with all its beauty and possibilities, finally belonged to them.

Psychologists define euphoria as one's emotional attitude of personal invulnerability and an "all-is-well" mental set. The euphoric individual experiences an intense feeling of health and vigor, is full of grandiose ideas, spectacular plans, and idealistic macro-scenarios for the future (English and English 1958). For the person going through a euphoric stage, real-life individual problems or obstacles seem small and insignificant. Moreover, they are typically ignored or neglected. The future is great and awesome things are definitely set to happen tomorrow.

Many Russian writers have captured the experience of societal euphoria at times of grave calamity. Poet Fedor Tyutchev wrote: "One is blissful who came to this world in its death-throes." The great national poet, Alexander Pushkin, conveyed the feeling of shared elation in one of his *Little Tragedies* called "The Feast in the Time of Plague," in which he vividly contrasted the gruesome agony of a dying city with the ecstatic euphoria of a small drunken crowd. Alexander Blok reflected the inspiration and destructiveness of the exhilarating revolutionary change in his masterpiece "The Twelve." With a great deal of sarcasm, Vassily Aksyonov conveyed the feeling of national euphoria in his novel *The Island of Crimea*. Whether these literary allegories came to the minds of educated Russians in 1989 or not, people were certain they were witnessing the collapse of the oppressive Communist order. In the end of 1988, Gorbachev began to dismantle monopolistic party control over all layers of social structure—from economic management on the national level to the regulation of individual travel abroad. In the Baltic republics and the Caucasus region there were fast-growing, powerful movements for national sovereignty and secession from the Soviet Union. The case in point was that the collapse of the old system, like a mountain avalanche, threatened to bury and crush everything in its path—statehood, the country's social order, the national economy and—most importantly for the unsuspecting Russian individual—his or her standard of living.

Gorbachev's Revolution: The Origins of Euphoria

The mythological foundations of the perceptions of the United States among the elite—primarily on the leadership level—help comprehend why, during the Gorbachev years, the balance of attitudes toward the United States swung from prevalent hostility to overwhelming pro-Americanism. At the highest political level, Gorbachev and his advisers jettisoned official ideology and, in the resulting vacuum, embraced a range of romantic, social-democratic, and liberal ideas (Geller 1997). Like their predecessors, they began with a highly ambiguous image of the United States: Even though it was hard to deal with the "war mongers" in the Reagan administration, it was possible to convince simple American people of the Soviet Union's peaceful nature and good intentions. In his foreign policy, Gorbachev strived to end the Cold War by forming a U.S.S.R.-American condominium. By the end of 1989, he peacefully presided over the collapse of the Soviet empire and during the Malta summit accepted American (i.e., Western) values as "universal" (Brown 1996; Baker 1995; Levesque 1997; Beschloss and Talbott 1993).

Many people from the new crop of reformers who supported Gorbachev came from the political culture of Westernizing liberalism; their values were shaped by the ideological and cultural divides of the 1960s and 1970s. Economist Leonid Abalkin believed it was a "generational phenomenon:" Reformers had lived half of their lives fighting with Stalinists and "absorbed with their mother milk the ideas of renewal and reform and grew up with them" (Abalkin 1995, 6, 10). For many of them, pro-Americanism was part of their social identity, a symbol of rejection of the Communist past and a promise of Russia's integration into the international community of developed nations.

Nevertheless, who could possibly be elated when the country was facing so many dangerous predicaments? By 1990, the initial social enthusiasm of the earlier years of Gorbachev perestroika quickly evaporated, as well as many consumer goods in state-controlled stores. The Soviet economy, substantially weakened by hidden inflation and completely disorganized by Gorbachev's misconceived and chaotic decisions, began to crack. Week after week, the ruble continued to lose its value on the unofficial exchange market. Barter trade became one of the most attractive alternatives in financial operations between enterprises. In a desperate and sudden move to keep inflation down in 1990, the government limited the amount of money one could withdraw from his or her bank account. Barren supermarket shelves and huge lines sporadically popping up near stores resembled the worst images of wartime. In the summer of 1990, cigarettes vanished from stores and street booths, thus depriving two-thirds of Russians of their favorite "bad habit." Amateur entrepreneurs in Leningrad and Moscow began to pick up cigarette butts on the street, stuff them in glass jars, and sell them to particularly desperate nicotine addicts. Crime became rampant. Extortion and burglaries flourished. To own a VCR or video camera meant to run the significant risk of being burglarized. People who kept valuable items in their apartments began to install additional locks and steel doors.

Meanwhile, faced with rapidly worsening social and economic conditions, most Russians blamed the government and the old Communist system for all the difficulties the country experienced. Mikhail Gorbachev, a man of enormous popularity in the West, became the object of visceral hatred at home; the calls for his resignation increased the fast-ripening popularity of so-called radical democrats. As a result, people gathered primarily around Boris Yeltsin. The country was in a state of anxious anticipation of a major cataclysm. Gorbachev's foreign policy assistant, Anatoly Chernyaev, captured this feeling in his diary in May 1989: "The crux of the matter is the collapse of myths and unnatural forms of life in our own society. The economy is collapsing; the image of socialism is disintegrating; ideology is already gone; the federation, i.e., the empire, is coming apart at seams; the party is crumbling. . . . Protuberances of chaos have already broken out. . . ."

At the same time, a feeling of euphoria was developing in the face of new frontiers. As Gorbachev's societal projects crumbled like sand castles, this euphoria did not evaporate from individual minds. On the contrary, it became a compensatory psychological reaction. In October 1989, for example, observing the rapid transformations in Eastern Europe and the German Democratic Republic, Chernyaev (1989) wrote down in his log: "A total dismantling of socialism as a world phenomenon has been taking place. This may be inevitable and good. Since this is the reunification of mankind on the basis of common sense" (Chernyaev 1997, 17).

The failure of Gorbachev's revolution "from above" provoked the rise of yet another syndrome among particular circles of reformers: an exhilarated sense of dependence on the United States and its rationality, order, good will, and, above all, the desirable financial assistance that was seriously anticipated. Before the signs of the collapse became obvious, the Gorbachev team pursued a highly ambiguous strategy of dealing with the Americans. Gorbachev believed in his personal ability to convince the U.S. President—and along with him the entire American society—of the peaceful nature of the new Soviet government's good intentions and pacifist politics. The Soviet leader aspired to end the Cold War through the reconciliation of the West and the East and the integration of the U.S.S.R. into the cluster of "civilized" nations.[1] This development, he hoped, would create all the necessary conditions for the successful completion of the domestic reforms he had envisioned. Moreover, according to Gorbachev's plans, if the Soviet threat was dismantled, then the opposing blocs— NATO and the Warsaw Pact—would lose their military and political significance. The fall of Communist regimes in Eastern Europe in 1989, in Gorbachev's opinion, was just a prelude to the dissolution of NATO. The geopolitical tag of war would find its logical end in a new philosophy of mutual and rational self-restraint, cooperation, and interdependence (see Beschloss and Talbott 1993; Kozyrev 1992).

Although by the end of 1989, the geopolitical foundation for Gorbachev's foreign policy laid in ruins, still, in recognition and payback for Soviet goodwill, he hoped to gain full U.S. support. In December 1989, when Gorbachev met President George Bush at Malta, the mood of Gorbachev's team was quickly shifting from pride of being representatives of the superpower to a new feeling of dependence on the United States. Gorbachev promised Bush not to use force in dealing with the issue of separatism of the Baltic republics. In return, he sought from Bush the promise to facilitate American loans and the repeal of the discriminatory Jackson-Vanik amendment to the U.S.-Soviet trade bill. In 1990–1991, the Bush and Gorbachev teams acted in delicate psychological and political tandem. The former knew perfectly well that the West had won the Cold War, but did their best to avoid strutting and gloating in a triumphal tone that could have hurt the Soviets.[2] The latter behaved as if nobody had lost the Cold War, and that the world was moving toward a new world order, one that was no longer bipolar and confrontational, but rather a humane confederation of partners.

Of course, Gorbachev and the people in his entourage noticed a growing American assertiveness. The Soviet leader was actually quite upset to see signs of the rising popularity of America and Americans in Eastern Europe and the Soviet republics. For example, at the meeting with President Bush at Malta, Gorbachev said in obvious frustration: "I am under the impression that U.S. leaders are now quite actively advancing the idea of managing the division of Europe on the basis of 'Western values'" (Gorbachev 1993, 196–197). His disappointment was echoed by Alexander Yakovlev, a leading liberal reformer especially close to Gorbachev, who challenged the idea that democracy, openness, and free market are typical Western values. Later, the course and outcome of the Gulf War made Chernyaev write in his diary in April 1991, that the United States was reaping the benefits of Gorbachev's new thinking, at the same time it created "its own" world order (Chernyaev 1997, 127). Yet, the Soviet reformers did not allow this sense of bitterness to overshadow their idealistic, euphoric anticipation. Gorbachev's foreign policy assistant believed one should not "flicker, trying to snatch a bit of American victory, attempting to partake of American glory." Gorbachev agreed: "Why should we fuss and bustle? It would not be fit. They will do without us anyway. We made our contribution" (112).

The more the United States used Soviet weakness to promote American national interests—including the integration of the reunified Germany into NATO—the more Gorbachev wanted a partnership with Bush. The Soviet leader keenly understood that any confrontation with the United States at that time would be deadly to his regime. Without U.S. sympathy and the support of his political leadership—increasingly assailed from the right and left at home—he had little chance to sustain domestic attacks. No wonder Gorbachev ignored multiple warnings from the KGB about the American "agents of influence" in Soviet elites and told the American ambassador that "the United States should know everything about the U.S.S.R." (Chernyaev 1993, 121). It was a relief for Gorbachev and his supporters—who still cared about the image of their foreign policy—that the United States acted in the Persian Gulf on behalf of a victim of aggression and with the support of the United Nations.

America Becomes "Radical Chic"

The warnings issued by the KGB about growing U.S. influence reflected certain new realities. The processes unleashed by Gorbachev continued to evolve in a direction that very few people anticipated. Thus, since 1988 the liberal and reform-oriented mass media became increasingly critical of Gorbachev. At the same time, the image of the United States conveyed by the media became increasingly favorable. The Cold War frame of mind and the ambiguous image of America as its major component, was falling apart. Momentarily, the rejection of domestic Communist authorities led to a rise in popularity of those foreign leaders who—in the perception of the educated Soviet public—opposed Communism, its uncultured zealots, and bureaucrats. As a result, Ronald Reagan and Margaret Thatcher, the most resilient enemies of Communism and favorable targets of official Soviet propaganda in the early 1980s, became the most popular foreign politicians among reform-oriented Russians.

The elections of 1989 propelled Russian liberals—traditionally the major carriers of pro-American attitudes—to their peaks of status and reputation.[3] Riding on the surf of their growing popularity, they successfully challenged the political and ideological monopoly of the Communist party. Still, a statistical minority in the Congress of Peoples' Deputies, they were becoming the almost unchallenged heroes. The most substantial boost to their popularity was provided by the increasingly independent mass media. Driven by a thirst for sensationalism and influenced by the editors' personal beliefs,[4] television and radio networks relentlessly promoted a new branch of Soviet reformist wannabes—previously unknown to the Soviet people. Tens of millions of people from the educated public, primarily the urban middle class, were ready to eagerly absorb new opinions and judgements. Because the Communist Party's ranks were paralyzed by Gorbachev's policies and the resulting confusion among Communists, these new liberal activists quickly moved to a position of ideological and cultural hegemony.

In this new ideological and political situation, the new opinion-makers and general public pursued extensive searches for new shepherds and oracles. The traditional Russian and Soviet neurotic and ambiguous yearning for a role model became increasingly focused on American society and

American democracy. During 1989–1990, scores of academic specialists in Moscow's think-tanks and Leningrad's academic institutes argued with a great deal of enthusiasm about which economic and political systems were best suited guide the Soviet Union into the post-Communist future. Both of us—the authors—attended those numerous debates. Some participants liked the French model, partly because this country's revolutionary experience was similar to Russia's, its strong presidency, and perhaps just because of the perennial advocacy of Russian Francophiles. Only a few mentioned Great Britain, despite the popularity of Prime Minister Thatcher among many Russians. Some scholars—for example, from the elite Institute for U.S. and Canada in Moscow—looked at Scandinavian socialism. Nevertheless, the social and government systems of the United States were by far the most popular ones.

Soon, less sophisticated radical democrats (many of whom were yesterday's ideologists at local schools and research centers, professors of Marxism-Leninism, etc.), those who rejected failed Communist idols, eagerly grasped another deity: Americanism. Russia, they argued, had enormous resources and an educated, multi-ethnic population, just like the United States. Russia, like America, stretches through several time zones. Its people are generous and hospitable, just like Americans are.[5] An eclectic combination of imperialist thinking, high hopes and expectations, and disappointment with gruesome Soviet reality, churned in many minds and led people to a seemingly obvious and optimistic conclusion: If these two countries are so similar, but America is so prosperous and Russia is not, the major reasons for Russia's backwardness are its wretched social and feeble economic systems. As soon as these systems are replaced, Russia will prosper, like America does. Why could we not put our society on America's fast track?[6]

The official U.S. policy was to deal primarily with Gorbachev and his entourage[7] and to avoid encouraging the disintegration of the Soviet Union. However, the Bush administration began to notice that the White House, instead of the Kremlin, became the focus of the attention, respect, and veneration of the opposition in the center and in many Russian regions. Jack Matlock, U.S. Ambassador in Moscow, took the initiative and began to stage frequent, informal gatherings in his residence, Spaso House. After 1989, certain bigwigs of the Moscow political and intellectual elite began to flock to these parties without asking for anybody's authorization—a daring action absolutely unimaginable five years earlier. A post-Napoleonic nineteenth-century classic mansion with white columns, the room where Khrushchev signed the book of condolences after Kennedy's assassination, a sizable ballroom where Moscow nobility used to dance before the 1917 revolution—was now the site for the pilgrimage of scores of elite sympathizers of the United States. Jack and his wife, Rebecca, played an important role in the lives of the Russian *Demorossy* (members of the *Democraticheskaya Rossia* movement) when they began to develop as an opposition force against Gorbachev. Perhaps an equivalent role was played by U.S. Ambassador Davis in 1981–1983 when he hosted meetings with Polish intellectuals and Solidarity activists in his house in Warsaw.

Soon Spaso House began to symbolize the meeting place where "progressive" circles gathered to chat. To be there meant to belong to the "right" group of the Soviet reformers.[8] Numerous Russian intellectuals, who sought to take maximum advantage of the U.S.-Soviet rapprochement, sought useful contacts, breathed the air of freedom, improved their English, and savored . . . American cuisine. The American embassy in Moscow became a safe-haven for all kinds of radical Russian preachers who, echoing Cato the Junior, promoted the idea that the Soviet Union—like ancient Carthage—should be buried. As early as 1990, these individuals appeared to be closer—both ideologically and psychologically—to the U.S. embassy than they were to the reformer in the Kremlin. The nationalist opposition and separatists from the Baltic republics, Georgia, and other non-Russian regions of the Soviet Union joined them. Gradually, these activities developed into an open challenge and an insult to Gorbachev's authority. Chernyaev recorded indignantly in March 1991: "[U.S. Ambassador Jack] Matlock, acting on [Secretary of State James] Baker's instructions, convenes 'a party caucus' at the Embassy consisting of the presidents of Soviet republics and chairmen of their Supreme Soviets. What a disgrace! [Gorbachev] became enraged. . . . We managed to derail Matlock's undertaking" (Chernyaev 1997, 116).

Smaller details and seemingly insignificant facts reveal the big picture of the developing pro-American orientation among many new Russian opinion-leaders. For instance, in July of 1991, Gavriil Popov, one of the most popular reformers of that period, first sent a signal about a possible coup to U.S. Ambassador Matlock and subsequently, American intelligence. Only after this contact was made, did the Americans pass the alarming information back to the head of the state—Gorbachev. Just a few months after these events, in December of 1991, Yeltsin and his advisers made the first call to George Bush to inform him of the end of the Soviet Union—and only then did new Russian rulers let Gorbachev know about the decision they made.

The defeat of the coup in August 1991 released pro-American sentiment in Russian society: It rushed like water through a broken dam. All the signs suggested that the United States was obviously becoming a powerful and benign friend of the Russians who came to the parliament building in Moscow to defend their freedom and to the millions of their sympathizers all across the country. Bush offered Yeltsin's team assistance in communications and asylum in the American Embassy in the event that the putschists defeated the resistance.[9] As a political officer at the United States' Embassy in Moscow recalls: "After the August coup to be American in Moscow was—as Shelly said about being young at the time of the French revolution—'very heavenly.'" During those days, Americans could even be embraced in the street by enthusiastic Russians—a sign of gratitude for President Bush's disapproval of the coup plotters and growing sympathy toward Americans.[10]

American Dream Reaches Russians through VCRs, Computers, and Travel

By the end of the 1980s, a swift change in the Soviet information situation started with the rapid expansion of the VCR on the Soviet market. Still extremely expensive, [11]*vidiki* began to appear, as Russians say, like mushrooms after the rain. Back in 1984, as an old notebook reveals, a representative of the Leningrad Regional Party Committee spoke to a group of political science professors and told them that according to official estimates, there were 1,700 VCRs in private hands in the four million population city. He also suggested that city officials would soon register every piece of video equipment in order to prevent any uncontrollable distribution of the anti-Soviet propaganda (personal information).

The promised "registration" never took place. Neither the astronomical prices, nor constant threats and rumors about the confiscation of all VCRs, nor the increasing numbers of violent video-related burglaries, could stop the VCR revolution of the late 1980s-early 1990s. Like in New York or Los Angeles, people got together to watch the Super Bowl on a Sunday afternoon in January—Russians in those days gathered together to "watch" a *vidik*. It was almost irrelevant what the owner of the new technology had to offer for the show: an action film, sci-fi episode, mystery thriller, horror movie, or erotic comedy. People were eager to see almost anything that came from the West.[12] American films—most of which were produced in Hollywood—became a convenient source of entertainment and knowledge. It also became "cool" for touring Russian pop stars to carry a VCR in their luggage on tour. In every city, they would find old and new friends who would bring to them a few videotapes with new movies. [13]

Practically all the tapes watched by Russians at that time were pirate copies. No laws existed then that guaranteed copyright protection. Russian distributors were able to sell videotapes with American movies long before these movies went on sale in New York or Los Angeles. Underground interpreters dubbed them into Russian—the voices of the two most industrious of them became as famous in Russian homes as the voices of television news announcers. Russians started to watch American soap operas and selected NBA games. Russian rock musicians began to record and perform some of their songs in the English language, in hopes of getting their own videos and being noticed in the West. [14]

Vidiki were closely followed by the first personal computers. While they facilitated word-processing enormously, they also played a prominent cultural role because they introduced the possibility to play computer games. Most of the games were produced in the United States and for the American market. Those who had access to computers spent a lot of time in front of the screen fighting in M-1 "Abrams" against hostile Red Army tank formations or piloting "F-16" or "Hornet"—with a generous supply of missiles—on a mission to bomb Libya or Soviet bases in Archangelsk or Murmansk. It was a strange situation, yet nobody acknowledged this absurdity. Those who had personal computers at work (not to mention at home) were envied by many. American computer games were hugely popular and greatly enriched some people's English vocabulary.

The period between 1988 and 1989 marked yet another mini-revolution. This one was in travel abroad. The old suffocating and humiliating procedures for granting an exit visa—i.e., the certificate of loyalty approved by the local party organization and the KGB—were revoked. Suddenly, it became difficult to buy an air ticket for trips abroad. Aeroflot, the monopoly state air company, had all the flights booked for months ahead. There were lines of desperate people on waiting lists to buy a ticket on any flight departing to the United States. Another problem was how to get more dollars in excess of the strict and puny state quota for the traveler. High demands for this currency inflated the exchange rates between the ruble and the dollar that then soared from 1:10 in 1990 to 1:100 in 1991. Dollars in Russia nearly became a second currency in person-to-person deals, trades, and other financial operations.

Many Russians, not just diplomats, high-level bosses, and a handful of experts were allowed to set foot on the soil of the New World. In the late 1980s, the Soviet "invasion" of the West progressed rapidly and uncensored by the government. Russian artists began to travel abroad to sell their paintings. After the scandalous escape of Alexander Mogilny, the first Russian hockey player to join the NHL, scores of Russia's best athletes rushed to the U.S. and Canada (Fetisov 1998). It was a time when visiting the United States no longer remained an impossible dream for tens of thousands of Russians. For example, hundreds of educated, young individuals from the Soviet Union visited America for the first time through the Yurmala-Chatauqua program, a widely publicized chain of meetings. Major Soviet universities launched exchange programs and scores of professors and students began exploratory journeys in Europe and across the Atlantic Ocean. Being a prerogative of the ministry of higher education for many years, foreign exchange programs were no longer under Moscow's intrusive control: Schools began to seek their own independent links with American and other Western counterparts.

Those who had only a dim perception of the United States could now relish the skylines of New York and Boston, marvel at the lives of the rich and beautiful in Santa Barbara and Miami. Travel overseas contributed palpably to the radicalization of thinking in the new Russian elites. It even became a psychological hurdle for many Russians who traveled abroad: how to cope with the multiplicity of choices and possibilities including a "pluralism in eating" as Soviet scientist Roald Sagdeev states visiting a steak house in Washington D.C. (Eisenhower 1995). For many of them, supermarkets in New York, Helsinki, London, or Boston were not only sources of goods. For most travelers, the obvious contrast between U.S. abundance and Russian poverty produced genuine culture shock.[15] Direct comparisons of Russia and the West—as many of them repeatedly suggested—further developed the already existing belief that the Soviet system could not create such a high standard of living.

Anger at a Soviet system that could not give such wealth to its people was combined with the naïve belief that Russia would quickly ascend to Western living standards as soon as the old Soviet system was destroyed. People were not surprised to see capitalist prosperity. They knew about the "horn of plenty." Most people knew that there was a substantial difference between Russia and the United States; however, they could not imagine that the gap between the countries was not insurmountable.

Most secret institutions and previously classified corners of America became accessible to Russians. Soviet military officers traveled to U.S. bases and command-and-control facilities in fulfillment of the program of mutual on-site inspections. Their job was to verify the INF treaty and to monitor nuclear tests. Marshal Sergei Akhromeyev, Gorbachev's personal military adviser, traveled to America in the summer of 1989 and admired the professionalism and good-natured spirit of his U.S. counterparts. A young Russian journalist, Artyom Borovik, whose reports from Afghanistan made him instantaneously famous, "joined" the U.S. Army for several months and published reports in the Soviet media on the training and life of GIs. These trips and reports hugely contributed toward the collapse of the Cold War militarist mentality in Russian society. It seemed that very soon Russian and American soldiers might become buddies and shake each others' hands—just as they had done in 1945, when they met at the Elbe river in Germany.

Yeltsin Embraces Americanism

Since December 25, 1991, the date when the death certificate of the Soviet Union was issued, the Yeltsin administration began to act openly and exuberantly on its pro-American beliefs and expectations of American help. During Yeltsin's appearance at the U.S. Congress in June 1992, he gave credit to the United States and praised it for helping Russia slay the dragon of Communism. His speech was a huge success, and Yeltsin was flattered by its reception (Ryurikov 1999, 62). A vital part of the official Americanism of the Yeltsin camp was the concept of maximum liberation of market forces: the ideas of Friedrich Heyek and the Chicago School of Economics. This theory had long been in support of the pre-New Deal philosophy of the minimal role of the state in economy. Yegor Gaidar, Petr Aven, Anatoly Chubais, and a handful of other young theorists of economics who, in a matter of a few months, would rule the entire country, were captivated by these free-market ideas. For instance, Gaidar, the forthcoming acting Prime Minister of Russia, believed that the only way to revive the Russian economy—and revive it quickly—was to destroy at once the old state regulations, and replace them with monetary ones. By the end of 1991, Gaidar and his group moved from seminar auditoria straight to the halls of power.

Faith in the free market had emerged already in the last years of Gorbachev's presidency. Initially, Gorbachev began to discuss Soviet economic and financial problems with the U.S. Secretary of State, James Baker, who, as former Secretary of the Treasury in the Reagan administration, did not shy away from pushing the Soviet leader toward market solutions. In 1990, two young and ambitious American economists, Jeffrey Sachs and Robert Allison from Harvard's Business School of Economics, worked with Russian economist Grigory Yavlinsky on a program of transition to a free market in 500 days. However, to their disappointment, Gorbachev never could fully grasp free market principles. In addition, there was some psychological resentment about following the American lead. Chernyaev mentioned in his diary one of the reasons for such resentment: "Sachs in his professorial way reproduces the mainstream American perception of us: if you [Russians] do not become like us, the U.S., you would not get our dollars!" (Chernyaev 1997, 140).

During the total economic paralysis of late 1991–early 1992, the Gaidar group and Harvard advisers became extremely close—in fact, they became a single team that perceived itself to be the savior of the sinking ship of Russia. Among many remarkable features possessed by these young Russian reformers in 1991 was their urge to implement their decisions fast. Moreover, the road chosen by the new Russian rulers and their foreign advisers precluded the process of gradual learning, patient self-education, and the cautious adaptation of certain foreign recipes in the process of Russia's transformation. Therefore, the invitation of American advisers, from all kinds of think-tanks and foundations, and their immediate arrivals to their temporary Moscow headquarters, was a development in the spirit of the proposed course and pace of Russia's economic reforms. The last months of 1991 and the first half of 1992 were an amusing and extraordinary time, when any American professor of economics or even an owner of a master's degree in business administration could easily enter the most top-level offices in Russian officialdom. Unfortunately, beside the tiny group of young economists—all of them were Yeltsin's collaborators—the new rulers of Russia were abysmally ignorant in economic matters. People, who at that time occupied positions of immense power and responsibility, knew very little about the nature of the "American way" they had chosen for their country to emulate. They looked at Gaidar and his team, and particularly at foreign economic and business consultants, as disciples look at their gurus. All in all, they were very much at the mercy of their American advisers.[16]

It is noteworthy to observe—now in retrospect, of course—that many Americans, who advised Russia in the first heady months of the Yeltsin administration, came from the ranks of those who professionally specialized in the furious struggle against the Soviet Union. Most of them were from right wing, conservative, anti-Communist, and Cold War oriented institutions. Perhaps it is not an exaggeration to imply that the main criterion for the measurement of the reliability and credibility of any American institution, organization, or individual was the record of their anti-Soviet attitudes. The more anti-Communist and anti-Soviet a group or a person in the United States was, the better suited they were for the new Russia. Indeed, various specialists from the Heritage Foundation, American Enterprise Institute, Foundation for Democracy—to name a few—were having their field day in Russia.

In the twisted logic of Russian liberal reforms, the die hard anti-Soviet "hawks" turned out to be better allies than American liberals. What were the reasons for such a choice? American liberals, from a Russian standpoint, wholeheartedly supported the Brezhnev *détente* instead of suffocating Communism with a resource-draining arms race. The liberals did not seriously challenge Russian expansionism all over the world. Moreover, many American liberals and Democrats developed a relationship with the wretched Brezhnev regime that continued to systematically abuse human rights. Next, American liberals adored Gorbachev and his perestroika— something that was certain to antagonize a "true" Russian reformer of 1990, and likely most Russians. In fact, many Western experts from the left, with their search for a "third way" for Russia and an inherent antipathy toward American capitalism, were treated by Russian radicals as a waffling Quixotic bunch on the same bandwagon with Gorbachev: They were all apparent political failures!

Reliance on the West and the United States reached its peak at the same time. The disastrous economic and financial situation in Russia seemed to justify this attitude of dependency and entitlement. Gorbachev, during his last months in power in 1991, desperately waited for the magical assistance package from the World Bank and the IMF that would act as a financial launch pad for economic reforms. The United States, however, no longer believed the Soviet leader was capable of managing the situation. Therefore, Gaidar and the young reformers were determined to demonstrate to the Americans and the West that they (and only they), unlike Gorbachev, meant serious business.

Radical reformers believed that the country should get substantial credit for defeating the hydra of Communism in their home for at least three reasons. The first reason is because such a bloodless victory saved the west billions of dollars that would otherwise have been spent on the arms race. As happened after World War II, when the United States assisted both Germany and Japan to become democratic and prosperous, post–Cold War Russia also expected to receive a generous, helpful, hand from the United States (Malashenko October 1999).[17] Second, because the return of Communists and nationalists would turn out to be more costly to the West than the scares of the Cold War, the West should secure its own safety by investing in Russian capitalism. Third, Russia's economic collapse—in the event that urgent help was not delivered to Russia—would cause a crisis of global proportions. The West, it was believed, had to realize that there was only one alternative to a Russia that was economically strong, democratic, and friendly: a Russia that was strong in terms of nuclear warheads and either totalitarian or mafia-bureaucratic (Kozyrev 1992).

Overall, the pro-Americanism of Yeltsin's supporters was based on specific material reasons. They expected that a massive program of economic assistance, similar to the Marshall Plan, would be provided to a new democratic Russia. Even such cautious experts as Arbatov (1992), who was an advocate of U.S.-Russian rapprochement, while holding critical views about the United States, suggested that he would welcome a thorough examination of the Russian economic situation by the United States. Reasons? Americans knew better what needs an urgent repair in the economy. American help would also be needed in reorganizing key Russian economic sectors: food production and its distribution, energy use and conservation, and the conversion of defense industry.

An "America First" Foreign Policy

What was happening with Russia's foreign policy? Preaching the concept of Russia's dependence on someone else in philosophical terms required a gifted personality at the head of the Foreign Ministry. Andrei Kozyrev became such an individual. In Yeltsin's picturesque entourage, Kozyrev was the most natural and persistent Westernizer of all. He was born in Brussels to a family of Soviet diplomats and spent many days of his youth in the West. He was educated, had good manners, fine language skills, important social connections, and a healthy dose of confidence—an erudite and liberal-minded young man who contrasted the stereotypical image of the "Mr. Nyet" of Soviet-era diplomacy.

Kozyrev turned out to be "Mr. Yes" in many respects. When he took the reins of Moscow's foreign policy, he had no practical experience for this particular job. Because many senior Soviet diplomats were compromised by their ambiguous behavior during the coup, Kozyrev preferred not to seek advice from the ex-Soviet foreign service. Instead he turned to American colleagues for counsel and guidance. He did everything, in words and acts, to win the trust of Washington's policy makers.

Kozyrev's public statements and interviews reflected the consensus among the Yeltsinites. The most important task of Russian foreign policy was to become friends and partners of the United States. And how could it be otherwise? Russia's rebirth as a free and democratic country was necessarily linked to the creation of an effective market economy. To achieve these goals—and this was how the new rulers in the Kremlin perceived the situation—Russia needed official membership in the Western community. And the United States was the only power that could introduce Russia to the community where she should belonged. "The West is a natural ally of Russia," stated Russia's foreign minister in 1992 (*Izvestia,* 16 January).

The Yeltsin team—despite the fact that it helped more than anybody to destroy the Soviet Union—continued to espouse a great-power mentality and sense of national pride. But Yeltsin and his advisers felt that dependence from the United States was a necessary policy. Their attitude was summarized by the Russian Ambassador to Washington, Vladimir Lukin, formerly a leading researcher from the Institute for the United States and Canada Studies. "Just name us a 'great power,' for God's sake," he said, "then you can do whatever you like" (Simes 1999, 212). As Gorbachev did before them, the Yeltsinites firmly believed that the restoration of Russia, as a strong and democratic country, had to be the highest strategic priority of the United States. Gaidar wrote in his memoirs: "Strategically at that time the West had no task more important than to help [the Yeltsin government] to overcome this chaos as soon as possible, to create the foundation for restoration of functioning state institutions, to provide the capacity for the economic stabilization." The West, in his view, had no other alternative. "The question was being answered: What would emerge on the rubble of the socialist empire? Would it be something ugly, economically and political unstable, the source of constant threat to peace—or the commonwealth of young and growing market democracies that could become an engine accelerating global economic growth in the twenty-first century, and a reliable strategic partner of the West?" (Gaidar 1997, 180).

Unfortunately, such optimistic hopes of the new Russian leadership were based on even weaker grounds than the aspirations articulated by Gorbachev at Malta's summit. Despite all the confident statements made by the reformers, Russia of 1992 was indeed a poor and begging neighbor located at the border of a strong, stable, and prosperous West. Nobody in a "realist" cast of mind could ever imagine how a country such as Russia could carry out its foreign policy in a manner as predictable and efficient as the policy of the United States.

There were other important, underlying assumptions that fed the euphoric expectations of Yeltsin, Kozyrev, and other early architects and participants of Russian foreign policy. One was the sharp distinction that they drew between the old Soviet Union and a new Russia. They never tired of emphasizing that Russia liberated itself from the Soviet Union just as the other Soviet republics had. They believed that the end of the Cold War and the demise of the Soviet Union was a win-win situation for both Russia and the United States. Therefore, no nation should claim victory in such a chain of historic developments. Besides, the actual outcome of the peaceful ending of the Cold War was beneficial to all: the unification of Germany, the end of the bipolar confrontation, the breakup of the huge military Warsaw bloc and the totalitarian empire that glued that bloc together. Finally, Russia and the United States—like sparring partners after a boxing match—should walk out of the ring holding hands after a declared tie.

The official enemy-image, once a staple of the Soviet mentality, almost disappeared by 1992. Russia's Foreign Minister spoke about the necessity to convert the super-armed and heavily-manned military into smaller, mobile, rapid-deployment forces that served on a contractual basis. He ridiculed those in Russia who could not surrender the image of an enemy. He called their anti-American feelings an infantile disorder (Kozyrev 1992). NATO, in the cautious opinion of the Russian minister, would transform into a mechanism for consolidating the Western democracies. This organization will never expand eastward, or if it does, the bloc would embrace Russia as a full member (Kozyrev 1995).

Another underlying assumption supporting the new Russia's foreign policy was the vision of a multi-polar world, not a world of American hegemony. Moscow experts became self-assured that not only bipolarity, but also a hegemony by one superpower would become anachronistic in the new interdependent world. Some of them even theorized why "unipolar world hegemony" would become an antiquated concept. First, American public opinion would not support the military hawks' aspirations. Driven by electoral concerns, any incumbent U.S. president would abandon such unpopular hegemonic ideas. Second, the world hegemony of one country would be difficult to justify. Indeed, if there were no enemy overseas, why should a nation be so preoccupied with power? Third, any superpower would face an increasing risk of resistance from other countries, a prospect that is not acceptable in a contemporary world. Fourth, world domination is a waste of money and human resources. To put it simply, it is too costly (Arbatov 1992).

Finally, there was an assumption that military power and the use of force in international relations had become an outdated phenomenon, the relic of an ugly past. There was a wide-spread and understandable post-Soviet aversion to the use of military force. In 1992, Yeltsin-Kozyrev foreign policy stressed a "new global order" of developed nations based on consensus and partnership. Disputed issues would be resolved through negotiations and compromise. Military force would be used strictly within the framework of international law (Kozyrev 1992).

Russian foreign policy of that period was a highly romanticized liberal utopia. Kozyrev's "Mr. Yes" personality was later criticized by many as that of an enthusiastic teenager looking up to his adult guardian, the U.S. State Department (Simes 1999, 213). However, this policy did not end soon. In fact, it lasted for almost four years.

Great Expectations

In 1988, the well-known liberal Russian economist, Nikolai Shmelev, criticized his fellow scientists for their endless theoretical discussions about the Russian economy: "We are fed up with all these 'isms.' The main thing [is]—to have sausage on the shelves!" (Gorbachev-Mlynar 1994, 69). This "give-me-something" reasoning could be found in the depth of the consciousness among millions of Russians who never could grasp the ideological clichés of official Communist propaganda. According to two Russian experts who analyzed letters sent by people to the editors of Soviet journals between 1987 and 1991, "from the kingdom of the golden devil the West transformed itself [in the minds of people] into the world where most any of the fantastic dreams of the *ex-Homo Sovieticus* could come true" (Zakharov and Kozlova 1993, 81).

The media revolution played a remarkable role in the reversal of public expectations. In late 1991, the Russian television and press became relatively independent from direct governmental control and inundated the country with advertising styled after Western examples. This new media, specifically the journalists and TV broadcasters, were now hasty to forget about the years of conformism and nauseating propaganda: They bashed Communism and the banned Communist Party. At the same time they demonstrated at every opportunity that they had democratic liberal credentials and behaved as if Russia had always been part of the "civilized" West. As the Soviet Union fell apart and the Soviet economy plunged into catastrophe, the media began to prepare the population for a giant quantum leap toward market capitalism.

During 1992, the media never wavered in its uncritical support of "shock therapy" and conveyed almost unconditional pro-American and pro-Western attitudes. The leading *Argumenty I Facty* weekly newspaper published 54 articles about the United States, its culture, traditions, and people. Thirty-two (59 percent) contained clearly sympathetic and positive information about U.S. policies, business, and domestic situations. Seventeen (32 percent) were gossip stories and reports about American celebrities. Only 5 stories (9 percent) were critical, covering some social problems in the United States. More importantly, American soap operas blended nicely with Russian television programs. Writers and poets, artists, choreographers, even music conductors appeared daily inviting all to invest their money in new, unprecedented opportunities. An obscure actor, Lyonia Golubkov, hit the jackpot, when he was featured in a series of advertising snippets about a man "like all of us," who began to save money as an investor in a mutual fund. The viewers watched, transfixed, as Lyonia's drab apartment transformed into a first-class loft; then he became surrounded by attractive women, drove a nice car, etc. As the culmination of the series, Lyonia was on his way toward the United States as a wealthy tourist.

One important and often overlooked factor that advanced a pro-American sentiment among Russian people was the so-called *Sovok complex,* a psychological syndrome of inadequacy, haplessness, laziness, and lack of culture.[18] Russians could attach this label to anything "Soviet" or "socialist" that resembled the days of the Soviet Union[19] and people's overall dependency on the state. This was an attitude of dependence with crippling laziness, lack of initiative, and—at the same time—aggressive urges to "grab the biggest piece" of anything available. Frequently mentioned in newspaper editorials and reports, in research monographs (Gozman and Edkind 1992; Lowenhardt 1995, 6), mentioned by politicians (Burbulis 1992, *Argumenty I Facty,* 31, 2)—*Sovok* represents something distasteful, primitive, and provincial in Soviet or Russian life in general, and subsequently, in Russian character.

How was this unfavorable self-depiction related to the vision of the United States? It is likely that people idealized America and Americans—among many other reasons—as something and somebody opposite to *Sovok*. The idealized American individual was perceived as a brilliant decision-maker, reliable and trustworthy, and, at the same time, generous and grateful (see, for example, Kozlov 1998). Therefore, the psychological, imaginary links between Russians and Americans could have provided, in some individuals, a self-gratifying feeling of defeating an embarrassing syndrome inherited from the old system. In other words, certain pro-Americanism could have appeared as a "by product" of a specific motivational force that underlined an optimistic spectrum of Russian public opinion in the late 1980s and early 1990s. The American image became a convenient model that signified the legitimacy of a belief in rebirth, improvement, and self-actualization.

Pro-American euphoria was produced both by the romanticism of Gorbachev's new thinking and the reflections developed after the bloodless victory over the Communist regime. Above all, however, such optimism was induced by unrealistic expectations of "becoming the West" overnight. In the long term, the newly emerged Russian elites, as well as many ordinary people, could not escape severe forthcoming economic, social, and psychological problems. In time, it became clear that there were no easy solutions to these problems, and that the radical policies of "shock therapy" only aggravated a deep systemic crisis in Russia. In the time of an unavoidable social hangover, new frustrations, old suspicious, and even hostile attitudes toward the United States were bound to come to the surface. The pendulum swung too far in one direction—it was only a matter of time before it swung back.

Chapter Three

Russia in Great Depression

American leadership, official and private consultants, have been deeply involved in the implementation of Russian economic reforms. They arrogantly assumed a large part of responsibility for radical transformations of the thousand-year-old way of life of a giant country. This preordained that failures and excesses of reforms would be perceived in Russia as linked with American participation, and this would inevitably reflect itself upon foreign relations with the United States.

Alexei Arbatov, member of the liberal "Yabloko" party
and head of the Defense Committee of the Duma.

I ndividual frustration is a potent catalyst of human behavior. Caused by the devastating economic situation and further aggravated by societal turmoil, the human emotion of acute dissatisfaction becomes a powerful motivational force in history. When millions of individual aggravations amass, they may create the motivational background for great evil. One such case in the twentieth century became known as the "Weimar Syndrome" in Germany. Mass public frustration that grew as a reaction to the devastating policies of a weak republican regime led to the meteoric rise of Adolf Hitler and his National Socialist Workers' Party.

This and other much-studied cases of amazingly rapid transitions from an unstable democracy to the depth of darkest totalitarianism reveal how people's frustration over soaring inflation, unemployment, rampant crime, and other domestic problems lead to the search for external targets or "scapegoats." Political psychology identifies at least two types of such external targets. The first cluster is comprised of a people's closest neighbors, with whom they may already have a long history of rivalry, prejudice, and hostility. The other type is a 'remote' but salient entity—it can be a country, ethnic, or religious group—that somehow gets associated in people's minds with the cause of their misery or a contributing factor to their problems (Koenigsberg 1992; Gozman and Edkind 1992; Volkan 1988; Erikson 1950; Adorno et al. 1950).[1] For example, in Nazi Germany, such scapegoats were Jews, then the "Judeo-Bolshevist" Soviet Union, and the "decadent" democracies of the West.

The crumbling of the Soviet Union in 1991 and the birth of a new, ideologically free, but politically weak and fractured Russian republic, caused many analysts talk about "Weimar Russia" (Yuriev 1992). Newspaper editorials relentlessly entertained this theme. As the authors can testify, conversations and provocative rumors on this subject began to circulate among the Soviet intellectuals in both capitals—Moscow and Leningrad—by 1990, when the vision of overwhelming national chaos became apparent. One of the authors remembers how his colleagues at the United States and Canada Institute in Moscow asked each other anxiously: "What do you know about Weimar syndrome? Could it happen to us?" In the same year, the prestigious literary journal *Novy Mir* published an anti-utopian novel "Non-Returnee" [*Nevozvraschenets*]. The author, Alexander Kabakov, depicted in dismally graphic terms the state of anarchy in Moscow and a triumphant general who entered the Kremlin in a tank.

For optimistic pro-Western minds, any discussion about a collapse sounded like a misplaced prophecy in a time of hope and optimism associated with the transition to a market economy and a democratic government. However, in 1992, the "shock therapy" implemented by the Russian government failed to achieve immediate reinvigoration of the economy, and the prices after the ending of state regulation rose four times in three months—instead of the promised 150–200 percent. Prices continued to climb with no end in sight. The government of Yegor Gaidar prevented hyperinflation by the summer of that year only by freezing most of the payments, including salaries and wages, and by lifting most of the state subsidies to the regions and industries. However, when, in the fall, the State Bank resumed some of the payments on the arrears, the beast of hyperinflation returned (Gaidar 1997). The promised rapid recovery turned out to be the longest depression in modern Russian history.

The gruesome social and economic situation in the country, aggravated by the economic reforms of the early 1990s—the miserable living standards of the vast majority of the population, corruption, organized crime, and inflation—caused deep societal frustration. The euphoria of liberation and the hopes of new opportunities, so pronounced at first, were bound to subside. Disappointment, unfulfilled dreams, and low social and political efficacy were becoming the dominant features of Russian popular sentiment and behavior. The government of reformers, widely called "the Democrats," quickly became the perceived cause of popular frustration. For many Russians, baby-faced Russian Premier Yegor Gaidar and the emotionless, red-haired Anatoly Chubais became genuine objects of hatred. As for a "remote scapegoat," the ready-made candidate for this role was the United States. In 1993, most sensitive American observers began to detect anti-American sentiments in their communications with Russians (Simes 1999, 213). In conversations behind the Americans' backs these sentiments appeared even earlier.

Throughout the second half of the twentieth century, America has been an object of admiration and hope for people in many societies around the world. It has also been a source of irritation and resentment (for a comparative analysis of anti-Americanism, see Thornton 1988). For example, in post–World War II Western Europe, and particularly in France, anti-Americanism was thriving. As one author noted, "the French, intellectuals especially, resented the very fact that they had been liberated by the Americans, resented their humiliated postwar status, and more particularly the need to go cap in hand to Washington for assistance with French reconstruction" (Judt 1992, 195). Tides and outbursts of anti-Americanism took place in China and Cuba in the early 1960s, some European countries during the Vietnam War, Iran during the anti-Shah revolution of the 1970s, Jordan and Syria during the airstrikes against Iraq in the 1990s, Indonesia in 1999, and many other parts of the world. Although such manifestations of anti-Americanism were caused by many dissimilar reasons, one of the most important contributing factors in these and many other cases were people's overall unhappiness with domestic developments and frustration over their lives in general.

In order to better understand the nature of contemporary anti-Americanism in Russia, let us examine briefly some political-psychological aspects of the Russian transformation.

The Aftermath of Shock Therapy

Yeltsin's government pushed rapid economic reforms without sufficient preparation and modification to Russia's social institutions (Melville 1999; Abalkin 1995; Shlapentokh 1996). Economic reforms launched in the early 1990s were not reinforced socially or politically.[2] The painful consequences of these changes fell upon the socially unprotected population. The fabric of Russian society went through a major stress test and the figures that reflect Russia's appalling difficulties speak for themselves. One major societal indicator—life expectancy—dropped from 67 years in 1994 to 57 years for men, and from 76 to 70 for women. From 1992–1997, the death rate in Russia was 4 million higher than the birth rate. Moreover, the birth rate continuously dropped. By the end of the 1990s, there were 3.7 million fewer children in Russia than there were in 1990. The number of suicides in the country is twice that of late 1980s, and reached the 60,000-per-year mark. For one of every 100 live births in Russia, there were 180 abortions performed (all data from Russian State Duma 1999). Russia's health-care system further deteriorated and was in dire straits. In the mid-1990s, the United States' taxpayer, for instance, contributed 2,700 dollars per person per year to health care. In the same period, the Russian government was spending only 9 dollars per person per year (*Argumenty I Facty,* No. 8, 5 February 1996). Many diseases that almost vanished during the Soviet years, such as tuberculosis or diphtheria, were back on a massive scale (Malashenko October 1999). The overall population of the country decreased by several million, despite the influx of over 4 million refugees from other areas of the former U.S.S.R. This was the worst depopulation of Russia since the Second World War (Ryurikov 1999, 21–22).

As a direct result of the reforms, main Russian industries were divided up among a few powerful clans who effectively gained control over key Russian economic industries and communication networks. The privatization of the raw material industries—the few enterprises in Russia that could generate hard-currency flow—created a class of extremely wealthy individuals who accumulated their wealth mainly through corruption, using their status, or both (Hough 1999). According to estimations of leading Russian and Russian-speaking oppositional politicians, journalists, and experts, the government in the country was a loose coalition of corrupt governmental bureaucrats, businesses, and criminal organizations. They virtually took control of Russia's society, as official state structures disintegrated and became increasingly inept (Melville 1999; Yavlinsky 6 June 1996; Zhirinovsky 22 May 1996; Shlapentokh 1996).

The standard of living of the vast majority of Russians—despite growing availability of products and services—was extremely low and continued to stagnate despite numerous and optimistic government forecasts. From 1992–1995, as a consequence of the economic reforms launched exclusively according to the plans of a few individuals in Kremlin,[3] the GDP went down 49 percent; real income fell 29 percent, and inflation was up 650 percent. More than half of all Russians in 1995 reported that they did not have any savings kept in a bank (CISS Index to International Public Opinion, 1995–96). Monthly per capita income in 1995 was 62 dollars, a bit more than the 40 dollars average in 1979. However, the comparison may be misleading, because in the 1970s, prices on basic goods and services were state-subsidized and fixed. Only about 50 percent of the average income was spent on food. In the 1990s, however, the amount of money spent on groceries was close to 90 percent (Shiraev 1999a).

Social inequality in the nation grew as rapidly as did new enterprises. Although the estimated number of the poor in Russia varies, the State Duma assessed their total in 1999 at 34 million—an amount 14 times higher than it was in 1990. During the initial two-year period between 1991 and 1993, the already-wide income gap between the richest 10 percent and the poorest 10 percent tripled. Overall, by the mid-1990s, the distribution of main resources among a select few groups of individuals in Russia was virtually complete (Bivens 1999; Rivera 1995, 65). At the same time, the period after 1993 can be flagged as the beginning of disillusionment with the free market and democracy—two grand pillars of pro-Americanism in Russia. America was rapidly losing its appeal among those in Russia who were optimistic and euphoric about this country and its policies just a few years earlier.

An optimist could argue that Russia's societal transformations have conceivably enhanced people's capacity to have a voice in political affairs, greater interest in political life, and a growing sense of control about the future. In fact, in the years of Gorbachev's liberalization (between 1988 and 1991), there seemed to be substantial progress in the search for an effective way for people to have their opinions heard at the top—not only through elections, but also through public demonstrations, petitions, campaigns of protest, and the like. There were powerful environmental and human-rights movements on the local level that made city mayors and regional party secretaries tremble. The level of political participation grew among the urban middle class (Yuriev 1992). Nevertheless, a few years later, a reversed trend toward increased political apathy and pessimism spread and the level of direct political participation plummeted.

Attitudes of indifference and depression stemmed directly from the range of unfulfilled expectations and hopes that enchanted Russians at the time of the Soviet Union's collapse. People wanted a new and prosperous life and they were often promised one by their leaders and popular experts (Gurevich 1987). This trend of disillusionment is confirmed in a number of surveys (for review see, Shiraev 1999; Wyman 1997; Grushin 1994). For example, a poll taken in 1995 showed that respondents who were not satisfied with their lives outnumbered those satisfied by a ratio of 8:1 (*Segodnia*, 2 August 1995). Only 13 percent of the people in Russia looked to their future with optimism (Shlapentokh 1996). More than half of the respondents thought it would be irresponsible to have children with the future so uncertain (*Argumenty I Facty*, No. 18, 1992, survey by Sluzhba VP). General pessimism about the future may stem from feelings of low confidence in the ability of people to control their present (Gozman and Edkind 1992; Yuriev

1992). In the media, the reflections of people's pessimism and disappointment became mixed with continuous mockery and an ironic, sarcastic depiction of reality. [4]Common in the media became the theme of inevitable disasters and overwhelming social cataclysms (Shakhnazarov 1996; Grushin 8 October 1994).

In the avant-garde of criticism were, predictably, the leaders of the political opposition to the Yeltsin administration. One such voice, the leader of the liberal Yabloko party, Grigory Yavlinsky, called the Russian social situation during the transformation "the senile dementia of extreme poverty that presses heavily upon every man" (Yavlinsky 6 June 1996). With the exception of a few periodicals loyal to Yeltsin, newspapers blamed the reformers in the Kremlin for the "misery of millions of Russians," accusing them of committing "robbery against our national pride," describing the reforms as a "national catastrophe" and the "destruction, rape, deception, betrayal" of the country. Trust in government institutions, after a brief rise in 1989–1990, spiraled down again in the 1990s (Wyman 1997, 63–73; 125–27). [5]

It is true that the old Soviet paternalistic legacy still held many Russians in its grip. It was very hard for many people—especially for the older generation—to act on their own and live without expecting to being taken care of by the state, trade unions, and local government offices. While younger people took their new life chances with relish, ambition, and energy, older generations felt uncertainty about a new life. Unable to cope with rapidly changing social conditions, many of them readily embraced nostalgic ideas as a convenient safety blanket. America, as a principal supporter of the painful Russian transition and, in a way, an intrusive foreign advocate of the change, did not evoke positive feelings of optimism and gratitude in the minds of these Russian citizens (Chuprov and Zubok 1996; Shiraev 1999a).

At the same time, not only older and paternalistic-minded Russians suffered from these changes. Those who were willing and able to work under new conditions, soon discovered that the promised prosperity did not come through hard and honest work. The privatization unleashed by the Kremlin reformers went on without established rules. Soon, the absence of fair regulation became the main feature of Russian business life in general. The impudence of the new Russian rich, the virtual impossibility for smaller business to work without threats, extortions, and bribes, the lack of any legal defense for employees—all these conditions led to the predictable popular belief that freedom could engender the enrichment of a few, but not a decent life, democracy, and civil liberties for the rest. "We idealized freedom. We thought of freedom of speech as the key to prosperity," wrote Russian poet Yevgeny Yevtushenko about those times (1993). Beside freedom of speech, Russia needed institutions, legislation, and implementation of the law. There was a grievous lack of these structures, and no systematic effort by the government to deal with this situation.

The Marshall Plan that Never Came

The United States did not make a systematic effort to help Russia. The first priority of the Bush administration was the safety of Soviet nuclear arsenals and their non-proliferation. Most of the rest, including economic assistance and advice on how to run businesses and build new institutions, the administration left for private companies, non-government institutions, philanthropic foundations, and individuals to manage.

Yegor Gaidar, the head of the first Russian government under Yeltsin, recalls that his cabinet of ministers was preoccupied with two urgent tasks: how to make money work and how to eke out an existence until the next harvest in the fall. Moreover, any talks with the United States were suddenly complicated by the presence of many political and financial obstacles. Deputy Secretary of the Treasury, David Menford, even threatened Gaidar: If the Russian side did not recognize all the financial commitments of the U.S.S.R.—the United States would halt shipments of grain to Russian ports. In response, Gaidar writes, he promised to appeal over the heads of Western governments directly to Western public opinion (Gaidar 1997, 138). At last, after much haggling, the Russian government agreed to continue servicing Soviet debts. Grain export from the United States continued. Gaidar complained later that, at that time, the West "lacked a leader capable of fulfilling an organizing, coordinating role similar to the roles that H. Truman and G. Marshall played in the reconstruction of post-war Europe." He made some predictions about Russian-Western relations: "Much depended on how the West would behave: whether it would believe in the seriousness of Russian reforms, whether it would be able to size up their prospects not from the angle of an accountant, but from the viewpoint of social and political strategy" (181; 143–144).

The White House did not come up with such a strategy. In 1989, when epochal changes in Eastern Europe and the Soviet Union began, President George Bush's actions were seriously limited by the domestic budget deficit. He staunchly refused to borrow money in order to invest in the emerging post-Communist regimes. It was not only a question of fiscal conservatism, but one of classic political prudence: Bush, Baker, their advisers, and analysts never seriously considered any "Marshall Plans" for Eastern Europe or Russia. The lack of proper institutions and structures there, they reasoned, would doom any assistance to become a waste (Scowcroft 1999; Zoellick 2000). Instead of lobbying for the appropriation of massive governmental funds, Bush appealed to private foundations to fill the gap and help post-Communist regimes to create institutions of civil society. However, foundations and wealthy individuals like George Soros were not adequate substitutes for the role of the government.

Meanwhile, in retrospect, it is still striking to speculate how popular a large-scale "Russian initiative" could have been in the United States. The American public, to a great extent, was moved by the plight of its former enemy. Journalists' depressing personal reports and graphic images of empty store shelves and sad-looking old women selling wool socks at the edge of huge snow piles were compelling enough to make many people in the United States commiserate with an ailing Russia. In 1992, Russian consulate officials in San Francisco told us that certain compassionate individuals were offering to send small shipments of food baskets or warm clothes to the starving people of the former Evil Empire. The diplomats graciously declined the offers, arguing that no one was starving in Russia. Meanwhile, some help was delivered. Airlifted shipments of ham, chicken legs, and crackers were broadly advertised as crucial assistance to the poor, hungry nation. Unfortunately, it was not up to the scale of the situation. Another kind of help from America was expected in Russia.

Perhaps the Bush administration made correct assessments about what was needed in Russia from a capitalist, economic viewpoint. Nonetheless, in psychological terms, the absence of a large-scale rescue-like initiative proved to be a political mistake. Older Russians still recalled that back in 1942–1943 the United States, instead of opening "the second front" in Europe, sent to Russia—in these people's perception—only canned food. Now, in 1992, instead of a big initiative to boost the morale of the nation that rejected and defeated Communism, the Americans were sending chicken legs. People in Moscow began to call these shipments, with a tinge of irony, "Bush's legs." They were as thin and small as the pillars of American policy toward Russia.

Russian reforming liberals had to face reality: There were no massive financial and technological infusions coming from the United States. The amounts and favorable consequences of the anticipated monetary assistance from the West fell short of even the most conservative expectations by the most cautious experts (Pushkov 1995). The amount of American assistance to Russia was about one billion dollars during 1992–1994, and only gradually, when the speculative financial boom started, began to climb (only to plummet in August 1998). Overall, it amounted to ten billion dollars overall from 1992–1998 (Krasnow 1999), and was far from what Russia had counted on. Assuming that the whole ten billion dollars went directly to the Russian people, one can calculate that over the six-year period, each Russian individual received about 70 dollars in American aid.[6]

Continuous failures on the domestic front, coupled with many unfulfilled expectations about the West had a sobering effect on those who counted on the new Western would-be allies. Disappearing mirages of massive American and European assistance put Russian leaders in a frustrating predicament later when it became clear to them that the help would not materialize in the future. Gradually, it dawned upon Russian liberals that the Russian economy needed to rely only on its own resources.

In the eyes of millions of Russians, the West flinched from its initial interest—and maybe it did not have such an interest in the first place—to help develop Russia into a strong and independent country. America, according to the views of the growing number of opinion-makers in Russia, wanted to keep their country weak, confined within its territory, and without the right to extend its influence to the other ex-Soviet republics (Zyuganov 1995; Barkashov 1994). Among many opposition leaders, who converged their criticism, there was a strong belief that the United States was the country that benefited most from the collapse of the U.S.S.R. During the 1990s, the left-wing and nationalist opposition's politicians constantly blamed America for attempts to keep Russia away from "honest" economic competition (Lebed 13 May 1996), refusal to give Russia most favored nation trade status, and, as it was already mentioned, provide any real financial help. Moreover, a special mode of anti-American perception was further crystallizing: The powerful and rich America was witnessing Russia's devastating downfall; nevertheless, America did not help when its government had all the means and power to do so. America did not spend a pinch of its resources or power to give Russia a hand.

In Search of a Scapegoat

An angry person is less likely to look for a peaceful settlement of conflict. By the mid-1990s, the language of angry Cold War assertions about America was back in the media and interviews with opinion-makers. "It is utterly incomprehensible where it comes from, this aggressive, servile anti-Americanism that prompts journalists to present the public with a grossly distorted, vulgar picture of events," wrote a concerned Russian journalist (Abarinov 1996c).

Students of political psychology testify that individual or public discontent may arise not only from objective conditions, but also from the subjective feelings of being blocked, deprived, or mistreated by others. According to the relative deprivation theory, an individual may develop negative feelings toward a group of people when they have something that this individual does not, but feels that he or she is entitled to have (Bernstein and Crosby, 1980). The individual may also develop frustration upon realizing that his or her group (ethnic, religious, or professional) is not gaining as fast as other groups do (Sears 1996). Such frustration often causes prejudice, which is often viewed as an act of displaced aggression (Dollard 1939). The displacement occurs when the frustrated individual is not able to eliminate the source of his aggravation. This person may look for somebody against whom to blame or vent frustration. Furthermore, such a search may become a form of psychological obsession and be used to engage other frustrated individuals. Overall, the real source of frustration is not eliminated. Instead, people begin to fight against "windmills" (Shiraev and Tsytsarev, 1995).

As soon as an enemy-image is created, people may try to look for further justification of their feelings and actions. Cognitive theories of cross-national prejudice imply that people tend to form convenient patterns of perception and they are reluctant to change these patterns. Furthermore, this process of categorization allows people to classify, or even pigeonhole other people and entire nations into groups. Having an "enemy"—even though the enemy may exist only in their imaginations—may help some individuals to boost their own self-esteem (Tajfel 1982).

Despite a popular belief that aggression eases hostility and plays a psychotherapeutic role in conflict, it has been found that aggression often leads to a feeling of disrespect for the victim of aggression or prejudice. Why does this happen? When a person does something harmful to another individual, it sets the aggressor's cognitive processes in motion toward justifying that act of aggression. A good way for some people to justify an angry reaction is to make a nasty evaluation of the victim. "They deserved the bad thing that happened to them because they are terrible human beings" (Levy 1997; Aronson 1995).

In this light, it is plausible to see why the growth of frustration with the United States was caused, in part, by the powerful self-fulfilling beliefs about mistreatment, abuse, and deception committed by Washington and people associated with America. "Our country is suffering because she was put down on her knees by the enemy." This theme, manipulated by European Nazis and Fascists in the 1920s and 30s, reappeared in the Russia of the 1990s. Political opposition did not hesitate much and expressed very negative opinions about foreign intentions in Russia: "There are forces in the West who are willing to finish us off while we are almost bedridden. . . ." (Zyuganov 13 June 1996). Newspaper headlines, like "Licking Uncle Sam's Boots" (*Narodnaya Pravda,* 3 January 1993) were common in the Communist and ultra-nationalist press. Pro-government newspapers, even though they were more restrained in their expression of disappointment, conveyed the same anti-Western and anti-American mood. *Rossyiskaya Gazeta,* for example, used a set of dry statistical arguments to convey an angry message. It published a table entitled:"What do they feed us with from abroad?"The table displays that among 407,000 ton of poultry shipped to Russia from the West, 39 percent was spoiled or arrived after the expiration date. Likewise, 50 percent of imported meat, 60 percent of tea, 67 percent of alcoholic beverages, and 86 percent of children's food was not acceptable for consumption (2 June 1995).[7] More often, mass-circulation, mainstream newspapers published articles about the U.S. failure to provide economic assistance to the country—even in popular moderate newspapers, the articles started to resemble diatribes (*Argumenty I Facty,* No. 2–3, 1994).

Georgy Arbatov, a long-term student of Russian foreign politics, made a cautious prediction in 1992 about the possible linkages between Russia's continuous economic failures and social disappointment with the reforms on one side, and the rampant growth of anti-Americanism within the society on the other. He called Western and American economic assistance to Russia a matter of urgency. He implied that more economic failures would certainly discredit the Russian government in Moscow and would undermine its political strength among voters. However, in his view, a massive economic malfunction would also discredit the United States. He referred to the growing "grumbling" among Russian people that the West was trying to turn Russia into a banana republic, poor and deindustrialized. At that time, Arbatov called these and similar assumptions about the destructive role of anti-Western paranoia. However, he did not rule out the idea that such paranoid ideas could one day dominate Russian public and elite opinion (Arbatov 1992). Very few people, including Grigory Arbatov himself, perhaps, anticipated how accurate his predictions would turn out to be.

Down with Advisers!

It is easy to give advice when one side appears to be wise and victorious and the other plays the role of a polite student. Unfortunately, the Russian side was increasingly reluctant to be such a gracious student. The role American advisers played in the development of the Russian transformation—and more importantly, the unfavorable perceptions of their roles in Russia and by Russians—contributed to the already faltering image of America and its policies.

The irritation caused by American "helpers" in Russia had been accumulating since the beginning of the 1990s. It peaked right after the financial crash of August 1998, a crisis that had a profoundly sobering effect on the entire Russian society (see Chapter 6). Seemingly omnipotent financial corporations and banks collapsed like houses of cards. With the final departure of packs of frustrated foreign investors, the last hopes for foreign help faded. Communists and nationalists screamed their lungs out about America's perfidy and an international plot implemented against the struggling country by foreign governments and international corporations. Even moderate commentators were singing the same tune and maintained the view that Russia's difficulties were self-inflicted by the Russian "Reaganomics" copied from the United States. Never mind that both denationalization and privatization were economic policies implemented by Russians. These plans were enthusiastically recommended and even forced upon Russia by leading American experts. As an unfortunate result, the policy based on these outrageous plans brought the incipient Russian democracy and society to the brink of a major disaster. [8]

The perceived arrogance of American "teachers," and their "our-way-or-the-highway" approach caused serious and unpleasant resonance among the vast majority of Russians, including policy observers and opinion leaders. In short, Russians clearly showed that they did not like to be lectured on right and wrong behavior, especially when the lecturers failed to make a positive change in people's lives. Moreover—in the eyes of many people—the mentors from overseas made their lives worse. An illustration of what Russians could hardly tolerate in America's attitudes toward their homeland may be taken from a statement made by Sam Gejdenson, a Democratic Representative from Connecticut, during the Congressional hearings in 1999. He said, for example, and this was quoted by the Russian media, "We should have a policy that both engages Russia and provides penalties when they fail to live up to the agreements that we bring to them." Such a mandatory course of action preached by one side is exactly what Russians tried to avoid and resist (Wilson 1999). Yeltsin's infamous "son-of-a-bitch" reaction at the Istanbul summit, after President Clinton suggested that Russians should be grateful for America's role in saving Russian democracy in 1991—is just one vivid example that the Russians were frustrated with lectures on the definition of good behavior and what Russia and Russians should do.[9] Anti-American rhetoric in such cases stems from a distorted self-image. This image is based on the denial of one's own shortcomings, and helps people find a reason to explain the cause of their difficulties.

Russians have an old saying: "Entering someone's cloister, avoid preaching your own faith." Expressing a unique combination of ideological fervor on one side, and expert arrogance on the other, American advisers were no longer perceived as saviors, but rather as unwelcome guests who dictated new rules of behavior to their hosts. There is little doubt that only good intentions—and of course, generous honoraria—led many American specialists into the Russian land. The problem with the Russians themselves at the helm at that time was rather non-linear: They rejected the old rules of the Communist past and did not know themselves how they wanted to live. The point is, they also did not want to be taught about their own lives.

Frustration over the role of the United States in the failing Russian transformation was growing among even the most pro-American group of Moscow's well-connected and liberal opinion leaders. While recognizing their own mistakes in the initial phases of Russia's transformation, they found it much more rewarding psychologically to share this blame with America. As the most committed defenders of the pro-Western course, they felt abandoned and betrayed by the United States and its consultants. A leading Russian expert and a member of the Yabloko party, Alexei Arbatov, summarized the overall situation with the U.S. mentors and their role in Russia's economic reforms. "American leadership," he wrote, "official and private consultants, have been deeply involved in the implementation of Russian economic reforms. They arrogantly assumed a large part of the responsibility for radical transformations of the thousand-year-old way of life of a giant country. This preordained that failures and excesses of reforms would be perceived in Russia as linked with American participation, and this would inevitably reflect itself upon foreign relations with the United States" (Arbatov 1998, 6, 8). Director of the Institute for the United States and Canada, Sergei Rogov, intoned that after the collapse of the Soviet Union, Washington took the role of an economic and political mentor for Moscow upon itself. As a result, the United States should share, to a great extent, the responsibility for Russia's failures in the 1990s (Rogov 1998, 102).

Moral? American models were declared unworkable on Russian soil. A sense of disappointment with them was one of the reasons why anti-American attitudes were becoming more salient in people's minds (Shatalov 1995). A popular sentiment grew that despite all the ills, the "old" socialist economy functioned. However, the new capitalist economy didn't work at all.

Criticism against American mentors was also based on the popular belief that Harvard-educated advisers did not know Russia well enough to give any legitimate advice as to how to save the country and restore its economy. They had little knowledge about Russia's customs, practices, communications, and infrastructure. Moreover, they merely tried to install American principles of capitalism in the quite different—from what they were used to—economic and cultural environment. Michael Carter, the World Bank's veteran and chief representative in Russia, agreed publicly that the international community had initially been too simplistic in its approach to creating a market economy in Russia. One of the reasons, in his view, was the advisers' imperfect knowledge about Russia and some other misunderstandings. Achieving sustained growth in Russia was not just a matter of controlling the money supply, stabilizing the exchange rate, and inspiring major progress in privatization. He pointed to attempts to create a short-term fix instead of a long-term commitment as the major mistake of the West (Carter 1999).

In the Russian people's view, Washington was responsible for giving support to Yeltsin's "*grabatization*" (the pejorative popular slang for "privatization"). As a result of these actions, Russia nose dived into great social havoc. Another mistake was attributed to certain over optimistic Russian reformers and their expert American advisers, who allegedly put too much emphasis on macroeconomics, and underestimated the significance of microeconomic factors (i.e., the role of institutional structures), and factors such as unfriendly political and economic cultures, societal norms, skeptical and cynical public attitudes toward law and many other social intangibles. For example, Russia's rampant corruption—one such hurdle—became an almost indisputable element of Russian reforms (Malashenko October 1999). Because of corruption, the only two categories of people that directly benefited from foreign assistance were the new rich and some government officials.

The envy-sensitive Russian individual witnessed how the United States and the West swiftly embraced the most prosperous cohort of Russian entrepreneurship. Called the "oligarchs" by the media and people on the street, these individuals (i.e., Berezovsky, Gusinsky, Viakhirev, Potanin, and Khodorkovsky, to name a few) accumulated enormous fortunes in the early 1990s by grabbing fat pieces of the state economy, laundering budget money, and avoiding taxes. Resented by most people in the country, these robber barons clashed in a ruthless and cynical struggle for power. As a result, the Russian people witnessed only the most unprincipled and cynical aspects of so-called free-market policies. As former CIA director, James Woolsey, (1999) mentioned, the capitalist economic system introduced in Russia was modeled—in the eyes of the public—not on Silicon Valley, but rather on the Chicago bootleg market of the Prohibition.

Furthermore, in the eyes of the average Russian person, America helped to install in the Kremlin offices, and promote to the top government positions, a group of the most notoriously ruthless individuals who were responsible for the most devastating domestic policies. "Current leaders of the United States provided substantial political support to the group of [Gaidar-Chubais] who used it for implementation of the course that proved to be disastrous for Russia," implied the director of a think-tank in Moscow (Rogov 1998, 102). American support for the loans-for-shares policy of Anatoly Chubais was not merely imagined by the angry Russian individual. To a certain extent, that support was guaranteed by top advisers in Washington, such as Richard Morningstar, a coordinator of U.S. aid to the former Soviet Union and Deputy Secretary of the Treasury, Lawrence Summers (Simes and Saunders 1999). The Clinton administration and the U.S. media continued their uncritical support of Yeltsin, Gaidar, and Chubais, while denouncing their opponents—who were, meanwhile, steadily gaining public support and sympathy—as enemies of democracy. Even though the White House could not have prevented the degradation of the Yeltsin regime, this critical perception of the U.S. administration by the Russians contributed to mounting popular irritation with the United States.

Ironically, those who benefited the most in Russia from the Western financial help—i.e., government officials and business tycoons, supported by some politicians—also began to bear grudges against the United States. The sudden growth of anti-corruption rhetoric from senior U.S. officials in 1999 sparked confusion and irritation among top Russian rulers, who, for years, were able to "manage" these monies in the murky waters of the Russian banking system. A number of Russians considered this a sign of American mistrust toward their former partners, but even more people considered this anti-corruption oratory a relentless and deep-seated manifestation of U.S. and Western hostility against an independent Russia (Livshits 1999; Yavlinsky 1999).

No Weimar Russia?

Individuals who experience dissatisfaction over economic difficulties, lack opportunity in their lives, and have to deal with unfulfilled dreams may need an identifiable object against which to vent their frustration. Dissatisfaction on the societal level can be "redirected" and projected on some domestic and external targets—individuals, social groups, and countries. This was happening in Germany in the 1920s and 1930s. Russia was said to repeat this gruesome "Weimar" experience. The ominous shadow of the Weimar Syndrome had incessantly hung over the country's skies since the early 1990s (Rozov 1997). However, warnings and fears about the dangers of a fascist or nationalistic backlash did not become reality. Unlike Germany before World War II, the Russian transformation did not produce the fertile social and political conditions that might have caused landslide violence, aggressive nationalism, anti-Semitism, and—of particular importance for the case in point—fierce and virulent anti-Americanism.

Russians do not have anti-Western instincts, Kozyrev declared confidently (1995), referring to the average Russian individual. However, this opinion was true only to some extent. Popular psychological frustrations, in fact, grew in some individuals into consistently negative feelings toward the United States (for an analysis of public opinion see Chapter 5), though this was a far "softer" form of anti-Americanism than some Russian and American experts were afraid might emerge. The average Russian person accepted neither tough Communist rhetoric nor provocative nationalistic statements.

There were several reasons why the Russian "Great Depression" never naturally led to virulent nationalism and violent anti-Americanism. The main reason was Russia's capital city. Moscow, the social, cultural, and political center of Russia, weathered the hard times of the transformation much better than the rest of the country. In fact, Moscow almost became the land of great opportunities, the embodiment of the wild frontier and Klondike. Not only the traditional source of wealth—the federal budget—was in the hands of Moscow politicians and bureaucrats, but vast portion of the biggest banks and largest foreign ventures were located there as well. During the 1990s, money and wealthy entrepreneurs flocked to Moscow from all over Russia. All of this created a palpable "trickle-down" effect. As a result, Moscow turned out to be a place where hundreds of thousands could find better paying jobs. In the 1990s, people in Moscow spent two to three times more per capita than in Russia in general. In 1996, for example, the average employee's salary in Moscow was 145 dollars per month, which is about five times higher than in other Russian regions. Ford Motor Company suggested that nearly half of all Russians who can afford to buy its cars lived in Moscow. Muscovites, representing just 7 percent of the Russian population, paid 20 percent of the federal budget in taxes.[10] The dynamism of wild capitalism neutralized the sentiments of gloom and doom. "Moscow does not believe in tears," as a Russian saying goes. In the 1990s, Moscow began to believe in money.

Muscovites maintained more pro-Western attitudes than the rest of the country. The city did not and could not turn its back on the West and the United States (Shiraev 1999). For example, in a 1997 survey by the Mnenie Polling Service, less than 25 percent of Muscovites considered NATO an enemy. Nationwide opinion polls on the same subject showed more negative feelings against NATO prevailed in other Russian regions (MacWilliam 1997; see also Chapter 5).

Without the leadership of Moscow, the Russian provinces did not create any significant passionately nationalistic local movements. The revival of the Cossack militia-like formations in southern provinces could have instigated such movements (Laqueur 1994). Nevertheless, the new bearded Cossacks in their picturesque costumes turned out to be less frightening and belligerent than one might have expected. Their leaders were embraced in Moscow, became representatives for the Cossack movement, and quickly settled down in their bureaucratic positions. Mass societal burnout, the growth of apathy, and a low level of political efficacy contributed to the relatively low level of political participation, especially among the young. Facing enormous difficulties, millions of Russians were still able to manage their individual lives using their survival instincts and newly developed entrepreneurial skills.

There was widespread cynicism and lack of trust in any nationalist agitation and xenophobic preaching. It was almost a blessing—after the decades of incessant propaganda and persistent ideological indoctrination under the Soviet regime—that during the 1990s, the majority of Russians were tired of any new radical ideology. Meanwhile, there were obvious difficulties in the process of transition from Soviet self-identity to the new national Russian identity. This last circumstance was particularly crucial for the understanding of some principal aspects of contemporary Russian anti-Americanism. How this search for identity proceeded during the 1990s and where anti-Americanism fit into this process will be the subject of the next chapter.

Chapter Four

A Crusade for a New Identity

Russia's national spirit is anything but that of a defeated country.

Dmitriy Ryurikov, former top
foreign policy assistant to Boris Yeltsin

In the fall of 1993, Vladimir Lukin, Russian Ambassador to the United States, was visiting a small church in Chevy Chase, just 30 minutes away from his embassy in Washington D.C. He did not go there to pray. For the first time in the history of Soviet and Russian ambassadorship to the United States, he came to meet with representatives of the Russian émigré community. He talked before a small crowd about the reforms, nuclear disarmament, declined questions about Yeltsin's drinking, and readily drew perspectives for Russian-American cooperation. The dialogue was engaging. At the end, somebody from the audience said that with such an ambassador as Lukin was, America and Russia would finally become great partners. Everybody cheered. A few months later, Lukin was elected deputy of the Duma and appointed Chairman of the prestigious Foreign Relations Committee. A great Russian-American partnership did not become a reality. Moreover, Lukin, one of the most prominent supporters of the "soft" course in foreign relations in the early 1990s, started to appeal to Russia's greatness, its great-power status, and national prestige.

For millions of Russians, the fall of the Soviet Union and the sudden emergence of an independent Russia created an immeasurable psychological gap between past and present. Not long ago, they used to be citizens of a gigantic multi-national superpower, both respected and feared around the world. Who had these people become now? What was their nation now? What was their national identity now? The answers were not definite. The search for better answers started.

From a psychological standpoint, the individual's identity is a complex process referred to in the way the person recognizes himself or herself in connection with a particular set of features. As a result of self-identification, each individual's identity separates the person from some people and also connects him or her with many others. National identity is a unifying psychological phenomenon that develops within concrete territorial, conceptual, and spiritual dimensions. This type of identity bonds those people who accept it through common language, citizenship, ethnicity, religion, norms, and—most importantly—values (Barner-Barry 1999). There was not a systematic effort to find out to what extent new Russian anti-Americanism may be seen as an essential component of the Russia's search for a new national identity. In this chapter we attempt to do it.

The internal Russian metamorphoses of the late 1980s and 1990s caused anxiety in foreign observers. An overwhelming amount of western descriptions and assessments dealt with the seemingly growing threat of belligerent Russian nationalism (Devlin 1999; Sherman 1995; Sakwa 1993). For the West, the least desirable outcome of the Russian-identity transformation would be, of course, the rise of a new homegrown Hitler or Saddam Hussein. Serious attention, in light of these concerns, was paid to the various individuals whose behavior slightly resembled that of a potential nationalistic dictator. Indeed, frightening images of ostentatious personalities were popping out continuously through the 1990s. One after another they appeared near the main stage of Russian politics and continued to irritate western observers with their flamboyant behavior and histrionic statements. The searching light of Western media moved from the angrily nationalistic TV anchorman, Alexander Nevzorov, to the neo-Nazi Alexander Barkashov, to the rabble-rousing demagogue Vladimir Zhirinovsky, and the wannabe-Bonaparte, Alexander Lebed. The line of portraits in this gallery had no limit, and there were many attempts to hang a picture of Vladimir Putin at the end of it.

From Euphoria to Cynical Realism

During the euphoric years of 1990–1993, radical reformers and the media sought to establish an internationalist and politically liberal identity for the new Russia. As we wrote in Chapter 2, the pillars of this identity included Russia's equal membership in the community of the developed nations and—this was extremely important—a belief in a multi-polar world. Another part of this identity was the positive image of the West, particularly the United States as a supporter of Russian democracy and main contributor to Russian economic reconstruction. The search for this identity was stimulated not so much by philosophical ideas, but rather by the popular desire to distance the new and changing Russia from the Soviet Union, and by doing so please the West. In one apt comment, "Russian leaders thought that what had been called the evil empire should now be embraced as a republic of good that has no reason to quarrel with its former adversaries and can count on their general support" (Simes 1999, 209).

However, the internationalist liberal identity began to crumble even before it took shape, and a new set of beliefs began to emerge. These ideas would later constitute a collection of lasting components for a post-Soviet national identity. In this new identity, the United States apparently did not occupy a highly respected place.

"Americans do things here like they are at home. This [behavior] was impossible earlier. I assume that our security forces are moving under America's control," suggested a popular disgruntled general (Sterligov 1992, 1). General Sterligov used these harsh words in 1992; he was a political maverick and, at that time, his pessimistic and critical views were portrayed in the liberal media as an example of clinical xenophobia and paranoia. In early 1993, however, certain moderate, sophisticated Russians began to make a case—cautiously at first and then more decisively—that the only way to preempt a major anti-Western backlash in Russia was to develop an enlightened patriotic alternative to Kozyrev's foreign policy, one that was based on the notion of liberal internationalism. Vladimir Lukin, the first Russian ambassador to the United States, espoused this idea; he believed that Moscow should stop playing the enthusiastic teenager to Washington's grown-up. Russia had its own distinct interests and had to learn to behave like an independent power—albeit a weak one (Simes 1999, 213).

During 1993–1994 initial expectations of equal partnership with the United States quickly evaporated. Observing international developments, being bombarded by statements made by Sterligov, Zhirinovsky, Barkashov, Baburin, and other new Russian nationalists, responsible officials of the Russian Defense Ministry and the Ministry of Foreign Affairs began to send alarmed signals to the Kremlin, the essence of which were that the nationalists were correct: The West was no longer taking Russia seriously (Sidorov 1994). Yeltsin's top foreign policy assistant recalls that already, in the summer of 1992, Russian officials began to realize that the United States treated Russia as a subordinate nation (Ryurikov 1999, 62–63). The Russian reputation suffered a major setback in April 1994, when NATO airstrikes were launched against Bosnian Serbs near Gorazde without a word to the Russians. On various occasions, Russian and American economic interests clashed directly, for example, over

Russian trade deals with India, and the Russian side was the one to lose. Moscow's leaders kept finding new evidence that clearly suggested they were out of the game.[1]

Russian military officers and foreign-service officials were especially frustrated to see the process of "Americanization" of Russia's neighbors and allies that followed the destruction of the Warsaw Treaty Organization and the Council for Mutual Economic Assistance—the political and economic pillars of the socialist bloc in Eastern Europe (Ivanov 1996). Officials of the public in Ukraine, Kazakhstan, Georgia, and Azerbaijan preferred to seek contacts with Americans than with Russians. "Americanophilia" in those countries was linked to anti-Soviet and anti-Russian sentiments, and therefore had somewhat stronger roots than it had in Russia. All the Kremlin could see was that the former Soviet republics had drifted away from Russia and sometimes played "the geopolitical card" of Russophobia to attract American military, intelligence, and economic advisers, as well as to initiate profitable contracts with American companies. The Russian media pointed out, disapprovingly, that the United States spent 30 billion dollars to sponsor the anti-Russian policies of Russia's East European neighbors (*Negavisimaya Gazeta,* 27 July 1996, 2). Since 1993, Russian officials had begun to talk about Russia's "near abroad" that, by virtue of geographic proximity, decades-long ties, and scores of Russian inhabitants, was a natural part of Russia's sphere of interests. Negative American reaction to this rhetoric produced a round of angry counter-rhetoric. In a symbolic gesture, foreign minister, Evgeny Primakov, declared Latin America a region of Russian strategic interests. The meaning of this demarche was clear: If Americans claimed that Kazakhstan and Ukraine were areas of strategic importance to the United States, why couldn't Russia reciprocate with the same argument in America's own backyard?

Since 1994, Russian analysts and then public officials began to signal their distress with the geopolitical games that the United States played with the former southern republics of the Soviet Union (Ekedahl and Goodman 1997). They suspected that the Americans were set on displacing any Russian influence from this region. America was accused of supporting the ideas of the leaders of Georgia, Azerbaijan, Turkmenistan, and Uzbekistan—who were seeking to assert their independence from Moscow—to restore the ancient "silk route" that would allow them to circumvent Russia (Ignatenko 1994). Many American political elites publicly supported these developments as the legitimate struggle of fragile new democracies against the threat of Russia's neo-imperialism. For Russians, of course, these claims were reflections of sheer hypocrisy for these countries. In the Kremlin's view, they were anything but democracies; their leadership systematically disregarded human rights and installed regimes of personal authoritarian rule and corruption.

Especially sensitive to Russian officials became contacts between the United States and the Ukraine. Comments in the American press that it should be the strategic task of U.S. foreign policy to prevent the Ukraine from falling back into the Russian sphere of influence were considered a direct insult to Russia. Russian commentators pointed out the links between the CIA and radical Ukrainian nationalist organizations (that, among other actions, were allegedly sending volunteers to fight with the Chechen guerillas against Russian federal troops in the Caucasus).

It became clear to the majority of Russian officials that the optimistic expectations of the early 1990s simply would not come to fruition. There was an open struggle between Russia and the United States for the post-Soviet heritage. This struggle became a new stage of the geopolitical games of the past and Russia was clearly losing the battle. Something to which Russian officials had to adapt was the total domination of the United States as the sole remaining superpower. Three rival camps of experts, those who furiously fought against Communism (Solzhenitsyn 1996), those who pragmatically used the system for career purposes (Malashenko 1999; 1997), and those who sacredly believed in Communist ideas (Sterligov 1992), suddenly found themselves in agreement: Russia was no longer seen in the West as a major player on the international field. Indeed, this was an extremely disappointing revelation for those who believed in a different post–Cold War world.

In May of 1992, the daily publication, *Rossiyskaya Gazeta,* called the United States—after the long-time absence of such a phrase in the liberal media—"the world cop" (Busuev 1992). The image of Uncle Sam carrying a big stick was in American cartoons about Teddy Roosevelt; these cartoons were reproduced in all Soviet school textbooks during the Soviet times. Removed from the Soviet and Russian periodicals of the late 1980s, a belligerent Uncle Sam reappeared in Russian newspaper cartoons a few years later (Rodionov 1996). Increasingly often, Russian commentators began to lose patience as they saw *Pax Americana* gaining strength. The attitudes against the American domination were taking shape. The Russian press disapproved of and ridiculed American pretensions to rule the world with a big stick. In fact, anti-American resentment became a standard feature of the majority of Russian periodicals.[2] The rhetoric of the Cold War had been retrieved from the journalist archives of the early 1980s.

Euphoric beliefs that superpower status was atavistic and costly were replaced by the realization that, in fact, the costs benefit ratio of their aspirations for a global hegemony was quite favorable for the United States and its close satellites. There was no reason to capture a territory, hold it by physical force, risk the lives of American people, and gamble with volatile public opinion at home. It was just as effective enough to declare some regimes democratic and therefore "good," others non-democratic and "evil," and then impose American hegemony by appealing to the receptive allies. If a nation did not capitulate and continued to live by its own rules, a few bombs could be dropped to teach this nation a lesson.

Scores of Russian commentators began to recall what they had learned in school: American world hegemony is merely a logical extension of the doctrine of American exceptionality and predestination. American society, based on this ideology, and Wilsonianism—with its emphasis on free trade, global democracy, and national self-determination—is just a modern cover for American hegemony. Gleb Pavlovsky, a former human rights activist and dissident, who, since the mid-1990s had become a cynical supporter of Russian nationalism, argued in *Nezavisimaia Gazeta* that the end of the Cold War was a triumph of American propaganda over irresolute Soviet elites. These elites longed to share "universal values," while ignoring that those values were, de facto, the ideology of American world domination (Pavlovsky 1996).

On the basis of this reasoning, a growing number of Russian foreign-policy pundits began to imply that the American struggle against the U.S.S.R. during the Cold War era was actually a policy of Russophobia. This fear of Russia was caused not so much by anti-Communist beliefs, as by the fear of a strong and independent Russia. In the present-day context, this conclusion meant the following: No matter what Russia does, the United States will continue to prevent Russia's resurrection as a strong state. A strong Russia simply does not fit well in the White House's picture of the world (Kortunov 1998).

Growing alienation from Washington led observers to the disquieting realization that Russia had to defend its own interests from a position of weakness, if no' impotence. Longings for a multi-polar world became increasingly persistent, particularly when NATO unleashed the war in Kosovo (See Chapter 6). Several times in 1999—in April (in response to the NATO bombing of Yugoslavia), in July (during a summit of Russia, China, and three other Asian countries), in August (during a ceremony in the Kremlin), and in December (during a meeting with the Chinese leadership), Yeltsin repeatedly called for a creation of a new multi-polar world system based on the principles of international law and respect for other countries' national interests (Marshall 1999).

Another logical reaction to Russian weakness was the revalidation of military power—contrary to the concept of liberal internationalism that treated any military buildup as an atavism of the past. Increasingly, the same people who had criticized Soviet military superpower since the late 1980s, labeling it a costly burden, the Potyomkin village for squandering people's wealth, and the source of anti-Russian feelings abroad, began to wax nostalgic about it. The typical Russian official wished nostalgically to be respected as a representative of a great power, according to the saying, "If they are afraid of you, this means they respect you."

New Threats Outside and Inside

National identities may develop and thrive on the basis of outside threats and domestic "fifth columns." Both authoritarian regimes and democracies have always been the busy factories of nationalistic phobias. The Soviet identity was—to a remarkable degree—based on xenophobia and the denunciation of anti-Soviet elements in the society, particularly dissidents. However, belief in an outside threat seriously eroded during the Cold War and virtually collapsed under the ruins of the Soviet empire in the late 1980s.

There were certain forces in the new Russia that were interested in revitalizing the enemy image. As a rule, they were oracles who represented political opposition. They portrayed the United States and other Western countries as nations driven by greed and individualism. Accusations of western expansionism ranged from complaints about the cultural invasion of movies and music, to open dislike of foreigners. "Stereotypes of Western standards are being imposed on us," warned the Communist leader Gennady Zyuganov. "They are not in accord with the moral and cultural basis of the Russian people. They are trying to impose on us a style of behavior that does not fit in our character and our uniqueness" (Zyuganov 23 February 1996). General Lebed intimated that the West had not abandoned its ambitions to push Russia aside and exclude it from competition. "They calculated that it would be much easier, appealing, effective, and profitable to replace military expansions with economic and cultural expansion, which is what they did" (Lebed 13 May 1996). Vladimir Zhirinovsky echoed in his radio and television addresses: "Russia's troubles have always come from the West and today there are still coming from the West. Our money is going away over there, our people are going away over there, whilst nothing but poor-quality food, poor-quality medicines, and bad advisers who are helping to rob our country quickly are coming from over there. And war, danger, and aggression are coming from over there" (Zhirinovsky 22 May 1996). He continued in another interview: "Between May 1945 and May 1996 there have been 255 wars on the globe. The main organizer of those wars is the United States of America, the CIA" (Zhirinovsky 16 June 1996).

Yet, during the early 1990s, the mainstream elite and public opinion did agree not with the oracles regarding the external threat. In 1992, for instance, there was still widespread support of the landslide nuclear disarmament of Russia and the United States (Glukhov 1993; Kozyrev 1992). Most importantly, the military doctrine of the new Russia that replaced the defunct Soviet doctrine was virtually toothless. It was imbued with the language of pacifism and universal human values. Its main thrust was to be the inverse of Soviet military doctrines and to show the world that Russia did not intend to threaten anyone. The doctrine surely reflected pacifism of the public. Moreover, in October 1993, it took President Yeltsin a great deal of effort to motivate the military to engage in the mini civil war that erupted between the supporters of his presidency and the followers of the Supreme Soviet. Although Russian military detachments were regularly engaged in the various armed conflicts of the early 1990s (i.e., in Georgia's province Abkhazia, in Tajikistan, and in the Trans-Dniestr area), those events were considered casual and remote ethnic conflicts. As a result, they did not generate an overwhelming sense of public threat.

However, attitudes changed by the end of the 1990s—public opinion polls reflected a new trend of insecurity and the sense that the West, particularly the United States, could challenge Russian traditions and become a threat to Russia (see tables 4.1., 4.2).

The hard-liners—marginalized and generally ignored in the early 1990s—suddenly found a receptive audience. Provocative comparisons between Russian and U.S. military strategies and budgets, once the stock of the Communist *Pravda,* appeared in mainstream newspapers and on television.[3] Experts from prestigious think-tanks began to discuss international treaties. Thus, they started to portray the START II Treaty as inappropriate and dangerous for Russia (Surikov 1997). The opponents of this agreement argued that if the treaty between Russia and the United States were implemented, Russia would lose its nuclear retaliation potential. If this scenario unfolded, the United States would take advantage of Russia's military instability.[4] Numerous hints by American officials, politicians, and experts to approve the development of a new missile defense system did

Table 4.1 Attitudes toward Western Democracy. VTsIOM. National Sample.

Western democracy is incompatible with Russia's traditions	1995	1996	1997	1999
Agree	50%	52%	56%	55%
Disagree	28%	27%	14%	30%
Don't know/not sure	22%	21%	20%	15%

not go unnoticed in Russia. It was argued that if this defense system were built, the United States would gain the advantage in nuclear competition, which would lead directly to a substantial nuclear imbalance. Washington would then be able to inflict its will on Russia—the situation most threatening of all to many Russians. Overall, America's perceived military power resurfaced as the most significant external threat to Russia.[5]

Various political maneuvers in Washington were perceived in Russia from the same old angle: America poses a threat to Russia no matter what domestic political equations in Washington direct this country's foreign policy. It became almost cliché to accuse president Clinton of attempting to solve his domestic problems by blowing international conflicts out of proportion, like he did during the conflict with Iraq. Many Russian officials disliked Madeleine Albright—a former immigrant from Czechoslovakia—as the U.S. Secretary of State. Some interpreted her nomination to the post as a perpetuation of the anti-Soviet agenda of Dr. Zbigniew Brzezinski, who acquired quite an unpleasant reputation in Russia as the unflagging champion of not only anti-Soviet, but also anti-Russian causes. As a naturalized American, some said, Albright was especially inclined to be unduly alarmed by any signs of Russia's independence and assertiveness (Abarinov 1996a). Even in 1995, when Albright was still U.S. Ambassador to the United Nations, Yeltsin's top foreign policy adviser claimed that she just didn't like Russia (Ryurikov 1999, 63). Under the surface, there was also a profound public dislike of Albright's manners and style: She was considered by many (somewhat in contradiction to her émigré provenance) as too much a career woman, both arrogant and inflexible. It is interesting that the same Russians, who a decade ago, had lionized "iron lady" Margaret Thatcher for the same qualities, now believed that Albright was the living embodiment of Russophobia in the United States. When NATO's westward expansion began to take place, the average attentive Russian was bombarded by news comments that Albright was personally behind this process.

**Table 4.2 Western Attitudes toward Russia as perceived by Russians.
ROMIR. November 13–14, 1999. National Sample.**

The West wants Russia to be a "Third World" state, to become dependent on developed countries.	41%
The goal of Western countries is to break Russia apart, to destroy it as an independent state.	38%
The West is doing everything possible to help Russia become a civilized and developed state.	4%

Cold War rhetoric returned to the pages of hitherto ideologically moderate newspapers. For example, *Nezavisimaya Gazeta* published an article signed by an anonymous contributor stating that the U.S. State Department, the Department of Defense, the FBI, and the CIA were designing a plan to recruit Russian leaders and political activists, scholars, scientists, and top military personnel to Western countries. Moreover, the article identified a pro-American lobby in Moscow that included Burbulis, Gaidar, Kozyrev, Starovoitova, and Yavlinsky. The article stated that this group was under the direct control of American special services (Ivanov 1996).

The Russian Federal Counterintelligence Service published a report (FCS 1995) in which American research centers, foundations, and college departments were accused of "intelligence activities and subversion" in Russia.[6] The report implied that under the cover of research activities these centers' true objective was the implementation of U.S. foreign policy. Moreover, the American special services and the Pentagon covertly directed the functioning of these research centers. Using legal methods—academic conferences, exchange programs, and personal contacts—these organizations gathered important information about Russia's internal affairs, science, and defense. They scrutinized the Russian media for new facts and leaks. The report also implies that American Peace Corps representatives penetrated Russian provinces and set up their activities in populated regions such as Saratov, Vladimir, Nizhny Novgorod, and Krasnoyarsk. Peace Corps volunteers allegedly received secret assignments from American firms to study the Russian market.

The Americans were also accused of sponsoring public opinion surveys. American research centers allegedly gathered sensitive information about political and public movements and their leaders, and analyzed the political climate in an attempt to predict the social and economic development of the Russian Federation. While collecting open information, the research centers often attempted to obtain facts regarding Russia's state secrets. American research centers were accused in the report of stealing important Russian scientific discoveries and new technologies through grants and an open "buy-out" of research data. America was also blamed for the alleged sponsorship of the emigration of the country's best specialists.

According to the report, the U.S. Special Services were assembling a special network of correspondents in the Russian regions who were to provide the United States with additional information about Russia's internal developments. If the relationships between Russia and the United States were to deteriorate, these correspondents would become extremely valuable in sending information to the United States.

American research centers were also blamed for actively seeking to establish ties with the Russian oppositional non-Communist forces, such as

Yavlinsky's Yabloko bloc and certain other parties. The Heritage Foundation, for example, was blamed for its alleged attempts to influence the Russian State Duma. The Ford Foundation was charged with targeting Russia's young and "second-tier" politicians and cultivating in them pro-American attitudes. These new leaders would then support Western values—which would be regarded as treason—and simultaneously, enjoy the broad support of their voters.

As a measure of resistance, the Federal Counterintelligence Service did not offer anything new and different from what their Soviet predecessors had produced 20 or 30 years prior. The agency proposed a set of measures to oppose the U.S. Special Services in Russia. It encouraged the dissemination of the hackneyed rhetoric—based on new facts—about how dangerously close Americans were in the 1990s to the "vital" Russian state secrets. The agency also promised to fight against the "brain drain" from Russia by adopting new legislative acts. In addition to these wishful measures, the agency returned to one of its best strategies: to intensify the monitoring of trips abroad made by the Russians. There were, of course, self-promotional and pecuniary reasons behind these acts and statements. In a tight-budget situation, the best way to get funding and prestige had historically been to announce a new witch hunt. Moreover, the public had once again become receptive to calls for vigilance and the search for enemies.

The growing popularity of the concept of Russia's global struggle against the outside world and the internal "fifth column" affected a new search for the "Russian Way" and the "Russian Idea." This search—like fire in the dry steppe—spread fast and captivated the minds and hearts of the Russian New Right—elites and bureaucrats—including those in foreign policy and security sectors.

The Rise of Neo-Conservative Ideas

With the demise of liberal internationalism, its former advocates began to search for new ideas and concepts. The eyes of some of them turned to France: The name of General Charles de Gaulle, who led France out of NATO's military structures, was very popular in Russian commentator's essays and articles in the second half of the 1990s. They referred to his slogans of independent foreign policy and "defense against all the azimuths," his vision of "Europe from the Atlantic to the Urals" with great sympathy. Gaullism became one of the few role models for Russia to emulate.

The idea of uniting with Europe against the United States was as old as many of the other ideas of the Cold War that fell short of their implementation. The resuscitation of this concept in Russia meant both the beginning of a retreat from the previous course, as well as a sign of desperation. Russians wanted to exclude Western Europe from the emerging image of a foreign threat. However, they did it as clumsily as the Soviets had done it in the past. During a visit to Strasbourg, Yeltsin announced to his European colleagues: "We don't need any uncle from somewhere else. We ourselves are capable of genuinely coming together in Europe and getting along just fine" (Sukhova 1997). It was no wonder that alienation from America in the 1990s coincided with the revival of the image of Europe as a friendly neighbor. The great cultural attractiveness of the old continent, combined with geographic proximity—in contrast to the culturally unsophisticated and distant United States—contributed to this phenomenon. Hundreds of thousands of Russians, mostly representatives of the new middle-class generation, began to travel frequently to Paris, London, Vienna, Prague, Berlin, Budapest, Venice, Rome, and other European cities. Europe satisfied the perennial Russian search for the cozy comfort of resorts, the old culture of historic cities, and their marvelous museums. And, of course, for those who wanted to flaunt their sudden wealth, there were plenty of opportunities to do so in Europe.

The juxtaposition between "us"—Europeans—and "them"—Americans—was one of the tools of Soviet diplomacy and propaganda in the days of the Cold War. In the 1990s, it resurfaced as a popular notion, widely shared by the masses of Russians. When asked if they wanted to visit the United States, typical young Russians now answered: "Why? There is nothing interesting to see there. I would rather go to Spain, Italy, or France instead!" This phenomenon differed from the obsessive search for role models. Rather, it was reemergence of the sentiment of the educated classes of czarist Russia that belonging to Europe and—most importantly—association with Europe, was an essential component of Russian identity.

At the same time, scores of principled enemies of liberal internationalism in Russia stepped into the intellectual ring and began to exercise their increasing influence in the debates about Russia's identity. The first important influential factor was the ideas of Russia's spiritual uniqueness and special mission. Some of the new philosophers returned to the distinguished Russian Christian Orthodox tradition (Rev. Bulgakov, Trubetskoi, Florovsky, and others). Others became preoccupied with the occult and mystical ideas (Blavatskaya, Gurzhiev, and Usspensky). Since 1991, the books of these authors, previously banned in the U.S.S.R., have become bestsellers. The reading Russian public who discovered them anew, was mesmerized by the ideas that seemed completely novel and revealed totally new ways of thinking and feeling about themselves as Russians.

The second source of neo-conservative ideas were the writings of "Eurasians" and their followers from among the so-called New Right.

These writings were not linked to history, religion, or mysticism. In the search for Russia's future, the authors of these works appealed to geopolitics and *ethnos* as the natural foundation of Russia's uniqueness and greatness. Geography was a powerful temptation for both the old and new architects of Russian identity. Indeed, a great chunk of Russian territory remained in Asia: Siberia and the Far East preserved for Russia the status of the largest country in the world, spanning through 11 time zones.

Where did these ideas of geopolitics come from? In the 1920s, a group of young émigré thinkers from Russia created the idea of "Eurasianism," claiming that the destiny of Russia lay not in the West, but rather in the East. This school of thought perished, but the tradition continued in the 1950s with Lev Gumilev—an historian and the son of famous Russian poets Nikolai Gumilev and Anna Akhmatova—who learned about these ethno-geopolitical ideas in Stalin's concentration camps. Many of his thick books became bestsellers in Russia in the 1990s. In defiance of Westernizers, Gumilev presented Russia as an heir to the Golden Horde and a super-ethnos of great potential and creativity.

The prominent luminaries of the New Right, Sergei Kurginian, and, in particular, Alexander Dugin, worked hard to adapt "Eurasian" concepts to the psychological and political needs of the new Russia. In the 1990s, Dugin established the New University in Moscow and, in his prolific writings, sought to synthesize geopolitics and a potpourri of mystical and religious ideas into the rationale that validated Russia's exceptionality. Geopolitics, which emerged in the writings of William Mackinder, Karl Haushofer, and Admiral John Mahan, among others, is based on an extreme form of realism that depicts international relations as the zero-sum struggle between the hinterland and sea powers. From a "Eurasianists" view, only the former preserve their true ethnic authenticity and, as a result, develop an organic state and a genuinely creative culture. The sea-powers, by contrast, depend on commerce and are the enemies of organic states, their ethnic groups, and culture. In the contemporary world, the United States became the unchallenged leader in this group and successfully imposed its way of life on others, promoting liberal internationalism or *mondialism*—i.e., a global order according to the Eurasianists' terminology. The pro-Atlanticism of NATO is regarded as a version of *mondialism*. From the viewpoint of Dugin, the victory of the United States and Western countries in the Cold War was also a triumph of *mondialism*. However, it is possible that the pendulum of history might swing back. Dugin, therefore, advocated the construction of a continental super-empire from Dublin to Vladivostok to act as a counterweight to America. Naturally, Russia would become the hub of the "Eurasian impulse" that counterbalanced the "Atlantic impulse." Moreover, Russia's disintegration would mean a catastrophe of global proportions (Dugin 1998; Lacqueur 1994, 206–207, 244–245).

In the manifesto of his eccentric online "Arctogeia Society," Dugin proclaims that the global order established by the United States was the last embodiment of Antichrist. He also claims that "geopolitics and Eurasianism are the universal language of [Russian] national identity" (see *www.arctogeia.com*). The eccentric and esoteric writings of Dugin could easily be ignored. However, similar theses and ideas have emerged in the discourse and writings of a growing number of Russian politicians, bureaucrats, and foreign-policy experts. In fact, this could be nothing less than the emergence of a Russian Neo-Conservatism that offers a new national identity for Russians, an identity that is neither Communist nor cosmopolitan; yet is anti-Western and anti-American.[7]

Geopolitical realities and economic profits favored the spread of the concepts of Eurasian geopolitics. They guided many Russians to set their sights on Taiwan, South Korea, and Singapore. In general, the attention was focused on the two giant neighbors of Russia—the People's Republic of China and India. During a visit to India in December of 1998, Russia's then-Prime Minister Primakov proposed the idea of a strategic triangle committing India, China, and Russia to joint policies of regional peace and stability. The idea of creating a strategic Axis among China, India, and Russia was publicly discussed again in the spring of 1999. A warm response to this and similar ideas, that were evoked in Beijing and Delhi, stimulated further development of the concept of Russia's Eurasian identity not only among theorists, but also among many practitioners working in the fields of foreign policy.

On the political front, another significant development was gaining strength. Now the growing popularity of the People's Republic of China arose among Russian elite opinion-makers. China was seen as Russia's potential strategic partner and, to a certain extent, a role model. Russian officials, pundits, and opinion-makers, with admiration and jealousy, observed the successful rise of China. After several decades of bitter ideological hostility, there were many economic and pure political reasons for Russia to seek the normalization of its relationship with its giant neighbor. As soon as the euphoria of liberation from Communism began to evaporate, one could hear it said in Moscow that Chinese leaders had turned out to be wiser and more prepared for transition than Yeltsin's reformers. Some regretfully longed that Russia had emulated the Chinese way during perestroika.

Russia and China, the two former Communist allies-turned-enemies, found that they faced many similar problems. In particular, they were both threatened—although to different extents—by ethnic separatism. They both had to find their own respectable places in a global community dominated by the United States. In the past China, played the "Soviet card" to achieve rapprochement with the United States. Now, Soviet officials openly played the "American card" to point out to Beijing that there could be and should be a strategic alliance between Russia and the People's Republic of China. For example, Yeltsin, during one of his visits to Beijing, referred to the United States as a country that dictates its terms to the entire world. In his opinion, Russia and China should not tolerate this situation (Abarinov 1996b,d).

The rise of Neo-Conservatism—the new underlying philosophy of Russian identity—was illustrated in a most dramatic way in the writings of a few leading Russian foreign-policy experts. They had espoused the ideas of liberal internationalism in the early 1990s only to become disillusioned later with its main postulates. Sergei Kortunov, former arms-control expert in the Foreign Ministry and an adviser to President Yeltsin, published two articles in 1998 in the prestigious Russian journal "International Affairs." In the first article, called "Russia's Way: National Identity and Foreign Policy," in which he borrowed heavily from the arsenal of the New Right and Neo-Conservative concepts, Kortunov denounced the theses about Russian and Soviet imperialism as the reason "for political and economic pressure on Russia" in the hands of the United States and the West. Under contemporary conditions, American claims of "Russia's imperial ambitions" regarding the countries of the Commonwealth of Independent States is "a brazen lie." The Americans and the West sought to prevent political and economic integration of post-Soviet space and "encouraged new national leaders" in the CIS "to move away from Moscow." Kortunov turned the table, accusing "American geo-politicians" of the continuous effort "to use the victory in the Cold War and the Soviet Union's disintegration to further promote American interests in Europe and elsewhere." He asserted that the "national sentiments of the Russians are rooted in a bitter disappointment with Western policies: The West failed to appreciate all the sacrifices of the Russian nation" in the name of ending the Cold War (Kortunov 1998, 141–149).

Under the obvious influence of the main ideas of "Eurasian" geopolitics, Kortunov recognized "a genetic tie between the national interests [of Russia] and its ethnic foundation." He further implied: "Russia's future existence depends on the continued existence of the Russians, their spiritual and moral principles, and their gene pool." He concluded that "only the might of the Russian state" could ensure such interests. The aim at restoration, according to Kortunov, is the creation of "the Russian *imperium*" as a "supra-national and meta-historical" entity (Kortunov 1998, 150–161).

Kortunov set a new record of theoretical anti-Americanism (one that appears in mainstream professional publications) in the second of his two articles, in which he claimed that, for the United States, the Cold War was not a struggle against Communism, but rather a fight against Russian imperialism. Russia was tempted to deny "its historical territory"—the same goal that was already set once in history by Hitler. As a result of the territorial disintegration at the end of the Cold War, Kortunov claimed, Washington managed to achieve something that the Third Reich had failed to accomplish. From the critics of Gorbachev-Shevardnadze and Yeltsin-Kozyrev foreign policy, Kortunov picked up the currently popular thesis that the United States continued the Cold War against Russia after Kremlin decision-makers thought it was over. "By early 1998," he wrote, "the ring of geopolitical encirclement, based on pragmatic, utilitarian interests [of the United States] and detached from the postulates of the new thinking, has tightened around Russia." Kortunov appealed to the Russian political elite—both liberal-democratic and Communist—to recognize that an orientation toward partnership with the United States was a severe mistake. Kortunov concluded that the adoption of Western values and the acceptance of an American Cold War "victory" over Russia would be tantamount to the negation of centuries of Russian history and the Orthodox idea (Kortunov 1998, 143–151).

Another cry from the heart came from Yeltsin's former top foreign-policy assistant Dmitry Ryurikov. A professional Soviet diplomat who was stationed in Afghanistan and other hot spots, Ryurikov joined the camp of Russian reforming "Democrats" and renounced the Soviet empire. However, by the mid-1990s, Ryurikov became bitterly disillusioned with the idea of liberal internationalism. The final stage of his reorientation came when NATO attacked Kosovo (see Chapter 6). In his treatise, written in the spring of 1999, he castigated the "New World Order" or NWO (also read: *mondialism* or "Atlanticism"—the authors) as "an effort of a powerful political elite to install new international rules of behavior that suit primarily Western interests." "Disguised under the universally popular slogans of democracy, human rights, and lately, *globalism*," continues Ryurikov, this [NWO] is nothing else but an effort "to subject the world to the will of the elite." Ryurikov was pragmatic enough to stress that cooperation with the United States would remain in both Russia's and America's interest. At the same time, he emphasized that a certain part of the American establishment clings to the idea that the Cold War against Russia must end victoriously to ensure that Russian military capabilities are reduced to zero, to change the "current Russian administration and replace it with one faithful to the ideas of 'democracy and reform,' to extract compensation, and to ensure, generally, that the defeated party will never again be able to rise as a challenger" (Ryurikov 1999, 50, 65).

Ryurikov's understanding of Russia is shaped by the same concept of "Eurasian" geopolitics. He is unable to accept the popular belief that hundreds of years of Russia's great history went down the drain with the collapse of the U.S.S.R. He supports the postulates of Neo-Conservative writers like Dugin (who invented, by the way, a new academic "discipline" called *conspirology*) and cannot come to terms with the triumphalist theories that Russian reforms alone could have caused the destruction of the Soviet Union. There should have been a foreign conspiracy against Russia. He also recognizes a "fifth column" inside today's Russia. This group of conspirators consists of so-called reformers who do, in reality, support NWO. They act like new Bolsheviks, brainwashing people with the help of mass culture. They try to change Russian "laws, minds, political and individual behavior, and political tradition." He singles out George Soros and denounces his nonprofit enterprises in Russia by calling them "enemies" of Russia's sovereignty and "agents" of the NWO (Ryurikov 1999, 13, 33–34, 66).

Ryurikov's views are a blend of mystical historicism and confrontational attitudes. Russians, he writes, follow in the footsteps of their ancestors and fight against attempts to dismember the country and bring it under the New World Order's rule. The stakes are as high as they were during "Russia's battles with the Mongols, Napoleon, or Germany. If Russia wins, the consequences may be as significant as the victory in the Second World War." Ryurikov's path to victory in this war is the adoption of the Russian national idea. The lack of a national idea between 1992 and 1998 is his explanation for the misfortunes of the transition period. During that time, he argues, Russians were forced "to accept a national idea of vulgar consumerism" (read: the American way of life—the authors). However, in his opinion, the national idea for Russians should state that "the Russian people can survive only by building a strong state that is fair to its citizens." Despite the fact that Ryurikov attaches to this "Russian idea" attributes such as democracy and civil liberties, his preference clearly lies with a strong state that can impose law and order. His final verdict is firm: "Without [law and order], Russia will disappear as a nation" (Ryurikov 1999, 40–45).[8] Apparently, Vladimir Putin ran his electoral campaign and began his tenure as president under a similar banner.

Benign Nationalism or Exceptionality with Missiles? [9]

Ten years of collapse and depression took their toll on some of the most educated and pragmatic Russian thinkers. Their pride and patriotic feelings were badly wounded during the transformation. Their hopes for Russia as a Western-style liberal democracy and democratic illusions were burned to ash. Some of these people, who, back in 1993, wanted to pre-empt the advocates of ultra-nationalism and develop an ideology of "enlightened patriotism," slipped deep into the pit of ultra-nationalism. Their paranoid ideas, frustration, and overall state of disorientation led them to the camp of the New Right.

At the same time, up until 1999—events in Kosovo and Chechnya changed the situation—Russia's search for a new national identity failed to produce any angry or violent reactions against "others." There were no bitter enemies at home or in the international arena. A natural explosion of patriotism did not happen in Russia. Patriotic hymns are heard only during occasional Communist rallies or small nationalist gatherings. Russian flags are almost never displayed in front of private houses. Yeltsin's national appeal to the Russian people in April 1997 to buy domestic products and services had no effect at all, and only the collapse of the ruble in August 1998 gave an unexpected boost to cheaper domestic production. It is possible, as some argue, that a new wave of Russian nationalism—considering the rise of Neo-Conservatism and anti-Americanism—was not as pernicious and dangerous a malaise as was anticipated. From a broader historical angle, it was rather an inevitable development. There are several reasons in support of this argument.

Frustration over the growing power of the United States, the loss of Russia's Cold War "great power" status, the exclusion of Russia from important policy-making, and an absence of substantial economic investments into the Russian economy—these negative developments from a Russian standpoint—caused a new trend in the Russian search for identity. As we stated earlier, it did not result in terrorism or militant anti-Americanism. There were no boycotts of American products and enterprises. Instead, a growing and dominant new trend in Russian identity formation appeared. It was the idea of disengagement from America. Russia, according to this view, still had the opportunity to gather the broken pieces of its national spirit and the state. The country still had resources to fight its political and social ills. During this process—in the beginning of the twenty-first century—the United States will have very little influence on Russian domestic affairs. Therefore, America will eventually lose priority on Russia's shopping list during the forthcoming restoration (Malashenko October 1999). Such isolationist ideas do not necessarily suggest that Russia should back off and reduce its contact with the West and the United States. Quite the contrary, isolationism means pursuing solutions to domestic problems as the most urgent and the imperative priority for the Russian people.

Isolationism, however, also meant the unavoidable surrender of Russia's great-power status, a development that few people wanted to occur. The growth of great-power attitudes among Russian elites was also caused by certain social developments within the country—above all, by the rise of the new middle- and upper-middle classes of Russians. By the mid-1990s, most of them needed a strong state that could guarantee their rights and protect their property. Earlier in the 1990s, social instability allowed many of them to acquire wealth and prominence. Now they wanted stability and societal validation of their status.

Literature, as is often the case in Russia, is a reliable barometer of new social and cultural trends. Russian writer, Viktor Pelevin, who became one of the most recognized authors of the 1990s, used his characters to articulate some of his ideas, wishes, and yearnings. One such character, a bodyguard named Vovchik who became a gangster in the criminal environment of the Russian entrepreneurship, explains his view on the nature of a new Russian idea. (The "Russian idea," of course, is a concept to which people in Russia attach different meanings. In general, this concept reflects the essence, the central feature of the Russian nation and culture.) Vovchik explains why he needed this idea. Above all, he says, he hates foreigners, particularly Americans and Western Europeans, who believe they are superior to him and his friends. "They think we are culturally inferior, like animals with money. But we are, in fact, Russia. An omnipotent country! It sends shivers down my spine if I even think about this. . . ." Vovchik and the new masters of Russia—whether they were educated or not—began to feel an acute need for respect and esteem from others. They needed a validated social status. They wanted to feel that they were better and smarter than their Western neighbors. Russian nationalism and a distinct nationalist identity became the natural foundation for this validation process.

For decades, even before the Soviet period in history, millions of Russians had developed a sense of inferiority regarding the West. This sense grew stronger after the 1950s, when Russians began to believe that they were not only poor, but also backward and unsophisticated in comparison to Western people (Chapter 1). During the 1990s, a reverse trend began to take shape. Many Russians, particularly those who began to enjoy higher living standards, realized that Russian education, science, and culture were not as backward as they had formerly believed. The complex of "sovok" was partially replaced by self-induced feelings of self-worth and greatness. It is unfortunate that this change in self-perception was readily exploited by the apostles of Neo-Conservatism and the New Right philosophy. However, the development of high self-esteem may be considered as the inevitable by-product of a nation's rebirth. One could hardly expect Russians to start respecting others, if they did not respect themselves.

Like many French individuals, today's Russia turned to cultural anti-Americanism in an attempt to justify the superiority of Russian culture and civilization over anything foreign. Talk to almost any Russian and ask him or her to compare Russian and American cultures. No matter how abstract and helplessly irrelevant this conversation may seem to some people in the United States—especially to those who embraced the value of cultural relativism—most Russians will defend cultural absolutism and try to convince you of the superiority of the Russian culture over America's. One of our Russian colleagues even asked us mockingly during one such discussion: "You are asking to compare two cultures. Does America have a culture?"

Russia, as a nation and a state, has a longer history than the young North American nation. Nevertheless, America has become a prosperous country and Russia has not. Many Russians mention that their country has made quite a few political and economic mistakes. However, Russian soil gave birth to the music of Pyotr Tchaikovsky and Igor Stravinsky, the books of Fedor Dostoevsky and Leo Tolstoy, the joy of the dance performed by Rudolf Nureyev and Mikhail Baryshnikov, and also to numerous scientific inventions and discoveries. Russians typically view themselves as exceptionally talented people who, unfortunately, cannot run their lives well. General Lebed explained this in two short sentences: "74 percent of all inventions in the world originated in Russia," he said. "They've either being stolen or bought from us, or we drank them or lost them" (Lebed 24 May 1996).

Many Russians like Hollywood movies, but are seriously piqued by Hollywood's stereotypical portrayal of their countrymen as either mafia gangsters, spies, wealthy villains, or well-meaning idiots (Kara-Murza 1996). Indeed, it is practically impossible to find an American movie that features a Russian character who is decent, intelligent, or kind. For most Russians, such depictions of themselves are grossly inaccurate. What Russians prefer to emphasize is their national character's collectivist trends, the closeness of their interpersonal relationships, and adherence to the spiritual tradition. These features are considered in Russia to be highly superior to American individualism, with all its emphasis on personal independence and choice. "The soul does not feel 'cozy' in America," confesses pop singer Masha Rasputina (1992). Her interpretation of why Russia has an advantage over America is simple: One can become rich in the United States but will definitely miss the "warmth" of Russian friendship and personal contacts. In other words, America is too cold for the typical Russian person.

Overall, could one view emerging Russian nationalism—and the resulting anti-Americanism—as benign phenomena? We do not think so. The rise of Neo-Conservative ideas may plant dangerous seeds that—if there is support from the state—may create enormous problems for Russia in the future. Fears of Russian nationalism should be linked to the nature of Russia's authoritarian past. Suspected links between authoritarianism and nationalism are heard from Russians themselves. Among them are liberal sociologists (Grushin 14 September 1994), as well as politicians and government officials of all calibers and ideologies (for example, Smolyakov 1997; Yavlinsky 6 June 1996; Zhirinovsky 22 May 1996). Another concern about Russian nationalism can be linked to specific features of the Russian cognitive style, often understood as *mentalnost,* or psyche. There are two features that bear recognition. The first is the extent of Russia's national obsession with the idea of being historically "special" or "chosen." The second is an emphasis on a strong state that overshadows freedoms and democratic institutions.

"Russia is a special world . . . a special type of civilization," stated Communist Zyuganov in *The Economist* (1996). The idea of Russia's special role in history—the nation's exclusivity— is appealing to a country that is enormously big and diverse. It is commonly believed that most of Russia's failures in the past were caused by the country's obsession with ideas "borrowed" from other nations. "Judeo-liberal capitalism" and "Judeo-Masonic socialism" brought Russia nothing but trouble, the destruction of its culture, and suffering (Gryzunov 1995). Neo-Conservative thinkers continue to push Russia toward "a third way" between capitalism and Communism, talking about a mysterious "vector of Russia's development" (Kara-Murza et al. 1995, 14). Russia, they claim, has its own problems that can only be solved by its own unique and home-grown methods.

These unique methods, however, are already well-known—a strong bureaucratic state blessed by its Orthodox faith, with an autocratic savior at the top. The essential third element of this "holy trinity" is the restoration of Russia's military strength—the country's intimidating power. A new national concept required the presence of a new military doctrine. In fact, such a doctrine was optimistically proposed by Yeltsin in his public statements during his uphill battles against Gorbachev in 1990 and 1991. Having neither the resources nor the political will to carry out such a transformation, the pledge of a new military doctrine remained an empty promise. However, by the late 1990s, witnessing its own embarrassing weakness in Bosnia and Kosovo, the Russian military elite apparently reached a threshold of tolerance. The concept of small, mobile, well-trained military forces fortified by an impressive nuclear arsenal—were the two pillars that appeared in the center of the new strategic thinking (Rodionov 1996). The difference between the late 1990s and earlier periods was Russia's capability to finance such a project.

There was a rare public statement, a media-covered interview, or discussion about Russia's greatness without a persistent verbal discourse about "the nuclear button" in the country's possession (Shchedrov 1999). Russia is like a street-tough thug who avoids fistfights, but threatens everyone with a concealed gun instead. More and more often, it was declared that Russia could maintain a military balance only by relying on its overwhelming nuclear superiority. By 1997, outcries about the steps that should be taken to maintain strategic parity with the United States became as common as calls for disarmament in the early 1990s. Experts and commentators openly discussed why Russia should accelerate the manufacturing of SS-18 missiles, the most destructive missiles in the Russian arsenal (called R-36M2 by Russians). Moreover, such calls were supported by speculations over the production cost of these rockets in an attempt to emphasize that such a military build-up was not only possible, but very likely to happen (Surikov 1997). These and other ideas about Russia's military might became a desirable development around which a consensus between both public opinion and the political elite was suddenly established (Mikhailov 1999).

The Unfinished Process

Even the harshest Western critics of Russia have to admit that during the worst and most tumultuous years of the Russian transition in the 1990s, the ghost of militant, anti-Semitic, swastika-carrying nationalism fell far short of expectation. In short, it failed to materialize. It is indeed a factor of major historic importance that belligerent Russian nationalism has not become the major ideology of any strong political movement or party. Favorable conditions for nationalistic unrest never reached critical mass. Russia's working people cared primarily for their daily bread. Only a few of them paid attention to their national identity—how pundits in Moscow distinguished themselves and others as an ethnic group or nation.

The main opposition political force—the Communist Party of Gennady Zyuganov, who carried about one-third of the popular vote in the elections of 1996 and 2000—has taken advantage of nationalist slogans, particularly during electoral battles. Yet, his party's program and ideology have been largely based on a cautious blend of Russian patriotism and an old, Communist-style internationalism. More importantly, many leaders of the Communist Party cherished the dream of the reintegration of the former Soviet countries, and the resurrection of "the International," i.e., a union of Communist parties in the newly-independent states around Russia, particularly in the Ukraine. The leaders of the Russian Left understand well that if they adopt an explicit nationalistic platform, they would then foreclose on even a remote chance for this internationalist plan to come to fruition. A venerable veteran of the Communist leadership, Yegor Ligachev, told one of the authors in Moscow that Russian Communists face two rival ideologies—capitalism and nationalism (Ligachev 1999). This telling admission indicates that the Communist Party is not so much the main conduit to political nationalism as it is a barrier, at least as long as the party's old guard is in power.

If Russian nationalism did not receive the enthusiastic support of the masses during 1992–1998, as some had feared, why did anti-American attitudes continue to rise after 1993? The answer can be found if we backtrack for a minute to recap some important points related to the Russian search for national identity. The process of self-exploration and self-identification conducted by the elites resulted in a new concept of Russia's national distinctiveness. The cornerstone of this concept was a new Russian isolationism reinforced by skeptical attitudes about America and the Western way of life—they were regarded as unsuitable for Russia. People—who were tired of confrontations and fighting—could have easily embraced such isolationist and rejection-based attitudes: They are easy to understand, they created a sense of unity, and therefore, could have served as inspirational sources (Devlin 1999). The Russian concept of national identity also promotes attitudes of self-efficiency and freedom from foreign sources of help: Only Russians can understand Russian problems, and only Russians would know how to solve these problems (Malashenko October 1999). In this context, the interests of the theorists in Moscow think-tanks and the media and the concerns of ordinary people commingled. "Now everything is dictated by America. . . . America sent used clothes to us, as though we're an underdeveloped country," complained a frustrated World War II veteran in his letter to a popular weekly (*Ogonyok,* No. 12, March 1998). Russians did not want to be treated as a second-class nation. They wanted to believe that they still had enormous potential, represented a great nation, and were respected by others. The philosophy of isolationism based on a blend of Russian exceptionality and moderate anti-Americanism became a very suitable recipe for the post-Soviet Russian identity.

Many in the West, including adherents to the Kantian notion that democracies rarely go to war against each other, believed that the development of democracy in Russia, combined with economic revival, would prevent a nationalistic backlash. Democratic development, however, is a process that is based on political struggle among different interest groups. At a time of economic depression and continuing hardship, Russian politics became a major catalyst of anti-Americanism among Russian elites and the general public.

Chapter Five

Anti-Americanism within a "Democratic Polity"

In proportion as the antagonism between classes within the nation
vanishes, the hostility of one nation to another will come to an end.

Karl Marx and Friedrich Engels.
The Communist Manifesto. Sec.2.

In January 2000, a Russian colleague sent us an email from Moscow.
Sharing with us her personal news and recent updates she stated, with
a great deal of bitterness, that she had hoped to work for the campaign
team of Vladimir Putin. She had gained experience and connections working for Yeltsin's associates in the 1990s, and sincerely believed that she had
a good shot now as a campaign associate. However, as she wrote, there was
one significant flaw in her resume: She, a Russian citizen, was the graduate of a U.S. university. This three-year educational experience overseas and
a political science degree apparently made her unacceptable to her potential employers. Frankly, she explained, she had anticipated such a reaction.
A rare politician in Russia wanted to associate his or her name with the
United States. It had become a major political liability. American image
had become the hostage of Russian internal political games.

Foreign policy in democratic societies is generally developed in response
to pressures from various domestic interest groups. Foreign policy is expected to be responsive to the influence of political opposition and public
opinion in general. The desire to be elected or re-elected creates pressing
incentives for politicians—by not falling too far out of step with the me-
dian voter—to be aware of both supporters and political opposition. As a
result, the adoption by the ruling government of a certain foreign-policy

line may be based on yielding to opponents in some domestic issues. Conversely, some political gains on the domestic front may be leveraged—under the pressure of opposition and public opinion—for both short-term actions and long-term doctrines concerning foreign policy issues. Therefore, a country's international relations may often depend on the strength and weakness of the government's domestic political opponents (Putnam 1988; Everts 1996).[1] Foreign-domestic tradeoffs are especially common in countries where governments are unstable and cannot rely on a shaky party coalition in the parliament (Sobel 1996). The traditional democratic "left wing"-vs.-"right wing" political struggle on the national level typically directs the course of foreign policy from a more nationalistic to a more cosmopolitan orientation, from isolationism to interventionism. Many examples of such links between internal political factors and a country's foreign policy doctrines are found in the Israeli-Arab conflict in the Middle East, discord in Northern Ireland, Bosnia, and many other cases (see also Holsti 1992; Shiraev and Zubok 2000).

The domestic struggle for power was prominent in the Soviet Union before 1991. However, there were only a few instances when this struggle affected foreign-policy doctrines—it happened, for example, in the interregnum after Stalin's death in 1953. Leaders from Khrushchev to Andropov used the "enemy image" of the United States to consolidate the ranks of the bureaucracy and political elites. The long-term ban on factionalism inside the Communist Party developed strong inhibition among Soviet *apparatchiks* to challenge the authority of the General Secretary of the Communist Party and his political course. Mikhail Gorbachev skillfully exploited the enormous inertia of this psychology when he took a drastic turn toward rapprochement and then "convergence" with the West. The apparent opponents of this course were silent, even as late as the fall of 1988 (Gromyko 1997).

Only further political liberalization started by Gorbachev and continued by Yeltsin unleashed foreign policy debates among different political forces within the country and vastly increased domestic political pressure on foreign policy. Andrei Kozyrev, Russia's first Foreign Minister after the breakup of the Soviet Union implied, for example, that the changeable nature of the international situation dictates the need—on the executive level—for regular updating and clarification of Russia's foreign policy based on a search for the broadest consensus of the country's public and political forces (Kozyrev 1992). We will see later, how in the 1990s, slowly but surely the search for such a domestic consensus resulted in the establishment of an anti-American doctrine that began to dominate Russia's foreign policy by the beginning of the new millennium.

How and why did domestic political factors influence the development of an anti-American core in Russia's foreign-policy doctrine in the 1990s?

Did the lack of a "real," western-style democracy in Russia contribute to anti-Americanism? To what extent were the interpretations of Russian-American relations among Russian elites affected by domestic politics? In particular, what issues—domestic and international—became catalysts for anti-American trends in Russian politics? To begin, we turn now to discussing certain features of post-Soviet Russian public opinion in relation to some key domestic and foreign-policy issues.

The Public Opinion Factor

During the 1990s, the majority of Russians did not pay much attention to the nation's foreign policy. International affairs were not at the top of their everyday concerns (Mikulski 1995). Scores of domestic problems preoccupied the average Russian citizen to a greater extent than any important events abroad. People in the country had to deal with events such as the breakup of the Soviet Union in 1991, the parliamentary coup of 1993, the two military campaigns in Chechnya, the parliamentary elections of 1993, 1995, and 1999, the presidential elections of 1996 and 2000, the financial crisis of 1998, and above all—the unpaid salaries. "The average Russian thinks about his salary and prices. He is not in a position to think about foreign policy," implied Viktor Kremenyuk (1997), Deputy Director of a prominent Moscow think-tank. Indeed, according to *Izvestia* (13 October 1995, 6), 72 percent of Russian citizens in the mid-1990s attached personal priority to domestic problems, and only 18 percent to foreign ones. According to the newspaper, the relationship with the neighboring former Soviet Republic of Ukraine, for example, was viewed as more important than ties with the United States.

However, based on disinterest with what was happening around the globe—and this is characteristic of public opinion in most democratic societies—Russian attitudes toward the West and the United States were becoming increasingly unenthusiastic and lukewarm. This shift was already evident in the surveys conducted between 1990 and 1994. Despite some fluctuations and diversity of opinion, the perception of a growing threat from the West and the United States was obvious (Chuprov and Zubok 1996, 138; Shiraev 1999b).

What general features of the Russian people's attitudes about America and its policies stand out in surveys? (See Tables below).

To begin, the results of several surveys published in the 1990s do not give the analyst legitimate opportunity to accurately compare the dynamics within a ten-year period of both pro- and anti-American attitudes. Without a doubt, there is little empirical information about the types of attitudes that Russians held about the United States in 1985—opinion polls of this kind were rather atypical for Soviet-era social studies (Shlapentokh 1988;

Table 5.1 Attitudes about the United States (1998–1999). VTsIOM. National Sample.

	12/1998	05/1999	08/1999	09/1999	12/1999
Very good	13%	2%	5%	11%	10%
Rather good	54%	30%	45%	50%	50%
Rather bad	17%	30%	23%	19%	20%
Very bad	6%	24%	10%	5%	8%
Don't know	10%	14%	17%	15%	12%

Table 5.2 Attitudes about Russia's Cooperation with the United States and other Western Countries. Public Opinion Foundation. National Sample.

I think this cooperation is . . .	June 23, 1999	September 23, 1999
Harmful to Russia	36%	22%
Helpful to Russia	39%	53%
Don't know	26%	25%

Table 5.3 Hostile Attitudes toward the United States. Public Opinion Foundation. National Sample.

December 1998	April 1999
28%	72%

Table 5.4 Attitudes about NATO enlargement. Public Opinion Foundation. National Sample.

Statement/Date	Summer 1999	Spring 1997
NATO enlargement to the east is a threat to Russia	66% (14% disagreed)	51% (34% disagreed)

Table 5.5 "What country do you think is a source of a nuclear war threat?" Public Opinion Foundation. August 1999. National Sample.

U.S.A.	Iraq	Iran	China	None	Don't Know
44%	14%	11%	10%	5%	27%

Shiraev and Bastrykin 1988). However, what is remarkable about the results of this and other polls, is that despite the fundamental change in the government's ideological stand that took place toward the West after Gorbachev introduced the "New Thinking" doctrine of international relations, and the apparent elimination of state-sponsored anti-American propaganda in the 1990s, the opinions of ordinary Russians about the United States and Western countries in general did not become more positive.

In fact, the pro-Western, pro-American euphoria of 1989–1992 was shallow. It never penetrated the depth of the Russian heartland. It never strayed from Moscow and St. Petersburg. Empirical studies show that people with internationalist and liberal views, the main values of the Protestant philosophy of life in general, are more likely to be found in two major Russian cities. In the Central and Southern areas of Russia, the old egalitarian and authoritarian Soviet-style attitudes always remained strong, and the plurality (often it was a majority) of people in those areas voted in 1993, 1996, and 1999 for the Communists and anybody else who avoided to say the word "democracy" often (Wyman 1997; Shiraev 1999b). Besides opinion polls, the traditional Cold War and anti-American attitudes of these people are exemplified in a series of published diaries and notes from the collection of the "People's Archive" in Moscow (Olshanskaya 1991).

As we stated in Chapter 2, the late 1980s and early 1990s were marked by people's optimistic beliefs in the almost unlimited opportunities of bilateral Russian-American and international cooperation. Such beliefs began to evaporate and morph into more pessimistic and frustration-driven isolationistic attitudes (Interfax 21 September 1995). This trend, however, did not mean that many Russians sought to quarrel with the United States. Very few people believed in the high probability of a major war between Russia and America (Kelley 1994). At the same time, almost one-third of Russians named the United States as a potential aggressor against Russia (Smirnov 1997). Although individual opinions about possible wars are contingent on immediate international developments—and we shall discuss this issue later—there is a clear link between this security concern of Russians and the old Soviet concerns about America.

In the mid- and late 1990s, the increasing numbers of Russians—from one-half to two-thirds—expressed their concerns about NATO enlargement, one of the major world developments of that decade (Interfax 30 July 1999). A further shift toward negative attitudes was caused, in part, by the events in Kosovo and in particular, the NATO bombardment of Serbian towns. It is essential to note, however, that this military campaign took place far away from Russia's borders in a country in which most Russians expressed little interest before the 1990s. And yet, the public mood became extremely electrified by U.S. actions and yielded a great deal of frustration and hostility toward America and Americans. Uncle Sam was blamed for starting and escalating the war in Kosovo (Centre TV, Moscow, 7:15 P.M., 18 April 1999; Radio Ekho Moskvy 3 May 1999; see also Chapter 6).

All in all, despite fluctuations—and at times substantial ones that were linked, as we mentioned earlier, to certain domestic and international developments—most opinion polls taken in Russia yield a minimum 20–30 percent of respondents who hold negative and extremely negative opinions of the United States, its policies, and influences. This sample of people—the carriers of anti-American attitudes—is overwhelmingly diverse; it contains individuals of different ages and social groups. In general, most anti-American attitudes are positively correlated with the support of Gennady Zyuganov and pro-Communist views. Nationalist attitudes also correlate with negative views of America. It is also likely that anti-American views are positively correlated with the respondent's age: the older a person is the more likely he or she will hold anti-American attitudes. In addition, urbanites from Moscow and St.Petersburg are more likely than other Russians to express positive views about the West, and the United States in particular (Shiraev 1999b; Chuprov and Zubok 1996; MMMM January 1993 and December 1991).

Without substantial evidence of extreme, violent, and persistent hostility toward the United States, so-called moderate anti-Americanism still remained an integral element of Russia's public opinion in the 1990s, an attitude carried by potential voters. In the Soviet days, this segment of public opinion had virtually no impact on the power struggle and the creation and correction of foreign policy. In fact, the vast majority of the Soviet people did not oppose the foreign policy or initiatives of Brezhnev, Andropov, or Gorbachev governments. People did not oppose the policy of *détente,* the claims about disarmament, or principles of international security. Most Soviet people were convinced that the Kremlin leadership knew better how "to defend peace" and many would stand firm against American "encroachments" and "provocations" (Olshanskaya 1991). However, these opinion-policy linkages changed with the introduction of free elections and the establishment of a parliamentary system. As a rule, if there is a public opinion base, there will be politicians who can and will represent these views on the level of elite politics. And such politicians had already appeared by 1993.

1993: Politics without Center: A "Pro-American" Line Endangered

In 1993, the struggle for power intensified in Russia, as victorious democratic groups gathered around two major camps. The leader of the first group was President Boris Yeltsin; the leaders of the second group were his recent allies, the Chairman of the Supreme Soviet, Ruslan Khazbulatov, and former Vice President, Alexander Rutskoi. The latter group was supported by the rehabilitated Communist Party and various groups of vocal nationalists and local leaders who demanded the restoration of the Soviet Union. This opposition was looking for any misstep, any unpopular action of the president and his administration to launch attacks on the government. Foreign policy was also under the opposition's surveillance. For example, the unfolding Bosnian conflict and Russia's diplomatic actions in this region in the early 1990s became targets of intense scrutiny from the oppositional camp. The main argument—used largely by Communists and nationalists—was that Russia would readily "bend" and do whatever the West dictated even though the actions discriminated against the Serbs, who were apparent Russia's allies.[2]

The constitutional crisis of 1993 worsened the already deteriorating political situation in Russia. Yeltsin wanted to break the deepening legislative-executive stalemate by holding a direct referendum on April 25, asking the Russian people whether they supported his government, the reform process, or early legislative or presidential elections. As the referendum neared, it became clear that Yeltsin wanted to eliminate any issue or hurdle that could cost him votes. As a result, certain foreign policy developments became dependent on the unfolding internal political situation. For example, appealing to the anti-Western sentiment of potential supporters whose votes he didn't want to lose, Yeltsin reportedly sought the postponement of any United Nations decision (obviously, from the Russian view, a decision that was under the direct control of the United States) on sanctions against the Bosnian Serbs until after the Russian referendum took place. As one prominent analyst put it, Yeltsin's government became "extremely vulnerable to national pressures from below," and did not want to be accused of helping the West to discriminate against Bosnian Serbs (Volski 1993, 22).

Apparently American decision makers were sympathetic to Yeltsin's request, as the vote to sanction the Serbs in Bosnia was postponed. Washington also slowed its efforts to secure a U.N. Security Council vote authorizing enforcement of the no-fly zone over Bosnia, largely because it feared such an anti-Serb move would undermine Yeltsin's chances to win the crucial referendum (See *U.S. News and World Report,* 5 April 1993). However, without waiting for the official results of the referendum, Clinton rushed to congratulate the Russian leader—whose platform got almost 43 percent of the popular vote—on his "outstanding victory." This action stirred up the resilient Russian anti-Yeltsin opposition. *Pravda,* a leading Communist Party newspaper, immediately warned the United States "against the temptation to interfere in our internal affairs. Russia is not a banana republic . . . it can never be a state someone keeps in his pocket. No such pocket exists" (Glukhov 1993, 3). This printed attack was supported by the same reasoning that made the opposition to Gorbachev turn for help to U.S. conservatives: "A friend of my enemy becomes my enemy too." Supporting their bitter foes—Yeltsin and his team—the United States was enthusiastically "blacklisted" by the Russian opposition. The United States' place at the top of this list was already reserved for many other reasons, as we saw earlier in the book.

Through the end of 1993, brushing aside a legitimate challenge of the opposition, Russian ruling elite continued to cooperate with the United States and other Western powers in the resolution of the Bosnian crisis. Gaining political strength after the referendum, and therefore ignoring for some time criticisms and accusations of "selling out" the Serbs, Yeltsin's government refused to use Russia's veto power to block Security Council resolutions designed to increase the pressure on Serbian President Milosevic. On June 4, 1993, Russia also voted for U.N. Security Council Resolution No. 836, which declared Gorazde a "safe area." This resolution, adopted unanimously by the Security Council, authorized "all necessary measures, through the use of air power, in and around the safe areas" in the Republic of Bosnia and Herzegovina to support UNPROFOR (the U.N. Protection Force) in the former Yugoslavia (*The Economist,* "Pax Russiana?" 19 February 1994, 57).[3] The opposition immediately interpreted those actions as the green light for a forthcoming U.S. invasion on the Balkans.

Political battles continued in Russia at the end of 1993. Yeltsin ultimately disbanded and laid siege on the recalcitrant Supreme Soviet; as a result, for a few tragic days in October, Moscow was literally on the brink of civil war. On October 4–5, government troops clashed with the paramilitary groups of the opposition, and Yeltsin sent tanks to shell the Russian parliament. Turner's CNN showed the scene of the battle to the whole world and to those Russians who could receive the broadcast from their local transmitters. Symbolically, CNN cameras were installed not far from a place—in front of the Supreme Soviet—from which Yeltsin's tanks were shelling it. The Clinton administration wholeheartedly supported Yeltsin's violent measures, despite the fact they evoked much revulsion among Russians, not only among the opposition to the Kremlin, but also some of its erstwhile supporters. The criticism did not affect Yeltsin's plans. Soon he abolished the old Soviet-age Constitution and introduced a new draft. This new Constitution granted the president power comparable to that granted to leaders of authoritarian regimes; it also significantly weakened the power of the parliament—as if Yeltsin wanted to ensure that the legislative branch would not again become the political counterweight to his executive power. In December, the new Constitution was put to a vote and, along with it, a legislature named the Federal Assembly was elected.

However, the results of the parliamentary elections of December 1993 shocked the government. The electoral outcome was not favorable to Yeltsin and, ultimately, his foreign policy course. Opposition forces, particularly the Communists and nationalists lost the mini-civil war of October. However, they won numerous blocs of seats that guaranteed them prevalence over a minority of reformist and pro-government deputies, scattered among many small parties and groups.[4] The most significant development was the electoral triumph of the Liberal-Democratic Party of Vladimir Zhirinovsky: The party won 22.9 percent of the party-list vote. Remarkably, most of those who voted for Zhirinovsky supported clear anti-American and anti-Western views (Devlin 1999).

Soon after the Duma convened, its new leaders immediately turned their attention to the conflict in Bosnia, the hottest topic on the Russian foreign-policy agenda at that time. Pressure was applied to the government, and the Foreign Ministry of Andrei Kozyrev was blamed for its allegedly pro-American course. On January 21, 1994, three Duma factions (representing the Communist Party of the Russian Federation, the Liberal Democratic Party of Russia and the Agrarian Party of Russia) issued a statement declaring any use of foreign military force in the republics of the former Yugoslavia unacceptable and demanded that all foreign troops, that were "brought there" by the United States, be withdrawn from its territory. Russia's representatives in the U.N. Security Council were requested by the Duma factions to take immediate steps to implement the parliamentary demands (Rodin 1994, 2).

This legislative demarche conveyed perhaps the harshest criticism yet leveled at the Russian government for its foreign policy by democratically elected legislators. In the Duma, attacks on Russia's feeble Bosnia policy escalated at this point and extended to vituperative personal attacks on Kozyrev (Kremenyuk 1994). The faction of the Liberal Democratic Party of Russia (LDPR), the largest in the Duma, warned in January 1994, that if the Ministry of Foreign Affairs failed to take a clearly "pro-Serbian" position in Bosnia and stand firmly against U.S. policies in the region within one week, the LDPR would demand the Foreign Minister's immediate resignation (Rodin 1994). Vladimir Zhirinovsky declared in February 1994, that he would not rest as long as Kozyrev remained a minister: "My mission is to remove him from the Russian government" (Baturin and Gryzunov 1994, 4). For a long time, the Kremlin ignored such declarations. Nevertheless, the opposition began to enjoy the increasing growth of public support outside of Moscow.

The year since December 1993 was marked by the end of romanticism in foreign affairs and the steady cooling of relations between Russia and the West (Mlechin 1994). Gradually, domestic turf battles began to have a cumulative effect on foreign policy.

A Correction of Course

Not only the extremist fringe and the Communist propagandists sensed that the West wanted to keep Russia on its knees and that it was time for Russia to stand tall in its international actions. Professional Foreign Service officials, particularly those who worked in the area of arms control and relations with former Soviet republics, began to speak privately that the American side had not quite behaved in the spirit of friendship and partnership that Yeltsin had proclaimed earlier. Some veterans of the "Gromyko school" of diplomacy, could hardly stand Yeltsin's political appointees to the Ministry of Foreign Affairs, and blamed them for their rosy idealism, ignorance, and their naïve desire to bend over backward to demonstrate to American officials the extent of Russia's good will (personal interviews). Facing growing pressure from opponents and hearing objections within its own ranks, Kozyrev and his closest entourage began to give more thought to how to refute accusations of the "pro-American" and "Western" thrust of the government's foreign policy. Gradually, the Yeltsin administration itself began to adopt various elements of the opposition's rhetoric regarding foreign policy. For example, after their electoral defeat, certain Yeltsin advisers and speechwriters (such as Dmitry Ryurikov and Liudmila Pikhoia) began to arm themselves with the opposition's slogans. "For some time now, it has been difficult to determine the origin of various statements made in the field of foreign policy—[foreign minister] Kozyrev or [Communist leader] Zyuganov," commented daily to *Izvestia* in a sarcastic tone in March of 1994 (Yushin 1994).[5]

For some time, however, despite all the apparent changes in rhetoric, Boris Yeltsin and his staff continued a firm course in cooperation with the United States and other Western countries. They invested substantially in a special relationship with the Clinton administration. Moreover, Yeltsin took pains to protect Kozyrev, who was widely regarded in Washington and other Western capitals as the live embodiment of the "new" anti-Communist and anti-imperialist foreign policy of Russia (Pushkov 1994).

The Russian intervention in Chechnya in December 1994—another domestic event—signified a new turning point for the Administration by toughening rhetoric and actions. By waging a successful war, Yeltsin apparently wanted to strengthen his nationalist credentials and neutralize the persistent arguments of the opposition. However, the outcome of the war gleaned the reverse reaction. The Duma angrily exploded. It was pointed out that the Russian legislature had not been formally informed in advance about the military action. Yeltsin was accused of not even explaining the purpose of the war. As a result, the responsibility for the military disaster became solely the government's. In self defense, the government's nationalistic rhetoric began to heat up (Simes 1994).

There was another important development in reaction to the Chechen war. Many conservative as well as liberal experts and politicians in the United States did not like Yeltsin's actions and criticized the war. Major television networks and cable companies in the United States aired reports revealing scenes of destroyed Chechen villages. This incensed Yeltsin and his entourage. Although the Clinton administration failed to take a firm position on the conflict, and Clinton himself compared the Russians' measures in Chechnya to Lincoln's actions against the separatist American South, there was a new crack in Russian-American relations. The past friendship between Russian "Democrats" and some Republicans and Democrats came to an end at that time.

The Fall of Kozyrev

In 1995, Russian oppositional forces, well aware of the support of their potential electorate, launched increasingly fierce attacks on Yeltsin, his Foreign Minister, and the government's entire foreign policy. Perhaps few other topics were more popular with Communist and nationalist columnists than the "pro-American" course of the Russian government. For Yeltsin—and this was becoming more apparent—Kozyrev increasingly turned into a political liability. Even liberal-minded observers accused Kozyrev of taking the good cause of rapprochement with the West too far, and thereby contributing to the reciprocal disillusionment they shared with the West (Pushkov 1995). Beside the Bosnian case, Kozyrev was blamed for condoning the American missile strikes against Baghdad in the summer of 1993.[6] Another nail in Kozyrev's political coffin was the fiasco with the 1992–1993 Russian-Indian deal to secure the delivery of cryogenic engines to India for missiles and associated technologies. The United States intervened to block this bilateral agreement, and the Foreign Ministry reacted with silent compliance. Most visibly, Kozyrev's reputation strengthened the claim of the opposition that the arms reduction treaties signed by Russia and the United States, including the important document START II, were designed to benefit the United States. This distrust expressed against America effectively blocked the ratification of START II in the Duma.

Disgust and contempt with Kozyrev's "weak-kneed" diplomacy grew among officials in the Ministry of Defense, the Foreign Intelligence Service, the Ministry of Foreign Economic Relations, and the Security Council's apparatus. For the first time since the polarization of the early 1990s, there was a palpable centrist mood in the Russian political and bureaucratic establishment. Those who expressed this mood began to call themselves *derzhavniki*. The word "derzhava" in Russian means great power and the imperial orb, an insignia of Russian czars. The priority of the *derzhavniki* was not Russia's integration into the Western community, but rather a new emphasis on domestic consolidation, restoration of the role of the state, and protection of Russian national interests. Among the *derzhavniki* were liberal young colleagues of Kozyrev, such as Andronik Migranian, Sergei Kortunov, Sergei Karaganov, and Alexei Arbatov. These individuals constantly traveled and lectured in the West. Nevertheless, they sensed very early that they would have to protect their vulnerable "pro-Western" flanks domestically. Even Kozyrev, at some point, began to timidly call himself *derzhavnik;* he clearly lacked credentials, however. Because his "pro-American" course was not of his invention, but rather an expression of Yeltsin's desire for friendship and partnership with Clinton and other Western leaders, the rise of *derzhavniki* contained a hidden menace to Yeltsin's leadership.

In October 1995, Boris Yeltsin, sensing the prevailing trend, publicly criticized Kozyrev for being too "soft" during consultations with the United States regarding the conditions for expanding the NATO bloc. Portraying the United States and Germany as Russia's new best friends, Kozyrev was never able to explain why NATO was so eagerly expanding into Eastern Europe. As commentators observed, the expansion struck a fatal blow to the foundation of Kozyrev's foreign policy (Pushkov 1995).

All in all, what happened to Kozyrev's diplomacy, i.e., Yeltsin's foreign-policy course between 1991 and 1995, was that it lost a significant portion of its domestic political base. Denouncing simplistically the "red-brown" coalition of Communists and ultra-conservatives for criticizing their policies, Yeltsin and Kozyrev practically overlooked the fact that the dissatisfaction with their diplomacy was rooted in a broad social and political base. With reluctant support in the Kremlin, and suffering continuous attacks from legislators and the extremely vocal anti-government media, Kozyrev did not have many alternative policies to consider. From the liability Kozyrev became a scapegoat for Yeltsin who, in the matter of fact, sanctioned most of the Kozyrev's actions. [7]

For the rest of his tenure, Kozyrev tried to sound tough in a calculated, but hopeless attempt to elevate his reputation in the eyes of the opposition. However, Kozyrev's sharply worded statements, that sometimes contained warnings and even threats, did not deceive the opposition (Pushkov 1995). The minister's earlier "romanticism" and resulting foreign-policy miscalculation could not be forgiven by Yeltsin's political adversaries, who began to play an anti-American card seriously.

Yeltsin was prepared to give up on Kozyrev in the fall of 1995.[8] When the December elections further strengthened the opposition to the government, with the Communist Party of the Russian Federation taking most the Duma seats, Yeltsin made another attempt to accommodate his critics and dismissed Kozyrev from his post as Foreign Minister on January 5, 1996. A majority of Russian lawmakers who were polled by Mnenie [Opinion] Service hailed Kozyrev's resignation and called for immediate corrections in foreign policy, despite the hawkish position Kozyrev adopted by the end of his tenure.[9] Yeltsin's decision to sack his foreign-policy quarterback showed the extent to which policy was being shaped to appease opposition forces. Yeltsin had long resisted pressures to remove Kozyrev and stuck with his much-maligned foreign minister for four years. But the 1995 elections, which demonstrated the growing strength of Yeltsin's critics and particularly Zyuganov—who would contest Yeltsin in the 1996 presidential election—pushed Yeltsin to succumb to the compromise he had formerly rigorously resisted.[10]

Yet, Kozyrev's dismissal did not substantially change the fact that the executive branch maintained essential control over foreign policy, responding to legislative critics only at its own behest and only in somewhat limited ways.

Primakov and Further Corrections

The rise of the new Foreign Minister, Evgeny Maximovich Primakov, was a turning point in the process of weakening the "pro-Western" course of the Yeltsin administration. Yeltsin's new appointee was a long-time adviser of the International Department of the Central Committee of the Communist Party. As a political appointee, he headed, in the 1960s, the Institute for Oriental Studies, and in the 1970s, the Institute for World Economy and International Relations. Gorbachev had included him on his team since 1985, and by 1990, Primakov was already Secretary of his Presidential Council and a Candidate Member of the Politburo. In 1991, Yeltsin appointed him—one of the few holdovers from the Gorbachev team—to head the Federal Intelligence Service. Primakov skillfully removed this organization from the deadly fire of the radical democrats, who called for KGB's blood. Thus, he earned the eternal gratitude of the Soviet intelligence and counterintelligence establishment (Daniels 1999). When Primakov came to the Foreign Ministry, he added to his team some intelligence officers who formerly worked for him.

Unlike Kozyrev, Primakov never burned bridges with Communists and nationalists in the Duma. Instead, he promised to put an end to the "naïve" and biased foreign policy of his predecessor. In his official rhetoric, he carefully distanced himself from anti-Americanism, but at the same time he deplored America's world dominance and emphasized Russia's need to cultivate alliances to counterbalance U.S. power. Most significantly, in his address to Russian diplomats in May 1998, he declared: "After a period of illusions and exaggerated expectations we are moving toward equal and balanced relationships with the United States" (p. 3). Yeltsin, himself, provided unreserved support for Primakov's search for a new foreign policy.

After two-and-a-half years in office, Primakov developed his reputation among the anti-Yeltsin opposition so effectively, that they enthusiastically supported his candidacy for Prime Minister in August 1998. The collapse of the Russian pro-American course of the early 1990s became an accepted reality in Russian politics. The situation inside Russia had shifted toward a harder line, self-efficiency, and growing self-isolation. As a consequence, anti-Americanism began to prevail. A small example illustrates the changes that were unfolding. During the early 1990s, Russia regarded the American economic embargo against Cuba an exclusive issue of bilateral American-Cuban relations. However, in February of 1996, when Senator Helms submitted a bill to tighten the embargo, it caused an uproar in Moscow and American policy was immediately indicted as interfering in the affairs of sovereign countries (Velekhov 1996).

The appointment of Primakov evoked a stony reaction in the United States. Many analysts branded him, simplistically, as a "KGB spymaster" at the helm of Russian diplomacy. This criticism, however, only contributed to Primakov's solid reputation among Russian political elites. This was the first time Americans bristled at the choice of a democratically elected Russian president and a freely elected parliament.

Presidential Elections of 1996

As in most democratic countries—with a few exceptions, of course—the rhetoric used by major candidates in the 1996 Russian presidential elections barely touched on international and foreign-policy issues. Remarkably, the opposition mentioned foreign policy more often than the president did and only in a critical way (Sigelman and Shiraev 2000, under review). However, most candidates, made a point to use anti-American arguments, thus distancing themselves from the official government course. Two major oppositional leaders—Zyuganov and Zhirinovsky—made clearly hostile anti-American statements (Zhirinovsky 14 June 1996; Zyuganov 15 June 1996). In the end of 1995, aware of the necessity to face the forthcoming parliamentary and, most importantly, tough presidential elections, Yeltsin's advisers convinced him to begin taking public opinion into account (MacKenzie 1995).

Obviously, the Administration had to continue walking the thin line between rhetoric and action designed for domestic and foreign consumption. Yeltsin's only reliable option was to maintain a moderate nationalistic course at home and, simultaneously, persuade the United States and other Western countries that he was the only alternative to a totalitarian revival in Russia. Perhaps it was seen as a correct decision that the Kremlin did not advertise Yeltsin's endorsements (made in May 1996) of German Chancellor Kohl and President Clinton at home. On the other hand, it was also logical to continue to receive western aid. For instance, the Yeltsin administration was eager to accept a 500-million dollar pre-election credit for the coal industry. Earlier in March, Yeltsin discussed with Clinton continued Russian purchases of American chicken legs (Abarinov 1996d).

Yet, under the surface, the electoral campaign and the way Yeltsin was elected did affect public perception of Russian-American relations. The great majority of Russians were forced to choose between Yeltsin and Zyuganov and obviously did not like this choice. Around 20 percent of the electorate were desperate for a third option. They did not want to return to Communism, but at the same time disliked what they regarded the continuing decline and humiliation of a great country. Therefore, many picked General Alexander Lebed as their candidate. Lebed entered politics almost by chance: In August 1991, he vacillated between the coup-makers and the Yeltsin camp, but eventually refused to cooperate with either side. In the early 1990s, he—as a military commander—protected Russians in a secessionist region of Moldova and immediately became the darling of many people in Russia. A number of veterans from "Lebed's Army" aligned themselves with the Supreme Soviet during the mini-civil war of October 1993. As the propagandist runner-up of the presidential elections, where he decided to run, Lebed published the book "*Za Derzhavu Obidno*" [I am bitter for the country]. The key word "*derzhava*" associated Lebed with the new political center, and the phrase itself came from a very popular Russian movie hero, who fulfilled his duty to the Russian empire and died in a battle against rag-tag Central-Asian bandits.

After the first round, when Lebed made a surprisingly good showing, the Yeltsin camp cunningly co-opted him and, it was widely believed, obtained his votes as well. During a brief stay in the Kremlin, Lebed declared the end of the war in Chechnya. He became popular among American pundits as a "strong-handed" man with whom the United States could do business. Actually, Lebed represented the same political force as Zhirinovsky did just a few years earlier. Now this force became part of Yeltsin's electoral coalition. Russia's evolution toward a tougher stance continued. Remarkably, this was the year when the Clinton administration began to push for NATO expansion.

NATO Enlargement

Shortly before the U.S. presidential elections in 1996, it was announced that three former members of the Warsaw Treaty Organization, Poland, the Czech Republic, and Hungary would become new members of NATO (Goldgeier 1999). In the eyes of the tough critics of Yeltsin-Kozyrev foreign policy, especially the Communists and nationalists, the announcement of the NATO expansion was a great vindication of their claims that only the opposition is capable of protecting Russia from foreign foes (MacWilliam 1997). The opposition received new evidence of growing multiple threats to Russia from the outside—chiefly from the United States. It is possible that certain American policies during the decade under review had contributed to this situation. The tough stance the United States took in its negotiations with Mikhail Gorbachev over the Interme-diate Nuclear Forces (INF) treaty and the future of the two Germanys led many individuals in the Soviet military and diplomatic establishment to believe that the United States had exacted too many concessions from the U.S.S.R. in the final days of the Cold War. The decision to expand NATO created even greater and more pressing concerns among opinion leaders and many ordinary Russian citizens.

The voices of opposition to NATO expansionism were heard in Rus-sia throughout the 1990s, and top Russian military commanders sent warnings about the appearance of the United States and its allies near Rus-sia's borders earlier in the 1990s. During his visit to France in 1995, Yeltsin correctly implied that NATO's eastward expansion was an extremely sen-sitive issue for Russia, especially on the threshold of the December elec-tions, in which it was generally believed that many voters would be drawn toward those candidates who espoused the idea of restoring national great-ness (Kalashnikova and Dymarsky 1995). On May 9, 1995, the Russian holiday marking World War II victory in Europe, the Duma called on Rus-sians to stage a day of protest against NATO expansion. Some members of the media reported in early 1997 that Russia's top generals sent a classified petition to the president in which they insisted on re-aiming some Russ-ian nuclear missiles on Warsaw, Prague, and Budapest, as an intimidating act of retaliation. Politicians who opposed the government lead anti-NATO rallies. In May 1997, the Popular-Patriotic Union of Russia, a Communist-led opposition alliance, sent groups of protesters to demonstrate outside the U.S., French, Italian, German, and British embassies in Moscow. The protesters carried signs saying "No to NATO Expansion" and "Hands Off Russia." Communist Party leader, Gennady Zyuganov, told reporters that his party's representatives in the Council of Europe's Parliamentary Assembly had launched a Europe-wide "No to NATO!" campaign. He claimed that socialists and social-democrats from many European countries had misgivings about NATO growth (Newsline on the Web; 6 May 1996, "Opposition Continues Protests against NATO expansion"). The United States and NATO were continuously charged with creating a *cordon sanitaire* around Russia's borders as an attempt to isolate the country from Europe (Lebed 13 May 1996; Volkov 1994; Fadeev 1994).

Many Russian politicians with internationalist reputations—commonly regarded as America's sympathizers—were forced to swallow the bitter pill of America's betrayal. Mikhail Gorbachev (1994), for example, accused NATO of unfair play and expanding far beyond its historical borders in violation of the gentlemen's agreements of the 1980s between him and George Bush. Both Yegor Gaidar, former acting Prime Minister and the leader of Russia's Choice Party, and Grigory Yavlinsky, leader of the Yabloko Party, repeatedly criticized NATO's expansion decision as dangerous. Moreover, Yavlinsky's faction in the Duma issued an angry statement against the expansion, claiming that it could lead to the disruption of military-political equilibrium in Europe and violate Russia's national and state interests (Mikheev 1994). Even the centrist newspaper, *Negavisimaya Gazeta* (15 January 1997), suggested that the expansion of NATO contributed to the development of mistrust and hostility between Moscow and Washington.

The culmination of the opposition's attacks against Yeltsin took place during the impeachment debates held in May of 1999. One of the accusations against Yeltsin was that his yielding to the United States caused enormous damage to the security and defense capability of Russia. The destruction of the U.S.S.R.—allegedly orchestrated by Yeltsin—allowed the United States and other NATO countries to conduct their foreign policy without regard to Russia's position. Doing NATO a favor, Yeltsin removed a 300,000 strong contingent of the Russian army from Eastern Europe. As a result of his actions, the United States was able to push NATO close to Russia's borders, and to conduct the barbaric bombardments of Iraq and Yugoslavia (Filimonov 1999). It was claimed during the debates that the destruction of the U.S.S.R. was designed by Yeltsin to serve the interest of NATO countries, and above all, the United States (Ilyukhin 1999).[11]

Gradually, "moderate" Russian nationalism became a powerful set of beliefs for a growing number of potential voters. Nationalism morphed into a political issue; anti-Americanism was transforming into a political commodity: It sold well to many potential supporters. Why was this happening? There will always be psychological justifications and excuses for self-defensive actions and we discussed these issues in Chapter 3. Nationalism is one such "justifications" in the individual consciousness, because it provides the individual with a sense of security. In this context, to be a nationalist, and therefore anti-Americanist, became a matter of common sense given the perception of growing intimidation from the West and the United States (Umbach 1996, 477). The nationalism of the elites became easily understood and embraced by the masses. The overall picture of the Russian political situation in 1995, in the face of NATO expansion, became not one of a "good" liberal administration under pressure from "evil" nationalists, but one of a nationalist government struggling to fend off other, more belligerent nationalists. For pure political reasons, after 1995, it was almost impossible to find a national-level politician who would risk calling himself or herself a "Westerner." This is a result that only a rare expert could have predicted in 1991: Pro-American orientations lost their appeal among the majority of the voters.

The War in Bosnia, the Resentment against America

As we mentioned earlier, the U.S. involvement in the Balkans and Russia's permissive policy toward U.S. actions in this region became a matter of concern and frustration on the side of the opposition from the beginning of the conflict in the early 1990s. The government's missteps in handling events such as the Western ultimatum to the Bosnian Serbs in 1994, the ensuing Russian decision to send troops, the agreement on military intervention in the fall of 1995, and the Dayton negotiations all provided easy fodder for critics. Moreover, later government corrections of course, which were primarily pro-Serbian, were interpreted by Strobe Talbott—at that time the U.S. Ambassador-at-large to the former U.S.S.R. and special adviser to the Secretary of State—as temporizing moves taken in Moscow to accommodate a substantial body of pro-Serbian public opinion in Russia. In fact, this opinion was not necessarily pro-Serbian, but rather anti-Western and anti-American (Shiraev and Zubok 2000).

The theme of the American presence in Bosnia was vocalized the loudest in radical opposition newspapers that began an unprecedented campaign of allegations against the United States. Washington was accused of conducting expansionist and barbaric politics in the heart of Europe.[12] By 1995, an anti-American flavor became an almost required seasoning to any public figure's public statements on international affairs. Thus, former Gorbachev top adviser, Alexander Tsypko, implied that the U.S. intervention in Bosnia had a clear anti-Russian motivation (*Ogonyok,* June 1995, No. 25, 73). In an article published by *Izvestia* in 1994, a renowned journalist angrily attacked the American government for disregarding Russia's "national interests" in Bosnia (Kondrashov 20 April 1994; see also Kondrashov 5 March 1994). The author, in a typical post-Soviet "take-no-prisoners" journalistic style, complained of the public degradation of Russia, which had been "spreading its legs" for the Americans.

NATO's January 1994 threats to bomb Serbian positions in Bosnia put the Russian government in an extremely vulnerable position, making its Western-oriented foreign policies, including its liberal policy in Bosnia, look like grave mistakes. Pressure to modify Russian policy to show more support for the Serbs intensified following NATO's air strike threats in early February. Zhirinovsky, leader of the LDPR, proclaimed that the Serbs were no longer alone, that his party would change Russia's foreign policy and send an army to help the Serbs, and even give them a new secret weapon (Gryzunov and Baturin 4 February 1994). An overwhelming majority of Duma deputies condemned the NATO ultimatum and demanded that the Serbs be supported (Bolshakov 1994).

Under continuous pressure from the opposition, the government finally began to modify its stance in the Bosnia conflict in a limited fashion starting in February 1994. As noted earlier, government rhetoric and certain actions began to shift, becoming less pro-Western and more pro-Serbian. Taking a harsh stance in the conflict for the first time, Yeltsin challenged the ultimatum and succeeded in thwarting NATO air strikes on the Serbs in Bosnia at least temporarily. Moscow's first challenge to NATO in Bosnia seemed to please some of those who had criticized the government for being beholden to Western interests and American interests in particular. After the accord was announced, and for the only time during the course of the Bosnia conflict, the relationship between Yeltsin and the Duma regarding policy in Bosnia was somewhat positive. The newspaper, *Segodnya,* even announced "the prospective emergence of a consensus" between the Duma and the Kremlin caused by a foreign-policy event (Volkov 1994, 1).

However, growing distrust of the West reached new heights in early September 1995 when NATO—once again—conducted a bombing campaign without Russia's prior notification. Then the U.N. Secretariat's approval of a secret memo relinquishing authority over the use of air power in Bosnia to NATO, which also occurred without consulting with all permanent members, further incensed Russia. This move was widely interpreted in Russia as a signal that NATO and the United States had taken over operations in Bosnia. Vladimir Lukin, chairman of the Duma's Committee on Foreign Affairs, complained again of the unfair treatment of Russia by the United States.[13]

These beliefs—rooted perhaps in Soviet socialization experiences, but largely in electoral concerns and public opinion approval ratings—became increasingly evident in Russian public discourse about the Bosnia conflict, as already shown. These concerns presumably came to modulate foreign policy to a greater extent than in previous cases.

Who will Benefit?

Maybe there are no serious reasons to overestimate the danger of Russian anti-American rhetoric and some anticipated unfriendly actions sponsored by Russians. In fact, they are just words, claims, and intentions. Often such statements are made either in anticipation of particular concessions from the West or for pure consumption of domestic pubic opinion. Moreover, assumptions about the danger of Russia falling into the hands of nationalists and Communists—common in the Russian political rhetoric of the 1990s—were often made in the form of warnings designed to frighten the West: "You better watch out! If certain things do not happen in the international arena, democracy will be threatened back here, in Russia."

In 1992, such "watch-out-for-us!" reasoning was used by the renowned Russian scholar, Georgy Arbatov, who urged the United States to deliver real help to Russia, instead of empty promises. Otherwise, he suggested, the Russian *reds* and *browns* (i.e., Communists and Fascists) would eagerly wait in the wings to destroy democracy (Arbatov 1992). There is no shortage of other examples of such warnings. Deputy of the Duma, Yevgeny Ambartsumov (1994), implied that Washington's actions in the former Yugoslavia were certainly going to provide additional strength to those nationalists and radicals in opposition to the Kremlin. In the same year, dangerous anti-democratic repercussions of American foreign policy were predicted for Russia by Yeltsin's special envoy in the former Yugoslavia, Vitaly Churkin (1994). Speaking in Prague against NATO expansion, former acting Prime Minister, Yegor Gaidar, implied that the shortsightedness of the United States and the West would play into the hands of Russian hard-liners and would help nobody in Russia except the radical nationalists (Reuters World Service, 16 January 1995). A warning statement about the U.S. and NATO policy in Bosnia was issued by Deputy Prime Minister, Sergei Shakhrai (1994), who, again, pointed at the links between international developments and the dangerous "domestic political situation in the Russian Federation." Assumptions about threats from abroad and Russian internal affairs were described in numerous newspaper publications at different times and by journalists of diverse political views (see, for example, Shchedrov 1999; Kondrashov 1996; Volobuev and Tyagumenko 1992).

As we mentioned earlier, foreign policy in democratic societies is responsive to pressure from various domestic interest groups, political opposition, and public opinion in general. The desire to be elected or re-elected creates pressing incentives in politicians to be aware of both supporters and opponents. Therefore, adoption of certain government foreign policies may be based on yielding to the opponents in other areas. Conversely, some political gains at home may be used as bargaining chips—under the pressure of opposition and public opinion—for particular actions in foreign policy fields. Therefore, a country's international relations—and Russia is not an exception—may often depend on the strength and weakness of the government's domestic political opponents (Everts 1996).

Criticism of the government by its political opposition is expected in a democracy, especially when the government is making mistakes. It was supposed to be happening in Russia, and, as was duly noted in an editorial in *The Christian Science Monitor* (27 September 1995), "political opponents of President Clinton, Prime Minister Major, and Chancellor Kohl daily do the same." As in most democratic societies, Russian political opposition tried to use each and every occasion to apply pressure on the government and gain momentum for forthcoming elections. In the Russia of the 1990s, the target of criticism and condemnation was Yeltsin and his administration. The ultimate goal of the attacks was to remove the president from power. Affected by the internal political struggle, the development of Russia's relations with the United States and the West was frequently used to promote the political interests of different groups and individuals (Glukhov 1993). Instead of being a stabilizing and constantly developing factor, relatively unaffected by varying political conditions, cooperation with the West was continually tied to various domestic issues—and more often—to the solutions of unmanageable internal problems. Ironically, apparent "solutions" to these problems unfortunately resulted in the strengthening of anti-American rhetoric.

It is a paradox that anti-Americanism was one of the unexpected effects of the competitive post-Soviet democratic political process. Unlike most European countries, Russian political debates were taking place in an extremely polarized and unstable domestic, ideological, and political environment, in which democratic principles of government were not supported by individual habits and democratic customs. The Russian elite had not developed a culture or tradition of compromise, balancing of interests, or consensus-seeking (Melville 1999). To make matters worse, the elites were convinced that only they—not the voters—had an exclusive right to draft and conduct foreign policy (Kremenyuk 1997). All of this increased acrimony and polarization—almost inevitable in cases when contestants have little intention to reach a compromise and shift instead toward more extreme positions than those they initially held (Moscovici and Zavalloni 1969). Pro- and anti-American attitudes became objects of manipulation and crude power politics.

Moral? Russian anti-Americanism is one of those unfortunate trade-offs of democratic society. Foreign-policy attitudes and actions—as well as attitudes and actions related to any other policy—can be bargained and traded as commodities. Apparently, Russian anti-Americanism had relatively high domestic value and there was no reason to keep it off the market. "The one bad thing about U.S. elections is sacrificing anything, including long-term national interests, to campaigning," former Russian ambassador to Washington, Vladimir Lukin, implied in a radio interview. "Some in [Russia] would like to copy that habit, but it is a bad idea. Like it or not, Russia and the United States will have to coexist and cooperate even after the polls," he added (Shchedrov 1999). Indeed, some find that one of the roots of contemporary Russian anti-Americanism grows in the soil of the democratic system itself: Too much attention is paid to "appropriate" image and potential foreign-policy setbacks, and too many concessions are made in anticipation of opposition criticism or—in the case of Russia—a Communist or nationalist backlash. On the other hand, some argue, an authoritarian government in Russia would not be influenced by immediate political concerns and would therefore maintain a pragmatic approach toward the United States. If there are only two pathways that Russian foreign policy has to choose from, this is not a very promising selection. The United States can do very little to influence any of these outcomes.

Chapter Six

The Eruption Against America:
The War Over Kosovo

America's and NATO's display of merciless strength and willingness
to execute those who dared to defy them was aimed at intimidating
anyone else who might fail to follow orders.

Dmitry Ryurikov, former top foreign policy adviser to Yeltsin, 1999

[The war] aroused the whole Russia.

From newspapers

"Honk if you are angry." This imperative to press a knob on
one's steering wheel was not provoked by a bumper sticker
or the road signs displayed by a group of strikers. In March
of 1999, thousands of drivers who passed the tall yellow building along the
ever-busy, major inner-city beltway, noticed the stars and stripes hanging
limp on the side of this building. Then the drivers furiously honked. Witnesses told us that in the 1960s, when a Moscow cabby was killed, allegedly
due to the negligence of the city police, hundreds of his fellows publicly
protested by driving through central streets and honking. In April 1989,
the motorists in Tbilisi—the capital of the Republic of Georgia—
expressed their anger in the same way, remembering the recent massacre
of civilians by Soviet troops. In 1999, it was the war launched by the
United States against Yugoslavia that triggered this massive storm of popular protest. When NATO aircraft began to bomb Belgrade, anti-American feelings in Russia suddenly and flamboyantly exploded.

The most active Muscovites started collecting signatures for impromptu petitions. Major newspapers and magazines were overwhelmed with letters and telegrams filled with anger and frustration over American actions in Kosovo. Elderly people who once—in the old Soviet days—were trained in throwing ink-cans against the walls of the Chinese embassy, now practiced these skills against Americans. There were many young people among the protest groups, which were comprised of some known troublemakers and the followers of the neo-Nazi party of Barkashov, college students, and scores of curious bystanders. An actor from a local film studio appeared in front of the U.S. Embassy in a knight's regalia, riding a horse, and carrying a bow and arrow. He took aim at the American flag, sent the arrow across the street and, before a group of stunned Moscow cops could do anything, stirred the horse and vanished. Moscow's criminal world, equipped with newer armaments, also left its signature on the people's book of protests. A Jeep Cherokee stopped in front of the Embassy and an unidentified man fired a bazooka into the front windows. Luckily, nobody inside was hurt.

Americans who lived in Moscow for years[1] and those U.S. citizens who visited their Russian friends in 1999, were stunned to discover that Russian revulsion over the war in Kosovo metastasized into their personal relationships. Some American colleagues began to complain that their usual popularity among the Russians had suffered a crushing blow. The infamous "And you, Brutus?" was felt in almost every email we received from our colleagues in Moscow and St. Petersburg. Old American and Russian friends whose relationships had been forged in Soviet times by the common enemy, the KGB and the Communist regime, now almost shouted at each other over their differences concerning the events in Kosovo (Joan Urban, private information). The playful tabloid of a group in the American community in Moscow quickly produced, obviously in self-defense, the manifesto "One-hundred and one reasons why NATO's war sucks" (*The Exile*, 8–21 April 1999, 62). One interesting sign though is worth noticing. The protesting Russians did not puncture the tires of Fords and Chevrolets on the streets and did not spill out Pepsi or Coca Cola—something that some Americans had done to the cars of Soviet diplomats and bottles of Stolichnaya vodka in 1983, when the Soviets shot down the Korean airliner because of a tragic mistake.

Many Russian public officials acted in unison with the public. Deputy Prime Minister Maslyukov called for the immediate shipment of weapons to Serbia. Communists in the State Duma requested the deployment of a military contingent in Yugoslavia. Several generals and activists of the Liberal Democratic party called for a military response to NATO actions (Yavlinsky 24 March 1999). The scale of public indignation and its unanimity was clearly unexpected and surprising for most foreign observers. However, these events did not grow out of nothing. They resulted from particular developments that were taking place in Russia prior to the 1999 crisis.

The Road to the Revolt

Any observer, particularly a Russian one who left Moscow in May and returned in the fall of 1998, right after the disastrous financial crash of August, would have immediately noticed the dramatic change in the overall psychological atmosphere and political landscape of the country. The perception was as if the society were going through the aftermath of a serious earthquake. One positive aspect of this change for foreigners, particularly for Americans, was the rapid growth of the value of the dollar and the devaluation of the ruble. As a result, retail prices in Moscow, once sky-high, plummeted: Most of the goods, services, and restaurant meals became cheaper by an order of three or four times. One could buy a hardcover book printed on excellent paper for one or two dollars, go to a first-class symphony concert for 50 cents, and attend a performance of the world-famous Bolshoi Theater for the price of a movie ticket in a typical suburban Cineplex somewhere in Ohio or Virginia.

Nevertheless, the majority of Russians paid dearly for these low prices. Virtually everyone lost in approximately three-quarters of their monthly wage (unlike in the United States people count their salaries by how much one makes a month). Millions of people had their savings disappear from their bank accounts for the second time since 1992. In just a matter of a few days, money that could have been converted into dollars was frozen, turned into non-exchangeable rubles, and then gone. One of the losers was Mikhail Gorbachev, whose foreign earnings—including a honorarium for acting in television commercials for Pizza Hut—had brought him a few millions. He had put this sum in a bank as the down payment for the construction of a new building for his Foundation on Leninsky Prospect. The bank then crashed and the money disappeared.

While the father of perestroika, with all his sources of income, could recuperate, the new Moscow middle class did not do so well. The average salary of Muscovites was around 600 dollars per month before the crash—3.8 times higher than the rate in the country—but it sunk to a bit over 200 dollars. The backbone of this social stratum—young, educated women working in private firms and companies—found themselves bringing home 300 or 400 dollars a month instead of the solid 1,000 or 2,000 they could and did make just a few months earlier. Among those who suffered were also Russian journalists, the very milieu that spawned and nourished the opinion-making environment in the Russian capital.

The 1996 presidential elections opened the spigot of "easy" money, and many of them started to get honoraria of 1,000 dollars and more per article. After the August 1998 crisis, they were forced to endure significantly lower compensation. One of the reasons was that the media suffered critically from the plummeting of advertising income, particularly in the first months after the crash. Writers and artists, the so-called creative intelligentsia from theaters, studios, and professional unions witnessed helplessly yet another debilitating collapse of their economic status. Under the new social conditions of capitalist, democratic Russia, one's financial decline and dire straits automatically presupposed a decline in his or her social status. The symbols of the "Russian dream"—a decent country house, a high-quality city apartment, a new car, a top-of-the-line stereo system, and trips to four- and five-star Mediterranean resorts were once again out of reach for most people.

Social clouds had gathered over Russia without the detection of sociologists and pollsters. Even though Japan, South Korea, and several other Asian countries were seriously shaken earlier, these events had not been considered a bad omen for Russian society. Now the question was: Who was responsible for such a fiasco? There were explanations needed as to who was accountable for such a rapid and spectacular collapse of the financial markets. The government of young technocrats, headed by Sergei Kiryenko, resigned immediately after the crash. However, this cabinet did not become a scapegoat: Kiryenko and his people had stayed in power for too short a period of time. The State Duma, the sensitive barometer of Russian mood, used the moment to voice renewed criticism of the "power party" in the Kremlin. As a result, the deputies of various parties and factions, browbeaten by Yeltsin's victory in the elections of 1996, resumed their attacks against him. Yeltsin, however, was smart enough to neutralize this mood by appointing Evgeny Primakov to the post of Prime Minister. A veteran of consensus-seeking politics, a profoundly reassuring figure, and typical centrist, Primakov was much disliked in the United States for his attempts in 1990–1991 to prevent the Gulf War and for acting as an unsolicited Soviet middleman between Bush and Saddam Hussein. In Russia, on the other hand, he was widely perceived as a solid father figure. With a small group of workaholic assistants, drawn mostly from the ranks of the Soviet intelligence, security services, and the military, Primakov quickly reached several gentleman's agreements with key opposition factions in the Duma, including the largest and most vocal—the Communist faction. The Duma decided to give Primakov the benefit of the doubt and the time to act. In reality, though, his hands were completely tied by Boris Yeltsin, who jealously watched his veteran Prime Minister and with irritation at his growing popularity. Primakov managed to push the first measures through the Duma designed to reduce the horrendously high taxes. Unfortunately, that was the end of prime minister's "New Deal." Days passed, and observers, particularly in the West, noted sarcastically that the Primakov government had managed to garner its support by doing nothing.

Quite unexpectedly to Russians, the United States bombed Iraq in December of 1998. At least three television networks aired footage of these scathing attacks. Immediately, the biggest Duma factions, including the liberals of the "Yabloko" party vehemently denounced the American military action. Vladimir Lukin, Chairman of the International Affairs Committee of the State Duma and the leading expert on foreign policy on the Yavlinsky team, implied: "It is absolutely intolerable for the world community [to give] an opportunity to one, two, or three countries to single-handedly condemn another country, announce a verdict, and then carry out the sentence." Such actions by the United States and Great Britain, in his view, were turning the world order into chaos (Lukin 17 December 1999). The Russian foreign ministry maintained a sullen silence for awhile, and then lodged a protest. This reaction indicated a sharp turn from the formerly tepid and reluctant support of the United States' and international sanctions against Iraq. Russia had apparently moved in favor of open opposition to the sanctions and overall U.S. foreign policy. For example, Grigory Yavlinsky, during a meeting with M. Albright in Moscow in January of 1999, talked at length about the necessity for both Russia and the United States to maintain peace and negotiate with each other. However, he—perhaps the most dovish Russian politician—decided to remind the U.S. Secretary of State that Russia had a missile defense system comprised of C-300s, which were more advanced than American Patriot missiles, and that it would take Americans at least three years to catch up with them (Yabloko Press Release, 21 January 1999, *www.yabloko.ru*).

Russia's political elites took the bombing of Iraq as a signal to mobilize. Apparently, there were several momentous developments in the offing in the relationship between Russia and the United States that bothered Russian politicians, security specialists, and foreign policy experts.

First, the implications of NATO enlargement dawned on the Russian elites only after a significant delay. The U.S. Senate voted for the admission of Poland, Hungary, and the Czech Republic to NATO on April 30, 1998. Surprisingly, this action evoked precious little protest in Moscow. However, a year later, the Clinton administration hosted a tremendous gala in Washington for world leaders in commemoration of the fiftieth anniversary of the North Atlantic Treaty Organization. For Russian leadership and the opinion-making elite, this was a deeply symbolic and highly unpleasant event. Even for those Russians who persuaded themselves that they hadn't lost the Cold War, it was hard to ignore the obvious connotations of the NATO gathering in the American capital. This was a celebration in which Russia had no seat of honor.

Second, there was the mentioned earlier financial crisis in Russia, and the way Prime Minister Kiryenko's cabinet chose to react to it by "defaulting" on state obligations, including so-called super-high-interest GKO bonds (high-interest, short term government bonds issued to banks). This measure elicited the quick and highly negative reaction of Western financial and business circles, particularly in the United States. Not only did thousands of small, risky businesses hurriedly flee Russia, but some very respectable firms, including Goldman Sachs of New York, lost their money, and their reputations as well. The Wall Street and world banking community were enraged at Russia, and many vowed that the country should be punished for its irresponsible behavior and singled out as a pariah for years to come. The IMF and World Bank shared these attitudes. Never, since the early 1990s, were the Russian government and private businesses completely ostracized and shunned by international economic and financial circles. The United States launched a series of measures to rescue South Korea, Thailand, and Malaysia where the crisis had already struck. Instead of asking themselves what Russia should do to encourage similar efforts of generosity, the Russian elites preferred to interpret Western aid to Asian countries—once again—as evidence of the double standard that the United States and its followers practiced in their relationships with Russia.

Finally, the woeful state of Yeltsin's presidency and the approaching presidential elections of 2000 opened a new round in the struggle for power. The anti-American card was a potent weapon in this struggle. The State Duma denunciations of U.S. actions in the Gulf were obviously just a rehearsal for the political battles that lay ahead. Among top officials and politicians who understood the nature of these struggles was Prime Minister of Russia, Primakov, the "wise man" of Russian politics and the veteran of the Soviet establishment. When he accepted his position in September, he declared that he would not run for president in 2000. Nevertheless, the situation emerging in Russia provided enough information to the careful observer to suggest that, despite his words, he would enter the presidential race. The yearning for a new leader who could guarantee stability was so overwhelming that Primakov became hostage to the situation. He seemed to be the only candidate who could garner support from the political center, the Communist opposition, and the vocal nationalist elements. His most well-known assets were his closeness with the Russian national-security establishment and his reputation as a staunch and principled defender of Russia's national interests, vis-à-vis the United States (See Chapter 4).

Sensing impending danger, Yeltsin, himself, and his close advisers began to plot countermeasures to undermine Primakov's growing popularity and, subsequently, his increasingly powerful position in the government. In the first months of 1999, Yeltsin stripped the Prime Minister of several important functions and made several humiliating public verbal attacks against him. Nevertheless, Primakov's reputation as the champion of a strong and independent Russia—a country unyielding under pressure from the United States—remained untarnished.

What was Behind the Revulsion?

The breakout of the war over Kosovo openly stunned Russian elites like no other political development of the 1990s. Most Russian experts—even those who were involved in the intricacies of the Yugoslav problem—did not expect the war to happen. As a matter of fact, despite all the disputes and scandals, Clinton was fairly popular among Russians. Prudence was his most recognizable virtue in the eyes of the experts: He was cautious and highly opportunistic, avoiding rash and impulsive actions. However, what he did in Kosovo was a shocker. When a former think-tank expert, and Russian Ambassador to a South American country learned that the war in Kosovo began, he just exclaimed: "What do these Americans think they are doing?" Most of his colleagues in Moscow were on the same emotional wavelength. In an interview with the radio station, *Echo Moskvy*, Grigory Yavlinsky called American principles of foreign policy "bulldozer style." In his view, Americans "crush through and break everything, and this style begins to irritate" (Yavlinsky 24 March 1999).

Primakov was on a government plane heading for New York and Washington for a long-delayed meeting with United States' officials. As the plane approached Canada, Primakov got a message from Vice President Albert Gore: After some indecision, Clinton decided to launch a preventive war against Milosevic. The Russian Prime Minister immediately tallied the possible domestic implications of these new international developments. Then he immediately ordered the plane to turn around and go back to Moscow. This gesture did not make sense from the viewpoint of Russia's international clout: It would have been better for Primakov to meet with Clinton and explain to him personally the nature of Russia's reservations. This demarche also damaged prospects of resuming the foreign financial assistance that the Russian government desperately needed. Some commentators, for example, from the respectable business daily, *Kommersant,* repeatedly criticized Primakov for this theatrical behavior. Yet, this small snowball of skepticism was buried in the avalanche of enthusiastic praise that Primakov evoked across a wide Russian political spectrum. His calculations and decisions apparently reinforced his political reputation as a tough opponent to U.S. expansionist actions.

The war was, above all, a sobering development that significantly distorted the vision of European security, for which the Russians strived. The United States, in one swing, violated several international covenants including the provisions of the Helsinki Act of 1975 that, from the Russian perspective, guaranteed peace, sovereignty, and territorial integrity for all countries in Europe. The war against Yugoslavia was also a violation of the "narrow" interpretation of the concept of national sovereignty in Europe. Many American commentators—among them Brzezinsky—explicitly called to put an end to the sanctity of the classical notion of sovereignty—a long-term axiom in international relations. From their standpoint, international force can be used to punish any "evil government" that imposes an act of genocide or similar crime against its own citizens. Translated into contemporary Russian—something Russian newspapers did not hesitate to do—this American demand signified the existence of the right of the United States to be a global cop and to punish—although hypothetically—the Russian government and side with ethnic separatists within the legitimate borders of the Russian Federation!

Second, the U.S. and Western European countries obviously far transcended the statute of NATO that envisaged the use of military forces only in cases of explicit aggression against one of the bloc's members. Again, many American observers used the outbreak of war to propose, with much zeal, a replacement for the outdated Cold War mandate of NATO with a new one and to use it as an authorization of police actions in areas outside Europe. From the Russian perspective, this meant the validation of the U.S. claim that it is a self-appointed global persecutor.

Third, the United States completely disregarded the role of the United Nations and its Security Council. The Clinton administration had gotten into trouble in Somalia, where the international peace keeping mission in 1993 led to disaster and the death of several marines. From that time on, the administration waged an undeclared war against U.N. General Secretary, Boutros Ghali.[2] In addition, the disastrous performance of the Western European countries in the U.N. peace-keeping mission in Bosnia in 1994–1995, confirmed to the Clinton administration that the NATO format, in which the United States has unquestionable leadership, would function much better than the U.N. format. The war over Kosovo was the first precedent where this new approach was tested. From the viewpoint of Russia—a permanent member of the Security Council—this policy was literally a slap in the face. While Russia could exercise veto power at the U.N. level, it had no leverage whatsoever in NATO policies, control for which Russian leaders obviously yearned and that Western allies were obviously reluctant to give. Indeed, during the debates on NATO expansion, the opponents and enemies of Russia in the United States warned that providing Moscow with any voice in NATO could create a dangerous predicament. Henry Kissinger complained about this situation in the spring of 1998: "Whoever heard of a military alliance begging with a weakened adversary? NATO should not be turned into an instrument to conciliate Russia or Russia will undermine it" (Goldgeier 1999, 113).

Those who were believed to be particularly cheated and betrayed by U.S. actions in Kosovo were the pro-Western and liberal strata. Although many of these individuals had long since become champions of a great Russia and adopted tough patriotic language, they, at the same time, quietly maintained a thread of understanding with Clinton, Strobe Talbott, and other members of the administration who were sympathetic toward Russia. In January 1997, a powerful player of Moscow politics, Anatoly Chubais, complained to Talbott that the NATO enlargement was making life very tough for the reformers. He said that Washington should compensate Russia for being excluded from NATO by, for example, providing it with membership in other prestigious international institutions. Fulfilling this request, Clinton announced, two months later, that Russia would be a member of the G-7. He also promised to work with Russia "to advance its membership in key international economic institutions like the WTO [World Trade Organization], the Paris Club [group of Western creditors], and the OECD [the group of advanced economies] (Goldgeier 1999, 112,114).

These commitments did not make much of a difference: Both poor and debt-ridden, Russia did not belong in the clubs of rich and prosperous nations. Yet, these promises served, like powerful drugs, to placate Russian elites and ease the painful consequences of NATO's enlargement. With the war over Kosovo, the soothing effect of such symbolic actions was over.

Russian liberals who implied that they had been betrayed by America behaved like an angry mob. They could not challenge their U.S. counterparts to a duel, like Musketeers in the good old days. Instead, they resorted to sniping and making caustic remarks in an effort to take revenge at Clinton and his administration for what they regarded as the breaking of a gentlemen's contract. Speaking at an international conference in early April of 1999, Vladimir Averchev, a member of the Yabloko party and a leading expert of the Duma's foreign affairs committee, suggested: "We were told that when we joined the world institutions we were joining a world of rules. Now we see that the rules are what the Americans want to make of them. The post–Cold War world of the past decade has ended. The U.N. Security Council is finished." Professor Yevgeny Yasin, a recognized liberal and former Minister of Finances, continued in the same tone: "Liberals now face a terrible defeat in the Duma elections later this year. The West has done something we thought impossible; it has united the country, in hostility to it." Yet another distinguished reformer, former historian, Yevgeny Kozhokin (1999), later appointed Director of the Russian Institute of Strategic Studies, implied that the humanitarian reasons given for the intervention were sheer hypocrisy. "The U.S President is weak and needed to prove himself. In his weakness, he is a tool of the military-industrial complex."

Mikhail Gorbachev, and a group of intellectuals around him, also denounced the war as a dangerous international precedent. They acknowledged the humanitarian motives behind the NATO attack, but believed that the chosen means were excessive, unnecessary, barbaric, and ultimately counterproductive. They openly criticized the American arrogance of power, and joined the chorus of those who spoke against the United States posing as the world's cop.

The reactions of the general public, unlike the elite responses, were more spontaneous and had a somewhat different underlying chemistry. In the weeks during the war over Kosovo, Americans came to believe that Russians supported the Serbs as if they were their Slavic and Orthodox brethren. American television commentators, in particular, opted for this type of explanation. Ironically, the Russian television programs that castigated the U.S. bombing of Yugoslavia and described the plight of the Serbs, also slipped into their own, anti-American linear mode: The United States was guilty, whereas Yugoslavia was absolutely innocent.

It seems, however, that the most powerful motives of Russian indignation laid far from historic sympathies, or ethnic and religious kinship with the Serbs (see Shiraev and Zubok, 2000; Shiraev 1999). Many Russians who were indignant over the war, were far from identifying themselves as either diehard Slavs, or committed Orthodox believers. Moreover, since the early 1990s, when all of Europe and at least the liberal circles in the United States had been following the tragic events in the Balkans, the general Russian public could not have cared less what was going on in the region. While the Communist-nationalist Duma, since 1993, produced a lot of noise about the events in the Balkans and the Russian media reported on them quite regularly (see Chapter 4), what was most stunning was the total indifference of Russian public opinion to the conflict and to what either side in it was doing.

In 1993–1994, the inaction of the United Nations caused the siege and suffering of the people of Sarajevo—a development that bears a certain resemblance to what happened to the Russian city of Leningrad in 1941–1942. Russian opinion leaders—except the Communists—did not notice this. Later in 1994–1996 the actions of the regime of the Bosnian

Serbs caused a shockwave of horror among Western journalists after the discovery of concentration camps, mass graves, and other unmistakable signs of a planned genocide against the Muslims. Widely televised events such as the shelling of the marketplace in Sarajevo and the fall of Srebrenica, made the American public angry at the ineptness of the U.N. peace keeping forces. Russian public opinion was generally untouched by these emotions.

It should be not interpreted, however, that the Russians did not sympathize with the Bosnian Serbs. There were regular, usually pro-Serbian, reports in the media. All of the major newspapers issued reports about Russian volunteers who went to Yugoslavia to fight for the Serbs. However, Russian public opinion was just completely self-absorbed and preoccupied with its own domestic problems. Besides, Russia, at the time, was experiencing its own dramatic predicaments, including the brink of civil war and the war in the Caucasus. The indifference to the Balkans was comparable to the general public indifference to NATO expansion and several "mini-wars" that took place on Russian territory and at Russia's doorstep.[3] After decades of global involvement, Russians withdrew into their crab-shells, and made it clear that they did not wish to be bothered (see Chapter 4).

In the end, the last act was more dramatic than logical. The general Russian public was like Rip Van Winkle, and simply slept through all the acts of the Yugoslav drama, only to awaken at the end, when the thunder of U.S. precision bombs finally caught their attention. And, like a trial jury that missed all the depositions of facts, the Russian public immediately passed a guilty verdict on the United States.

The Media Impact

All the negative trends that contributed in the previous several years to the development of anti-American attitudes suddenly converged in the beginning of 1999. The newborn Russian middle-class did not know most of what the concerned elites knew about the conflict. The middle class' reaction to the war was influenced primarily by the mass media. Major reports and reviews by networks and newspapers were pre-determined by the position of media ownership. And the position was clear. The government and financial magnates were among those who would suffer the most as the events in Kosovo unfolded. In particular, the news that Russia was shunned and even ostracized by international financial markets was especially depressing and humiliating to them, since, in a more immediate context, that meant that Russia's job market and personal fortunes would not rebound in the near future. The increasingly anti-American tone of leading Russian periodicals and tabloids became a reality.[4]

On the pages of the Russian press, Americans were portrayed as arrogant expansionists: They were drilling oil in Kazakhstan, making deals with Azerbaijan and Georgia, having joint military exercises on Baltic shores, and romancing the Ukraine. However, during 1998 and in early 1999, the news that most greatly affected America's image was neither IMF pressure on Russia nor NATO expansion. It was . . . the Lewinski scandal in the White House, which quickly approached an emotional peak during the impeachment hearings. Translated into Russian, the Starr report and other brochures describing the Clinton's affair were readily available in bookstores. Russian journalists continued to exploit this topic as a cornucopia of salacious and easy-to-consume stories. Russian public reaction to the Lewinski affair throughout 1998 and the beginning of 1999, portrayed an arresting psychological pattern: Russians were overwhelmingly and emotionally on the side of the U.S. president against Monica, and particularly against those in the United States who claimed that Clinton no longer had a moral right to remain in power. Of course, much in Russian authoritarian and sexist culture militated against a fair and objective approach to this affair. Nevertheless, there was a potentially important—although almost unconscious—overtone to this unanimous Russian reaction. They sided with Clinton as a human being and detested his opponents as false and insincere guarantors of moral superiority.

When the bombing of Yugoslavia began, a widespread opinion was expressed in the media—from respectable newspapers to racy weekly tabloids—that Clinton decided to fight a victorious little war away from American borders in order to rescue his presidential image after it was tarnished by the Lewinski affair.[5] The Russian media did not pay much attention to the plight of Albanian Kosovars and, instead, peddled the macabre vision of NATO planes using sophisticated weapons to deliver destruction, suffering, and death to the innocent women and children of Yugoslavia. In retrospect, it was perhaps the most vivid case of post–Cold War bias in the coverage of a war by Russian and Western media. Anyone with access to satellite broadcasting could have easily noticed a particular trend—that American and Russian journalists were covering the war as if it were two different wars. Both sides focused on one side of reality and exaggerated particular details out of proportion. American media continuously speculated about the genocide that was in the offing in Kosovo and consistently aired pictures of humanitarian disaster among the hundreds of thousands of displaced Kosovars. Russian media, in a contrast, showed destroyed bridges, houses, and apartment buildings. Reporters interviewed citizens of Belgrade, particularly women and children, who were begging for help and protection from NATO planes. Russian network anchors repeatedly branded pictures of the systematic destruction of the Yugoslav economic infrastructure "civilized barbarism."

Reporters in both countries exchanged a few hits, turning the media campaign into a small replica of Cold War psychological warfare. For example, in the first weeks of the Kosovo war, the American muck-raking journalist, Seymour Hersh, published a story in "The New Yorker" about Primakov. He alleged, that according to electronic data intercepted by the U.S. National Security Agency, Primakov received money from Saddam Hussein in exchange for nuclear-related materials. Russian Foreign Minister, Igor Ivanov, who worked under Primakov, immediately lashed back: The story was a ruse to divert attention from the "barbaric'" NATO bombing of Yugoslavia.

The polls showed that the overwhelming majority of the Russian public believed the story of the Russian press and completely disregarded the story circulated by Western media. This was striking in itself, given the old pattern, when many Russians preferred to trust any foreign voice more than their domestic commentators. Many Russians, not only in big cities, had access to foreign media and alternative channels of information such as Voice of America, Radio Liberty, and others that covered the events in Kosovo from an official Western platform. However, Russians were, in general, disaffected by what they heard in those broadcasts from overseas. According to public opinion polls published by ROMIR and VCIOM, the vast majority of Russians denounced the bombings. The Russian public reacted very nervously to the prospect of an escalation of military hostilities in Europe.

As the bombing continued, week after week, fear of war in Russian society became aggravated by the humiliating realization of Russia's international impotence. All the protests and demonstrations did not sway the United States in its determination to bring Milosevic down. The controversial editor of *Nezavisimaya Gazeta*, Vitalyi Tretyakov, a sarcastic manipulator of public opinion in Russia, wrote about "the arrogance of power in America and the balance of impotence in Russia." Tretyakov (1999) hastened to say that he was against ethnic cleansing, yet the lesson of Kosovo, in his opinion, was not about ethnic conflicts. It was about power. He implied: "What difference does my position make? Today all the decisions in the world belong to the United States. Not because [this country] is better than everybody else. Simply because it possesses the most power."[6]

The Russian elite, including foreign-policy pundits, sensed that for the first time they had gained the attention of the huge bulk of the Russian public. A barrage of emotional commentary in leading Russian newspapers and on television followed. In general, they repeated the same litanies on U.S. behavior and the American treatment of Russia as in the previous years, but now in more blatant language. On the same pages of *Nezavisi-maia Gazeta,* Dmitry Gornostaev commented on the Washington NATO meeting in which U.S. Secretary of State Madeline Albright planned a special session with the leaders of five countries adjacent to Russia: Leonid Kuchma from Ukraine, Petr Luchinski from Belarus, Islam Karimov from Uzbekistan, Geidar Aliev from Azerbaijan and Eduard Shevardnadze from Georgia. "It is a paradox that the leaders of states would be lectured by a mere Secretary," wrote Gornostaev (1999). "In her speech last December Mrs. Albright bluntly declared that the task of the United States was to control the processes that take place on the territories of the former Soviet Union. Apparently the meeting with the five presidents from the Commonwealth of Independent States would proceed along the same lines. . . . And all this happens in the absence of Russian representatives at the Washington summit."

Elites Draw Sober Lessons

As public emotions reached their height, anti-Americanism seemed to reach a somewhat dangerous stage, morphing from the level of the elites' games into a grass-root phenomenon, the development of which could have unpredictable consequences.

However, at this very moment, politics inside Moscow's inner circles again became the major factor that determined the further transformation of anti-Americanism. Boris Berezovsky (1999), the most powerful "oligarch" in the entourage of the President Yeltsin and, since the elections of 1996, the king-maker and gray cardinal of Russian presidential politics, was one of the first to set a cold, new, and realistic tone amidst the chorus of angry anti-American voices. The conflict in Kosovo, he wrote on April 23, is just one of many conflicts produced by "the contradiction between the growth of national self-awareness, on one hand (the Albanian one, in this particular case) and the need to preserve territorial integrity, on the other (i.e., Serbian national interests)." Berezovsky was specifically concerned that "the external extension of the conflict over Kosovo is the conflict between the United States and Russia." He admitted that Russia "contributed negatively to this conflict. From the beginning of the crisis, Russia assumed a chauvinist imperial position of one-sided sympathy, and then of direct support of Slavic brothers, thereby shutting itself off from the role of an umpire or guarantor. It is apparent that this position of Russia is the result of the inertia of an old state of mind that, unfortunately, is predominant even today in Russian foreign policy. The most articulate advocate of this state of mind is Evgeny Primakov" (*Nezavisimaia Gazeta,* 23 April 1999).

Berezovsky and his group were clearly concerned that the wave of anti-Americanism might have taken Primakov—their key political rival—to the Kremlin during the next presidential elections of 2000. In retrospect, this anti-Primakov strategy was the driving force behind many actions of the powerful elite group that obviously felt threatened by the prospect of losing much of their influence in Russian politics. One of the major themes of this course was to shelve the anti-American card and replace it with other ideas and policies that could mobilize and consolidate the nation's awakened consciousness. As we will see, one of the main consequences of these anti-opposition strategies would take shape during the forthcoming months, when an anti-terrorist war in Chechnya broke out in August-September of 1999 (see Chapter 7).

From the beginning, the anti-anti-American note picked up by Berezovsky's group did not seem to hold political promise, because of the lack of consonance between this course and the prevailing mood of the public, the media, and other segments of Russian political elites. However, the course of the war over Kosovo and its political context provided new food for thought, and, in general, this thinking supported Berezovsky's conclusion that outright anti-Americanism would be an erroneous—if not suicidal—course in Russia's foreign policy.

First, the United States demonstrated—and this was surprising to many Russians, including the military—its ability to win the war against Milosevic without engaging ground troops in the conflict. Deep in their hearts, Russian experts anticipated Americans to send body bags home from the Balkans. Under the pressure of these devastating developments—as it was thought—Americans would realize that their ambitions—whether imperial or humanitarian—had a very high price tag. The downing of a high-tech American bomber by the Serbs produced jubilation in some high-placed quarters in Moscow. However, this joyful reaction was prematurely expressed. By June of 1999, it became clear to many observers that the United States had chosen a safe strategy. They preferred to completely destroy the Yugoslavian economy rather than risk the lives of American soldiers. On the public level, this realization was simply more evidence of the immoral nature of contemporary wars: Some governments' efforts to protect one group of people could be achieved by the destruction of other humans. Meanwhile, for an observer on the elite level—and this became apparent in military circles—the war in Kosovo yielded new and very promising evidence: A local war can be won by a nation's government without losing its own people and subsequently suffering domestic fallout.

Second, the sustained and even enthusiastic support of the war by Western European public opinion and, in particular, by European centrists and left-wing political forces, came as a disappointing surprise for many Russian pundits. In the previous chapters, we implied that in the second half of the 1990s, the collective search for a new national identity led many Russians to reach somewhat contradictory conclusions: They thought of themselves as part of Europe; however, they did not want to be associated with America. Obvious and increasing distinction between Western Europe and the United States defied many realistic assessments and common sense. However, expectations of a rift between America and Europe were part of Russia's post–Cold War mythological system of beliefs. According to such expectations, European integration led some Russian strategists—along with certain pessimists in the West—to expect that a "unified Europe" would sooner or later defy the United States. Moreover, increasing tensions would develop between the American and European centers of power.[7] Some pundits also expected that the introduction of the euro as the common unit of European currency presented a great challenge to the monopoly of the dollar on the world's financial markets.

When the war broke out, these myths and expectations led experts to speculate that perhaps one of the real reasons behind the United States' decision to attack Yugoslavia (never mind, of course, humanitarian concern over the plight of the Albanians) was America's strong determination to bring Western European powers firmly under U.S. domination. In particular, the main objective of the White House in the war of 1999, was to neutralize the threat from the euro: By putting European finances under duress through war expenditures, such power would have weakened. The experts pointed at the continuing slide of the euro vis-à-vis the dollar as reliable proof of their correctness (Ryurikov 1999, 49). However, vehement support of the war by British Prime Minister Blair and Germany's "red-green" coalition of Gerhard Schroeder contradicted all these myths and mental schemes. Why, Russians asked, did Western Europeans want to participate so enthusiastically in their own political and financial subjugation by the United States? Were they duped by American propaganda? Had they gone crazy?

Only a few sober-minded Russian experts acknowledged that American-Western European ties were much stronger, and NATO solidarity over Kosovo was more overwhelming than they once expected and hoped. All agreed, however, that the United States was the only clear winner in Kosovo. From a military angle, the United States "succeeded in a *de facto* expansion of NATO to Albania, Macedonia, and Slovenia, and a virtual expansion to Bulgaria and Romania as well. The United States also consolidated its political and economic leadership in Europe" (Ryurikov 1999, 50).

The demonstration of American power provoked, despite Russian anger, a sobering effect. Along with this realization returned fears of Russia's isolation and its possible exclusion from the European community. Earlier, in 1996–1997, these fears had been among the primary reasons that explained the general acquiescence of Russian leadership and elites to NATO's enlargement. Journalist Marina Kalashnikova noticed in late May 1997 that, while some Russian elites looked at the Fundamental Act that Russia signed with NATO as a total defeat, others preferred to see it as a victory. Reflecting this latter viewpoint, Deputy Foreign Minister Nikolai Afanasievsky (1997) said that Russia managed to minimize the negative consequences of NATO enlargement and avoided stooping to overt confrontation with the West. In his opinion, Russia had escaped the chief threat—being isolated from European affairs, because the Fundamental Act requires that the West reckon with Russia.

After cries of Russia's betrayal by the West during the war over Kosovo, some Russian experts, particularly those in positions of responsibility in the Foreign Ministry, were swayed again by the threat of Russia's potential isolation. They grudgingly reasoned that Russian foreign politics could not be guided by rage and other emotions. As long as the split between Europe and the United States proved to be a myth, Russia had to work with both Europeans and Americans. The most sober-minded experts from the Institute of Europe, the Institute for the United States and Canada Studies, and the Diplomatic Academy at the Foreign Ministry began to publish serious, unemotional articles that reiterated these priorities of Russia's foreign policy.

The United States did not overreact to Russia's anti-Americanism. Despite cries for sanctions against Russia, aimed to punish it for its support of Serbia, the Clinton administration—to its credit—ignored these pleas. The White House also avoided using its financial and loan policies—for example, the pending issue of IMF assistance to Russian finances—to apply pressure to the Russian government. On the contrary, at the height of the anti-American wave in Moscow on March 28, IMF director Michel Camdessu arrived at Russia's capital with the mission to rescue Russian finances. The IMF, obviously encouraged by the concern of the White House, agreed to provide Russia with 4.8 billion dollars in fresh loans to help it stave off an all-out default and avoid becoming a financial pariah.

On the surface, it looked like Primakov's tough-policy line was successful. Speaking on the Russian RTR television network, the Prime Minister implied: "We agreed to cooperate, agreed that a new loan will be offered to us, agreed that next week a top mission will come here that will complete the preparation of an [economic] document" (Reuter from Moscow, 29 March 1999). The top level of the Russian government and the elites realized that their worst fears about U.S. and NATO intentions were unfounded, and that the West was not really interested in humiliating

Russia. This led them to consider the potential benefits of a political balance between Russia's independent, often anti-American behavior and its continuing desire for a beneficial relationship with the West. As Dmitry Ryurikov, former Yeltsin foreign policy assistant, frankly put it: "Russia must develop a very careful and balanced policy in financial and economic relations with the West in order to avoid becoming isolated and autarkic." He added: "This challenging task is feasible provided that political conditions are favorable for protecting and strengthening the country's integrity" (Ryurikov 1999, 57). Ryurikov meant not only international political conditions, but also, perhaps primarily, the domestic politics of Russia and Russian political leadership.

In addition to tough action in Chechnya (see Chapter 6), Prime Minister Vladimir Putin's first months in office after his surprising nomination to the second-highest executive position in the government was marked by several missiles test launches. These actions were viewed as part of Moscow's tough reaction to an anticipated U.S. withdrawal from the 1972 Anti-Ballistic Missile treaty. During a gathering of top-ranked military officials at the Plisetsk launching facility for intercontinental ballistic missiles, Putin told generals that in response to the U.S. initiative to renew its missile defense program, Russia would respond adequately and the response would not be as costly as the American defense program (Putin 14 December 1999). Then he observed the take-off of the new rocket, Topol-M, that later successfully hit a target thousands of miles away in Russia's far east. In fact, Putin—knowingly or not—renewed the old rhetoric of late Soviet foreign minister, Andrei Gromyko, in the late 1970s, who warned the West that the Soviet Union would undertake "less expensive but effective" measures to denounce NATO and U.S. plans to deploy medium-range nuclear missiles in Europe.

These were the first lessons that contributed to the process of a sober reassessment—on the elite level—of the benefits and losses of the anti-American "card" in Russian politics. The consequences of this reassessment were revealed in the second half of 1999.

Chapter Seven

Vladimir Putin and the
Future of Anti-Americanism

One should not forget that NATO and Europe are not the same thing. Russia belongs to European culture, but does not share the culture of NATO.

Vladimir Putin

Some Russians celebrated the end of the millenium with more than their customary exuberance. Little children expected "Grandpa Frost"—the Russian equivalent of Santa Claus—to appear at their doorsteps with bags of presents and surprises. However, nobody suspected that the biggest surprise on New Year's Eve would come from "Grandpa" Yeltsin. He appeared on television screens and, brushing off tears and pleading forgiveness, announced his resignation in favor of Prime Minister Vladimir Putin. New presidential elections, according to the Russian constitution and after some deliberation, were scheduled for March 26, 2000.

During 1999, like the year before, the president seemed to be permanently absent from the seat of power, withdrawn like a snail into its shell, far away from the world. He managed to alienate himself from his friends at home and those who had supported him abroad—the Clinton administration and the governments of key Western countries. In the spring of 1999, when Yeltsin repeatedly denounced the NATO war against Milosevic's Yugoslavia, his personal relationships with Western neighbors spiraled downward. The Western press continuously lashed out at the Kremlin: first, for corruption and money laundering, then for the war in Chechnya that began in September 1999 and caused an influx of hundreds of thousands of refugees. The last time Yeltsin saw the U.S. president was in November at the European summit in Istanbul. However, hidden inside the usual bear hugs, a conflict was brewing. Yeltsin came to Istanbul fuming over Western criticism of Russian activities in Chechnya. According to the Turkish and Russian press, Clinton, at some point, while seated at the big round table, reminded "his friend Boris" that, after all, he had no reason to decry U.S. and Western interference in Russian domestic affairs: In the past, such interference helped Yeltsin come to power and stay there. When Yeltsin heard the translation through his earphones, he turned purple. Rising from his seat, he muttered in rage: "*Ah, sukin syn!*" [Son of a bitch!].

Yeltsin's sudden resignation turned out to be the last of his unpredictable pranks. Yeltsin almost succeeded in stealing the thunder from the coverage of the millennium celebrations and the Y2K monitoring. He did not bother to call Bill Clinton in advance to warn him about the resignation; most likely the U.S. president learned the news at the same moment as television viewers in Russia did. Nevertheless, Clinton (2000) immediately mobilized to put a good spin on Yeltsin's decision. In Russia, he declared, "a pluralist political system and civil society, competing in the world markets and plugged into the Internet, have emerged from a totalitarian monolith that was closed off from the outside world and implacably hostile to our values and interests. No one deserves a larger share of the credit for this transformation than Yeltsin himself. For all his difficulties, he has been brave, visionary and forthright, and he has earned the right to be called the Father of Russian Democracy." In reality, Yeltsin's resignation bore striking similarities to Nixon's departure during the Watergate scandal. The Russian president left the stage with no remaining public support, hated and mocked by virtually all his fellow citizens. Yeltsin, like Nixon, obtained the pardon of his successor—an immunity pledge against any attempts to prosecute him in the future. In addition, the Russian president was suffering from the effects of alcohol addiction and was beleaguered by threats of crushing financial revelations.

In 1996, Kozyrev's resignation opened, with much delay, the road to defining Russia's national interests and a new foreign policy concept (Simes 1999, 215). The departure of Yeltsin allowed, with even more delays, the progression of Russia and its policies, both domestic and foreign, beyond the era of collapse, euphoria, and endless depression. The prevailing mood of the country's public and the dominant interests of its new economic elites pointed, among other directions, to a pragmatic if not friendly relationship with the United States. Yeltsin's successor, Vladimir Putin, was the man who could play the balancing act between domestic anti-Americanism and realist dictums that deterred a weak Russia from an open clash with America—the only remaining world superpower.

Patriotic Games

The lessons of the emotional anti-American eruption in Russia in March of 1999 were not forgotten by the Russian elites and, above all, the group of "oligarchs" who, since the elections of 1996, had vied for power and influence over the president. Boris Berezovsky, Anatoly Chubais, Roman Abramovitch, Vladimir Gusinsky, and a few other powerful individuals, often behaved like ruffians toward each other as if "when I show weakness to them, they will destroy me" (Soros 2000, 140). After the financial crash of August 1998, they united against a common threat. Despite their wealth, power, and influence, they lacked public support. Numerous allegations of corruption hung over them like the sword of Damocles. Because the main principles of democratic politics in Russia could not be abolished, they attempted to influence the 1999 Duma elections and the presidential elections scheduled for June 2000. At the same time, some leading Russian politicians responded to public demands and began to attack "the oligarchs" and, indirectly, "the family" in the Kremlin.[1] There was a distinct possibility that these politicians would succeed in bringing some of the tycoons to court for corruption and the theft of state property; they could also easily denounce them as an anti-patriotic group who kept their savings in foreign banks and enjoyed the support and favoritism of the West, particularly of the Clinton administration in Washington. The word *poryadok* [order] became popular again. It was already clear by 1999 that if someone managed to give voice to electoral slogans of law and order, anti-corruption, and anti-Americanism, this mix could be a winning recipe.

Two prominent politicians with the greatest potential to lead under these slogans were Yevgeny Primakov, Prime Minister from September 1998 until May 1999, and Yuri Luzhkov, the mayor of Moscow. Primakov relied, as we mentioned earlier, on a small, hard working group of professionals from intelligence and military circles who did not participate in the privatization orgy and were free of corruption accusations. In the context of anti-Americanism and patriotic values, Primakov's reputation was impeccable (See Chapter 5 and 6). In the spring of 1999, he tried to oust Berezovsky from the government (from the post of ambassador-at-large for CIS affairs) and even subpoenaed him on corruption charges. Luzhkov was mired in corruption allegations, however, he won the hearts of Muscovites by turning the Russian capital into a relatively clean and even glittering city.[2] Luzhkov was not liked in the United States: He was earthy and patriotic, supported by Moscow's big capital, and opposed to heavy borrowing from the IMF; he promoted "authentic Russian" businesses—like the fast-food chain Russian

Bistro to compete with American MacDonald's and Pizza Hut. In December 1998, he founded his pocket-party, the Fatherland, that attracted many members of the Moscow elite. Both Primakov and Luzhkov also established working relations with the powerful Communist party; Primakov, in particular, had only a few enemies and many friends in the Communist-nationalist majority of the Duma. The "oligarchs" had a real and growing threat from these people.

Although the "oligarchs" did not enjoy the love of the population, they were able to manipulate public opinion. Both Gusinsky and Berezovsky controlled major television networks in Russia. Through Tatiana Dyachenko, the latter had access to her father, Boris Yeltsin, and had perhaps more than an ample opportunity to describe to the president the dangers coming from Primakov and Luzhkov. As the following events later demonstrated, Yeltsin had his own concerns about how the "patriotic games" of these two politicians would affect the future of his presidency and the family. These concerns eventually influenced the outcome of the power struggle in Moscow. Since the beginning of 1999, Yeltsin had begun to strip the Prime Minister of his functions and, at one point, publicly humiliated him. In addition, Yeltsin never surrendered direct control over the three key instruments of power in Russia: the military, the police, and internal security. From the viewpoint of domestic struggle, the most important was not the military (that was weakened and demoralized), but the Ministry of Interior, headed by Sergei Stepashin, and the Federal Security Service, headed by Vladimir Putin. Both of these individuals were hand picked by Yeltsin in the summer of 1998. They were professionals of intelligence and counter-intelligence and owed their political careers to the president. Coaxed by "the family" and nagged by his own concerns, Yeltsin began to look to these men as possible successors who would be able to protect him from the revenge of Communists and patriots.

In May 1999, the president suddenly dismissed Primakov and appointed Stepashin Prime Minister and, it was hinted, possibly his future successor. Through the rest of the spring and summer, the intrigue-ridden Moscow was rife with rumors. Some believed Yeltsin would resign very soon, while others feared he would maneuver to announce an emergency situation that would enable him to cancel the presidential elections. Yet others suspected that Yeltsin would try to stay in power longer, using as a pretext the forthcoming political union between Russia and Belarus.

Luzhkov immediately proposed that the ousted Primakov become the head of his Fatherland party and successfully wooed many regional governors who could influence big chunks of local electoral votes. By August, the Primakov-Luzhkov alliance was a reality. On the opposite pole, two other former officials, Chubais and Kiriyenko, formed a new party called

Unity-All Russia in the hope to represent the Kremlin and "the family." It is remarkable, how the party titles in 1999 reflected the changed priorities of people: There were no more titles such as "democratic unions" and "reform alliances;" stability and unity became the main issues.

How did this patriotic politicking affect the attitudes and policies toward the United States? The theme of NATO's aggression against Yugoslavia maintained a powerful presence in the Russian attitude toward the West through the first half of the summer of 1999. The tension between Russia and NATO aroused the Russian public again in June, when Milosevic gave in, and NATO troops began to move into Kosovo, which was divided into zones of occupation. After hectic diplomatic efforts, the Clinton administration and its Western European partners agreed to let Russian troops in—despite protests from the KLA and other Kosovo-Albanian political factions. As a non-participant in the war—and it was another humiliating sign of Russia's weakness—Russia did not receive, as it wished, its own zone adjacent to the Yugoslav-Kosovo frontier. Suddenly, on June 11, a column of Russian tanks and 200 troops dashed into the heart of the British zone at the order Russian Lieutenant-General Viktor Zavarzin, the commander of a Russian military contingent in the area. They occupied the key airport in the city of Pristina and, for days, stayed put, surrounded by NATO forces. This was done in violation of all Russian-NATO agreements and the initial Western reaction was very negative. Yet, public opinion in Russia soared. Zavarzin was hailed by the media as a true patriot who saved Russia's face. Yeltsin promoted him to three-star general and made him Russia's military representative to NATO. Some compared this tiny incident to the heroic "anabasis" of the Czarist General, Alexander Suvorov, across the Alps in the early nineteenth century—a glorious episode of the Russian military campaign against France in 1799–1800. The Kosovo episode also revealed the mercurial nature of Russian attitudes toward the United States and NATO, reflected in simple transitions from a feeling of humiliation to euphoria.

It was easy to anticipate that America-bashing would continue. However, Prime Minister Stepashin, who traveled to the United States in July, behaved in a very conciliatory way. Whatever the reason for this attitude, the state of Russian-American relations appeared to be nothing but crisis-ridden.

War in Chechnya, Clash with the West, and the Rise of Putin

For Russians, the worst humiliation after the collapse of the Soviet Union was the defeat of the Russian troops in Chechnya in 1994–1996. America was not directly involved in this defeat; in fact, President Clinton refrained from exerting overt pressure on the Russian government to bring the war to an end. As we mentioned already, he defended publicly Russia's right to protect its sovereignty and territorial integrity, invoking the case of American Civil War. The Kremlin ended the campaign in Chechnya because it had clearly become a quagmire and an irritant to Russia's relations with the West. At the same time, the problem of Chechnya was not resolved. Chechen leader, Aslan Maskhadov, soon lost control over the region. There reigned chaos, crime, and local warlords who fought under the banners of independence and Islamic fundamentalism; some of them dreamed of establishing the Islamic Republic of Caucasus from the Black to the Caspian Seas. According to Sergei Kovalev, famous human rights defender and a bitter opponent of the war earlier in the 1990s, instead of an "independent Chechnya" there was a "black hole on the world map out of which bearded people driving Kamaz trucks and carrying Kalashnikov [machine guns] descended from time to time on the neighboring regions of Russia" (Kovalev 2000).

The analysis of the origins of the second Chechen war is not our task. However, the conflict's progress is related to two important developments in the second half of 1999. One was the rise of Vladimir Putin as the new leader of Russia. The other was the further worsening of the relationship between Russia and the United States. Further alienation from the West and the United States was provoked, in part, by Western protests against the indiscriminate use of Russian military force in Chechnya. It also occurred because Russian officials perceived those protests as part of America's geopolitics in the region that included the new independent states of Georgia, Azerbaijan, and Armenia. Georgia's and Azerbaijan's open policy of leaning on the United States, and particularly their plans to build an alternative oil pipeline from the Caspian Sea to Turkey, was a major source of concern and frustration for Moscow (See Chapter 3). Russia's influence, by contrast, was severely weakened by its defeat in and the loss of Moscow's control over Chechnya.

An official of the Foreign Ministry wrote in the summer 1998 that Southern Caucasus is turning in deeds, not only in words, into the zone of strategic interest of the United States. He warned that the idea of the pipeline project was motivated not only by economic concerns, but also by political considerations, namely to weaken Russia's positions in the region" (Chernyavsky 1998). Russian officials made the reasonable argument that some politicians in the United States and leaders in Georgia and Azerbaijan continued to play the anti-Russian card in the region, pointing at Russia's neo-imperialist threats. Independent American expert, Anatol Lieven, implied, for example, that many elements of U.S. policy in the region were indeed "unnecessary and even frivolous" provocations (Lieven

1999/2000, 74). It would be imprudent to suggest who provoked whom, given the tragic past, passions, misperceptions, and complicated politics in the Caucasus and Trans-Caucasus. It is clear, however, that both Russia and the United States were on opposite sides of this political situation. In 1998–1999, the potential for a direct clash of Russian and American interests in this area was perhaps greater than in any other place in the world.

During the summer of 1999, Russian leadership became convinced that it could no longer ignore the state of lawlessness and violence in Chechnya (Hoffman 2000). The U.S. demonstration of military force in Kosovo must have played a certain role in Russian decisiveness. If America could bomb civilians with impunity in another country, why couldn't Russia resort to similar methods to crush the bandits inside its own sovereign territory? In the early summer, Yeltsin ordered Stepashin to look deep into the Chechen problem. Part of the decision-making circle concerning Chechnya were also Director of the Federal Security Service Putin and Defense Minister Igor Sergeev. The geopolitical considerations of the great game over Caucasus and against the United States were almost certainly on their agenda. Four months later, in response to the anti-Russian campaign in the West, Sergeev declared on Russian television that the United States itself was trying to stir up the conflict in north Caucasus. He also implied that Western policy was aimed at ousting Russia from the Caspian region, the Trans-Caucasus and Central Asia. Russia had to defend its interests.

In August, a raid of Islamic guerillas from Chechnya into Dagestan—another ethnic region of the Caucasus and part of the Russian Federation—galvanized the Kremlin into action and brought to the fore Vladimir Putin, who became the main advocate of war as the only means to resolve the Chechen problem once and for all. In August, he replaced Stepashin as prime minister of Russia. According to insiders, Stepashin demonstrated frightening helplessness in dealing with the conflict, and this prompted "the family" to make a decisive political substitution. As Prime Minister, Putin placed his entire political career at stake by deciding to reconquer Chechnya. Later, he claimed that he made this decision only after mysterious blasts destroyed four apartment buildings in Moscow and Volgodonsk in September, killing 300 people, including children. Most probably, however, he would have pushed Russia to war anyway. In his interviews early in 2000, Putin disclosed that he realized the task was not simply crushing the Chechen bandits on their own soil, but rather stopping the processes that might eventually lead to the disintegration of Russia. "I was convinced that, if we had not stopped the [Chechen] extremists, then after some time we would have become a second Yugoslavia on the entire territory of the Russian Federation. It would have been the *Yugoslavization* of Russia" (Gevorkian et al. 2000). This was a chilling comparison between Russia and the country that had been recently bombed by NATO and forced to give up, de facto, a part of its territory. There is a risk of reading too much into Putin's words. However, for many Russian officials and elites, there were dangerous parallels between the case of Kosovo and the war in Chechnya. From their perspective, both the KLA and Chechen formations were bandits. Both tried to present themselves to the world public as freedom-fighters. And in both cases, they benefited from the world's (particularly American and West European) concern for the possible "genocide" of a civilian population in the midst of indiscriminate warfare.

Putin's gamble turned out to be the winning ticket. In contrast to the war of 1994–1996, now an overwhelming majority of Russians[3] expressed solidarity with Putin's determination to crush Chechen separatists. This support has remained steady since August 1999, despite the growing number of casualties among Russian troops in Chechnya. Chance and his firm behavior transformed Putin from an obscure functionary into the most popular politician of the country who, in March of 2000, was elected president.

This phenomenon dramatically revealed the consolidation of Russian society on the basis of authoritarian themes and images. This was a natural reaction to six years of experience with the partially or, at times, totally invalid head of the state. It also indicated a complete reversal of public fears and priorities. In 1996, the public was still predominantly anti-Communist and this helped Yeltsin's re-election. In 1999, the Communist menace was no longer credible. Instead, the main concern was the weak state and the real danger of national disintegration. The shock of the NATO war against Yugoslavia and the aftermath of the blasts in apartment houses in Moscow solidified public perceptions in a way no electoral propaganda could. The same forces in Russia that ensured support for slogans of law and order, anti-Americanism, and the struggle against corruption ensured across-the-board support for "Putin's war."

The humiliation of Russia that was an essential cause of the new anti-Americanism, could not be immediately redeemed by hostilities against the United States. For many Russians, however, Chechen fighters and their extraordinary resilience and challenge, were another form of national humiliation for Russia. Awkward remarks by Russian officials implying some kind of a link between U.S. interests in the Caucasus and the Chechen fighters were not just outrageous propaganda, but also cognitive schemes that indicated a possibly deeper link in the Russian psyche between anti-Americanism and ethnic intolerance. In a sense, the war in Chechnya became for Russian elites and the public an actual substitute for a potential confrontation with the United States and NATO.

The first three months of the Chechen war marked perhaps the worst moment in Russian-NATO relations ever. In the spring of 1999, during the conflict over Kosovo, the animosity irradiated mostly from the Russian side; American and Western opinion-makers and the broader public, preoccupied with Milosevic and the Kosovars, did not quite respond to Russian outbursts of anti-Americanism. In September-November 1999, however, certain influential segments of the American and Western European opinion-making elites and the public lashed back at Russia.

The ground for this animosity was fertilized by the financial scandal that erupted in September in the United States involving the Bank of New York. The bank was accused of laundering billions of dollars for the Russian "mafia"—corrupt government officials and entrepreneurs. This case, fully justified on the basis of facts, transformed into a referendum on the Clinton administration's policies in Russia. The Republicans attacked the administration for identifying America too closely with Yeltsin and his cronies, sacrificing democratic values as well as workable reform alternatives for Russia. At the Senate hearings on the money laundering in the Bank of New York, leading experts talked about the "kleptocracy" in Russia. Wayne Merry, of the Atlantic Council, said the United States became allied with some of the most ruthless, undemocratic, and rapacious people in Russia. "Eight years ago our reputation and prestige in Russia were supreme; now even the young see America as unprincipled and cynical" (Hearings, 23 September 1999). Former CIA Director, R. James Woolsey, intoned: "If one looks at the overall pattern, it is easy to see how ordinary Russians, who saw us in highly idealized terms just a few years ago, have turned so sour on the United States" (Hearings, 21 September 1999). Another expert, Dimitri Simes, lashed out at the administration's "unstinting support of Anatoly Chubais, the architect of the loans-for-shares scheme" and concluded: "Years of American support of the corrupt and ineffective Yeltsin regime have discredited the United States among ordinary Russians and led many to suspect that the United States seeks not to help, but to weaken. . . . Because of the high-profile involvement of the Clinton administration and international financial institutions influenced by the United States in Russia's transition, [the corruption and Russia's indebtedness] cannot but contribute to the growth of anti-American sentiment in Russian society" (Hearings, 21 September 1999).

Officials in the Clinton administration, who, in the spring of 1999, tacitly preserved good personal relations with their Russian counterparts, expressed their understanding, and worked behind the scenes to overcome Russia-NATO tension, had no option but to join the chorus of denunciation of Russian corruption. As a result, their "friends" in Moscow—first of all Chubais, Kiriyenko, Nemtsov, and others who had built their careers on close ties with the United States—appeared to be cornered, isolated, and hated both inside Russia and out. They and the

Russian media angrily denounced the anti-corruption campaign in the United States as just another example of America seeking to turn Russia into an international pariah in retaliation for the financial default in August 1998 and the country's opposition to the war in Kosovo.

In November, Chairman of the Senate Foreign Relations Committee, Jesse Helms (R-N.C.), Majority Leaders Trent Lott (R-MS.), and a number of other Senators, mostly Republicans, wrote a letter to President Clinton, calling Russia's conduct in Chechnya "a brutal assault on the core values of the OSCE [Organization for Security and Cooperation in Europe]." Zbigniew Brzezinski recommended that Russia say adieu to Chechnya and all other parts of the Russian "empire" (Brzezinzki 1999). He and a group of 34 dignitaries appealed to Clinton to support Azerbaijan and Georgia against Russian threat as a zone of America's "vital interests."

On the Russian side, old "friends" of the United States hastily reoriented their patriotic credentials by siding with Putin. Anatoly Chubais shocked Americans by supporting the war. He called the leader of the Yabloko Party, Yavlinski (the only presidential candidate who opposed the war), "a traitor" and branded Western criticism of Chechnya as "immoral" and "dishonest" (Chubais 1999). Yeltsin, as we noted earlier, went to the OSCE summit to face unanimous Western denunciation of the Chechen campaign. His most cherished diplomatic achievement—Russia's membership in the club of "G-7" developed nations, and its membership in various institutions of Unified Europe—were in jeopardy. However, the Russian president told NATO leaders what was on the minds of the majority back home: After the war against Yugoslavia, you have no right to criticize Russia over Chechnya (see *Johnson's List,* 19 November 1999). And in December in Beijing, during his last trip abroad as president, he made a comment on Clinton's harsh remarks about Russia's war in Chechnya that reminded some of Khrushchev's fist-waving. He roared indignantly into television cameras, pausing purposefully between words: "It seems he [Clinton] has for a minute, for a second, for half a minute, forgotten that Russia has a full arsenal of nuclear weapons" (Yeltsin 1999).

For the first time since the Cold War, anti-American and anti-Russian elements rocked the boat of Russian-American relations from both sides and threatened to throw it completely off balance. The ROMIR polling agency that surveyed 1,500 people in 40 regions of Russia, reported in late November that 41 percent said they believed the West was attempting to turn Russia into a third world country; more than 37 percent believed Western nations wanted to split Russia up and destroy it altogether. Less than 4 percent admitted that the West was helping Russia to become a civilized and developed nation (Reuters, 23 November 1999). A prominent opinion-maker (and Gusinsky's deputy), Igor Malashenko, went on the air with a warning that "big interest groups, groups of prominent Russian politicians" and the top military "have appeared interested in Russia's isolation from the West." Those people were gathering around Putin, he opined, because "they want to create in Russia a regime that could function without minding the West and then their interests will be guaranteed" (Malashenko 17 November 1999).

Perhaps the calmest voice in the Russian political world was that of Prime Minister Vladimir Putin. On November 1–2, he met with President Clinton in Oslo for the first time and took a nonconfrontational stance. In an interview on December 11, shortly before the elections of the new Duma, Putin was asked by *Financial Times* what could be done about the relations between Russia and the West. He replied that personally he "would not dramatize [the crisis in relations] and speak about a major retreat . . . to the Cold War era. At least, Russia most sincerely does not want this to happen. . . . The basic, long-term strategic goals and interests of our country can be attained only on the condition of our deep and constructive incorporation into the world community, on the condition of the development of partnership with the West" (Putin 1999).

While making these reassuring gestures, Putin relentlessly pursued his strategic aims in Chechnya. He excluded the presence of representatives of OSCE and other foreign observers from the area of warfare.[4] In December, the Russian Prime Minister praised Joseph Stalin's statesmanship in commemoration of the former Soviet ruler's anniversary and blessed the plaque in memory of Yuri Andropov on the façade of the former KGB building on Lubyanka Street. Of the two historical personalities, Stalin is known for talking softly to the West during the first years of the Cold War, while contributing to anti-Americanism behind the scenes. Putin is clearly not Stalin, but who is he? Is he prepared to improve relations with the United States by channeling feelings of national humiliation from fruitless anti-Americanism toward a process of constructive state-building? Or, will he quietly play the anti-American card, only when necessary, while using his intelligence officer's skills to avoid blame for confrontation between America and Russia? Russia entered the new millenium without answers to these questions, but with the man who rose from obscurity to power faster than any other leader in its history during the past century.

Putin and America: Three Options

Following Malashenko's November 1999 warning about Russia's isolationism, an observer from the moderate and pro-Western newspaper *Segodnya* noted with some anxiety that this policy could have disastrous consequences for Russia. "The international community has come really close to a kind of psychological barrier," he noted. "Having once over-stepped it, the West will no longer recognize any difference between Rus-sia and, say, Yugoslavia (or Iraq). All that can follow is international sanctions and high-precision bombing" (Odnokolenko 1999).

In fact, this analyst turned out to be wrong. By 2000, a realist approach was taking the center stage in Russian politics. The logic of this approach required some balancing between the conquest of Chechnya and the sta-bilization of relations with Western powers. Putin did not have to produce miracles to solve this dilemma in January-February 2000. Two factors worked in his favor. First, Russian troops, ignoring the shrill protests of the Western community, surrounded Chechnya's capital, Grozny, and—at great cost of human lives—captured what remained of the city. Although the war was entering another, potentially bloodier and more difficult stage, Putin could claim a partial victory and open portions of the war zone for Western observers. This decision was a concession to Western demands; however it diffused some tension. Second, Putin and his pro-war allies scored big in the Duma elections on December 19. The pro-Kremlin bloc, Unity (also called *Medved* [Bear]), hastily formed just a few months earlier, received an astonishing 23 percent of the Russian vote. The Union of Right Forces, established by Chubais and Kiriyenko with similar haste on the jingoistic platform, received almost 9 percent. The main rivals of the Kremlin and Putin—Primakov, Luzhkov, and their party, Fatherland-All Russia, received a disappointing 12 percent. Primakov, eviscerated by the pro-Putin media, and especially by the ORT network, failed to be elected Chairman of the Duma and withdrew his candidacy from the presidential race. The Yabloko Party of Yavlinsky, the most principled opponent of the war, barely scraped through the 5 percent barrier. The Communists re-ceived 24 percent—much less than in the 1995 elections.

These developments sent a clear message to President Clinton and other Western European leaders and their successors, that, whether the West liked it or not, it had to deal with Putin as the widely supported leader of Russia. And they responded with alacrity. In January-February, U.S. Secretary of State Albright, British Prime Minister Blair and some other Western politicians met with acting President Putin on Russian soil and stated publicly that the West was prepared to do business with him. Clinton, in particular, was willing to defuse Russian-Western tension and, since November 1999, had resisted strong public pressure to punish Rus-sia for its "misbehavior" in Chechnya. Having invested so much in a posi-tive relationship with Russia, the Clinton administration sought to undercut its critics from the Republican side. It also considered criticism of Putin's Chechen policy problematic: The United States needed Russia's return to participation in pan-European security and cooperation structures under U.S. leadership; moreover, the White House needed to rene-gotiate with Russia on the anti-ballistic missile treaty of 1972, so that the United States could deploy a limited anti-missile defense.

Putin won the presidential election with 52 percent of the vote in the first round.[5] The Clinton administration and NATO leaders unanimously expressed their satisfaction with the results. The brief honeymoon between the new Russian president and the West was doubly justifiable: Western politicians wanted to give Putin a chance and they were glad to deal with a robust and young Russian leader who appeared to be capable of making things happen.

Perceived improvement of Russian-Western relations did not mean that questions about Vladimir Putin and his future policies lost their impor-tance immediately after his first months in power. For that reason, we ven-tured to write about three possible scenarios for his Presidency, our views on the future of Russian anti-Americanism. Sure, the evidence available to us is still paltry and fragmentary. Current trends cannot be easily extrapo-lated. Besides, this method of analysis of political behavior has repeatedly proved to be misleading. Nevertheless, we believe it is important to spec-ulate on Putin's personal attitudes, the potential results of his policies, and see how they could magnify or diminish anti-American sentiments in Russia. So as not to risk the validity of such forecasts, we will assume that American and Western behavior toward Russia will remain nonprovoca-tive and largely cooperative.

In the first scenario, Putin easily defeats all kinds of opposition to his project of restoration of "vertical line of power" and becomes an au-thoritarian ruler within the constitutional framework. He remains free of deep-seated anti-American attitudes and refrains from using the anti-American card in his domestic and foreign policies. In the first months of 2000, some evidence pointed to this possibility. His first meeting with Clinton went well and, as Putin admitted later, he grew to like the U.S. president as an "open, sincere, and pleasant man." Putin relied on former KGB professionals, who spent a long time abroad and were not xeno-phobic (Gevorkian et al. 2000). Most importantly, Putin was not associ-ated with the pro-American policies of his predecessor in the early 1990s. The new president's strong showing in Chechnya made his patri-otic nationalist credentials unassailable. Therefore, Yeltsin's two mortal enemies—Communists and ultra-nationalists—will not be able to play the card of anti-Americanism in their future attacks on Putin that they did when attacking Yeltsin. Putin should have little use for anti-Ameri-can hawks. He did not appeal to anti-Americanism at all in his presi-dential campaign of 2000. His mandate from the very beginning was a strong state and suppression of local separatism, combined, in his own terms, with "the dictatorship of law." One could imagine Putin might become a milder and absolutely legitimate "version" of former Chilean leader, Augusto Pinochet. In this light, Putin would attempt to jumpstart the Russian market economy and promote ultimately liberal goals with authoritarian means. Anatoly Chubais and Petr Aven, two members of the initial reformers' team of Gaidar, supported Putin with just this particular scenario in mind (Zolotov 1 April 2000).

As one analyst put it, Putin's "pragmatic, cool-headed policy oriented toward Russia's interests (including the interest in a robust market economy) will present a far greater challenge to the West than Yeltsin's emotional oscillations between friendship and confrontation. Most important, he will position Russia in such a way that it does not bear the blame for confrontation" (Sokov 2000). As an example, Russia already claimed in the summer 2000 that the United States started a new round of "Star Wars" and that Russia had no other options than to defend itself militarily.

Putin's policies, however, if motivated by pragmatic reasons, could tear down some of the structural and psychological reasons for anti-Americanism in Russia. His strong-state policies and firm hand in Chechnya might diminish Russian insecurity and reverse the worst effects of national humiliation. If he succeeds in combining "moderate" authoritarianism with the preservation of basic civil liberties and the existence of an independent media, this might help restore to Russia the prestige of American values, such as individualism and materialism. If his emphasis on stability helps improve the Russian economy and lure foreign investments, it would diminish Russia's financial and economic dependence on the IMF and somewhat defuse anti-American sentiments as well.

In the second scenario, Putin appears as a "strong" man, but one who secretly harbors anti-American attitudes. As a result, his position, in combination with prevalent public sentiment, would be to corroborate Russia's pragmatic "realism" and redirect it toward more idealistic, ideology-driven schemes and calculations. Putin's murky KGB background provides some reason to surmise that he, on one hand, may like some American people; on the other, he is generally suspicious of the United States. As a loyal KGB officer without remorse or regret, he grew up in the atmosphere of the "old" Soviet anti-Americanism, which might have left deep imprints in his psyche. Perhaps he remained entirely free from the euphoric pro-American sentiments of the past. Besides, it is not clear what he may have learned about American society and whether he may be vulnerable to anti-American stereotypes. His alma mater—the Leningrad State University—has never been a bastion of liberal ideas and pro-Americanism in the 1970s–1980s. His teachers at the Law School were loyal advocates of the Soviet system.

Putin's obsession with the restoration of Russia as a great power, combined with his inexperience in international affairs may also leave him open to the influence of geopolitics and nationalism—advocated by the Neo-Conservatives. His interviews contain evidence that he advocates the idea of a Big Europe, including Russia as the future counterweight to the United States. "One should not forget," he said, "that NATO and Europe are not the same thing. I have already said that [Russia] is the country of European culture, but not NATO culture" (Gevorkian, et al. 2000).

In addition, Putin may share concerns that the United States is organizing plots against Russia, as it did in the Caucasus. In November 1999, for example, Putin was in complete solidarity with Defense Minister Sergeev at a major meeting of the Russian military and told military commanders that the United States was determined to weaken Russia and control the energy-rich Caspian Sea basin (*The Moscow Times,* "Kremlin Rattles Nuclear Sword," 13 November 1999). In February 2000, obviously with Putin's instructions, Foreign Minister, Igor Ivanov, declared at the Council of Europe: "Attempts to oust Russia from the Caucasus, and there are such encroachments, can lead to very negative consequences. . . . Our country historically played the stabilizing role in the Caucasus" (Ivanov 2000).

Ominously, Putin encouraged a domestic attitude against any independent opinion that runs counter to his "patriotic line." Such people may quickly be denounced as "traitors." For example, he ignored the vigorous campaign of Western opinion leaders and certain Russian journalists to release the detained reporter, Andrei Babitsky (his name was mentioned earlier). In his pre-election interviews, he called him a "traitor" (Gevorkian et al. 2000). According to Anatoly Kovalev, "Today, the human rights workers and organizations [in Russia] are considered the country's primary internal enemies, a fifth column that is supported by Western foundations (read: secret services), and is conducting subversive activities against Russia" (Kovalev 2000, 7). On the eve of the election, Putin's staff treated ABC *Nightline* anchorman, Ted Koppel, rather haughtily presumably in symbolic retaliation against a report of his that questioned the freedom of the Russian press (ABC *Nightline,* 24 March 2000).

If the second scenario plays out, Putin's brief honeymoon with the United States and the West will be replaced by another period of tension and acrimony. Even though the Russian leader continues to demonstrate pragmatic, conciliatory gestures, it is unlikely he will hardly conceal his "real" self for long. Many "ifs" about civil liberties, economic revival, and the pacification of the Caucasus would make Putin's project of the restoration of a Great

Russia a very uncertain enterprise, susceptible to sudden changes in priorities. With inevitable failures on this path, it will be likely that Putin will use anti-Americanism as an instrument to channel domestic frustrations. Unlike in the Soviet Union, the majority of the populace will be likely to support the anti-American course of its leader, because this time it will be based not only on the state propaganda, but also on the "new" psychological foundation that emerged during the 1990s.

Finally, in the third scenario, Putin fails to become a strong leader of Russia, but rather continues to react erratically to domestic and international crises and challenges. As time goes by, there is a growing number of instances in which Putin did not reveal leadership's instincts and capabilities. He did not shake off decisively his dependence on various groups that helped to promote him to power. When push came to shove—for example, during the arrest of the media magnate Gusinski and after the tragic incident of the submarine *Kursk*—Putin revealed a chief who personally controls everything, did not even break his summer vacation to be close to the dying seamen and take charge of the rescuing operations.

All this may fathom an impotent and reactive, rather than authoritarian and active, style of Vladimir Putin. In this case, his personal preferences with regard to the United States will not play the same prominent role as in the other two scenarios. Perhaps there is some truth in the jocular comment of one Russian observer that Putin is just a man with the personality of a mid-level official and the skills of a judo-wrestler.

If this scenario becomes reality, nationalist forces will become disillusioned with Putin's "strong hand" and begin to search for a stronger and more nationalistic leader. The attacks on the Presidency for its inability to resist "American expresssionism" and "U.S. interference" will likely resume. The lack of decisive improvement in economic areas will signify a continuation of Russia's "depression"—with the resulting waves of people's despair and the psychological need to bash the wealthiest country in the world. Against this backdrop, it will not be unthinkable that a new fringe personality will appear in Russian politics to lead a strong coalition armed with nationalist and anti-American slogans. Needless to say, this will mean a lot of trouble for Russia itself and the outside world.

Conclusion

Russians have a traditionally ambivalent view about the West; throughout history they have been inclined to choose a particular Western county against which to measure themselves. In the twentieth century, it was America's turn to be such a country. During Stalin's reign, attitudes about the United States were based on the fortified pillars of Communist ideology, reinforced by the generally limited access of the Soviet people to America. Stalin saw the United States—the Soviet Union's ally during World War II—as both a partner and a worthy opponent. Since the 1940s, the vector of the nuclear-arms race pierced the heart of Soviet-American relations. At that time, the wave of the Gallup poll revolution could not penetrate the Iron Curtain, and there is little empirical evidence to indicate what the ordinary Russian citizen thought about America and Americans. Certain archival documents and literary sources suggest that these attitudes were ambivalent. The Soviet people admired America's enormous achievements in the field of economics, but at the same time resented—and this was a direct result of government propaganda—America's ruling elite from big corporations, the Pentagon, and the CIA. Krushchev's Thaw enabled Russians to have limited access to information about the United States as well as its ideas, products, movies, and music. A new generation of Russians, called *shestidesiatniki,* brought to society a fresh breeze of romantic idealism and the relentless optimism that prepared the ground for pro-American attitudes among Soviet intellectuals. Still, throughout the Brezhnev years, the United States was considered to be a major opponent of the Soviet Union and the government encouraged this attitude among the vast majority of the Soviet people. The coming of Gorbachev signaled a major shift in Soviet foreign policy and attitudes about the West, an alteration that was initially designed to provide all the necessary conditions for the successful restructuring of the economy and the further refinement of societal institutions. Gorbachev needed to significantly improve the country's bilateral relationship with the United States to secure the successful implementation of his domestic agenda. This new-thinking policy, proposed by Gorbachev in international relations, was, in fact, an attempt to secure reforms at home.

It was the beginning of a euphoric stage in Soviet-American relations that lasted for almost five years, despite the developing societal chaos, economic collapse, inflation, corruption, and a growing number of other devastating problems. In the eyes of many Russians, the main cause of the country's inability to compete with the world's richest powers was the Communist system itself, the system against which the United States had fought for many years. Discredited in the eyes of millions of Russians, Communism symbolized everything that held Russia back from becoming a civilized society. On the contrary, America represented the future, and symbolized great new opportunity, unlimited potential, prosperity, and happiness. Gorbachev, especially after the summit on Malta in 1989— where he agreed to major geopolitical changes in Eastern Europe and virtually signed on to the end of the Cold War on America's terms—truly expected the United States to establish a bipolar balance by reducing its own military threat, dismantling NATO, and giving up a wide range of expansionist policies around the world. Gorbachev, and then Yeltsin, both hoped to receive substantial economic and financial aid from the West, a second Marshall plan that would inject a healthy dose of initiatives into the crumbling economy and guarantee sustained economic growth for years to come. Yeltsin also anticipated substantial help from the United States and other Western countries for slaying the dragon of Communism.

The events that followed the failed coup in August 1991 demonstrated the rise of pro-Western and pro-American attitudes among Russian elites and ordinary people. The new diplomacy, represented by Kozyrev, was based on a set of uncritical pro-American attitudes and assumptions. In effect, the new Russian military doctrine was toothless. The Kremlin saw the world as multi-polar, sought Russia's inclusion in the most powerful world organizations, anticipated being treated as an equal partner and a great and capable nation. Many Russians also believed that a quick reorientation of the country, according to Western standards, might help them turn their lives around. Revolution in the fields of information and interpersonal contacts guaranteed many people access to Western sources, gave Russians a great chance to travel abroad, and feel they were members of a world civilization.

The renewed growth of anti-Americanism among Russians was, in part, a reflection of the economic collapse and enormous difficulties that Russians encountered in the early 1990s. The economic doctrine, brought inside the Kremlin walls by a group of young, ambitious reformers, embodied radical principles of market capitalism. Their plan called for the implementation of a certain monetary policy designed to provide shock therapy to the Russian economy and then revive the country in a matter of months. A group of American economists was especially close to the founding fathers of Russian shock therapy. However, instead of achieving instantaneous prosperity, the Russian economy took a dive. Inflation soared, prices skyrocketed, the government was unable to guarantee protection to its citizens, crime became rampant, and social disenchantment with the course of the reforms grew after 1992. The expected massive influx of American assistance never materialized. There was no Marshall plan prepared for Russia and the realization grew that the country needed to solve its problems using its own—already drained—resources. American advisers, maintaining their ideological belief in the principles of macroeconomics, had made a serious miscalculation by failing to carefully appreciate Russian microeconomic context: the lack of social institutions, the nature of Russian bureaucracy, Russian egalitarian attitudes, and the lack of a democratic form of government. In the eyes of Russians, the old Soviet system suffered from serious flaws. However, the new Russian system created new problems. Store shelves filled with goods did not reflect societal prosperity because such goods were not available to the majority of Russians. Instead, the reforms produced a state of frightening inequality in Russian society. One of the psychological consequences of the Russian collapse in the early 1990s was the sustained growth of anti-Americanism. America—with its perceived attitude of indifference toward Russia's troubles, arrogant advisers, and unattainable wealth—became a scapegoat, the cause of Russian troubles, the country that willingly let Russia fall to her knees.

The development of massive disappointment with the United States and the West coincided with the beginning of a search for a new national Russian identity. Great-power status was effectively lost by the end of the 1980s. Economically, militarily, and diplomatically, Russia could not compete—as a major force—on the international playing field. Its role was downgraded and it was eventually ignored by the Western powers. History gives examples of how national humiliation coupled with devastating domestic collapse sparks explosions of xenophobia and fascism. Indeed, the rise of Russian chauvinism and nationalism became apparent after the collapse of the Soviet Union. Two specific groups became carriers of the great-power ideas. The first group was represented by several, mostly disjointed, radical nationalist formations. The second group was the Russian Communists—who were relatively organized and unified. Despite their many ideological differences, nationalists and Communists were among the main carriers of anti-Americanist attitudes that, by 1993, were shared by approximately 30–40 percent of Russians. By the late 1990s anti-Americanism was given another chunk of fertile soil on which to grow. These were ideas of the new Russian Right, who in the beginning of the Russian transformation, were the liberal-minded democrats who supported the West. Their theories represented a sophisticated blend of ideas about Russian exceptionality, the country's special Eurasian status, and the exclusive way that Russia should follow as the "chosen" country. The main principles of American capitalism were declared genuinely foreign to the Russian people, who were "destined" to be more spiritual, more collectivist, and more educated than the average American.

Meanwhile, despite many gloomy predictions, Russian anti-Americanism never became virulent and never assumed a sustained violent form. There were several reasons for this. First of all, the Russian nationalists movements—potential carriers of violent anti-Americanism—were not supported by overwhelming public opinion and did not become a major political force in Russia. Pessimism, low political efficacy, and deep-seated motivation to take care of their own personal problems kept the vast majority of Russians from active political involvement in any of the nationalist movements or groups. Moreover, there was never a single charismatic individual capable of unifying the Russian nationalists. The other major oppositional force—the Communists—were very cautious about embracing any radical nationalist ideas and did not want to sacrifice the basic principle of internationalism. The advocates of the new Russian idea also fell short of attacking America and calling for resistance against American "invasion." They were preachers of a new Russian isolationism that stood for detachment rather than active opposition to the United States.

Domestic public opinion played a specific role in Russian foreign politics, especially regarding the United States' actions in Europe. In any democratic country, the forces of political opposition use everything available to them to keep pressure on the government. Foreign politics are not excluded from this process. As expected, in the case of Russia, a course chosen in the early 1990s evoked active and persistent criticism from domestic political opposition. Anti-Americanism was used as a political card to achieve particular domestic goals. In attempts to maneuver and bargain with political opponents, the Yeltsin administration shifted, to a certain extent, its position in relation to the United States. Each time a correction was made, the concomitant attitudes became harsher. The fact that Russia maintained a clear pro-Serbian position during the conflict in Bosnia should be regarded as less an expression of pan-Slavic solidarity than a reaction to the anti-Serbian policy of NATO and the United States. Russians—those who were aware about the conflict—were more preoccupied with their country's inability to play a major role in that conflict and effectively counterbalance the efforts of the United States, than with their desire to help their Serbian brothers. Several significant developments of the 1990s, and, in particular, the fall of Foreign Minister Kozyrev and prominence of Evgeny Primakov, indicate how Russian policy toward the West fell hostage to domestic political considerations. Because of the nature of Russian domestic political battles, any democratic government in Russia could potentially become vulnerable to the attacks of its political opposition and would therefore need to avoid developing a reputation as a "softy." This avoidance could cause an occasional outburst of anti-Americanism. Ironically, the more authoritarian the Russian regime is, the more it will be capable of maintaining a stable and pragmatic policy toward the United States. This may come at a cost that some American observers are reluctant to accept: Certain principles of liberal democracy in Russia would be ignored until "better" times.

Two events of 1999 have affected the course of Russian-American relations and shaped many Russian people's attitudes toward the United States. The first event was the U.S.-led NATO military campaign against Serbia. Slobodan Milosevic, who did not enjoy the overwhelming support of the Russian people, suddenly found firm backers in the Kremlin and throughout Russia. As in the case of the war in Bosnia, Russians were especially irritated by the arrogant and irresponsible actions of Washington against a sovereign country. Suddenly, the major NATO expansion of previous years—that went virtually unnoticed by the Russian public as the expansion was happening—became a major issue. America was, once again, called an aggressor and a potential threat to Russia. Anti-Americanism shifted from being a convenient card in political games to a widespread phenomenon. Criticism directed against the United States crossed party lines. Even cautious optimists like Yavlinsky began to issue anti-American statements and warn against the dangers of American politics. Public opinion polls yielded a steady 60–70 percent level of anti-American attitudes. Negotiations over several agreements in nuclear and military fields were virtually stalled.

However, the events of the summer and fall of 1999 resulted in further corrections in Russian attitudes about the West and America. The Russian government began a military invasion in the region—provoked by the aggressive actions of Chechen warlords, supported by an enormous anti-Chechen campaign in the Russian media, and backed by virtually each and every major political leader in Russia. Suddenly, another convenient scapegoat fell into Russia's lap and America was effectively replaced from the top of Russia's list of immediate concerns. Chechen separatists became the new "external-internal" enemy. In the course of the conflict, Vladimir Putin, the newly appointed—and later elected—Russian leader, was given the rare opportunity to demonstrate that his country was still capable of carrying great-power status. It appears, that for the time being, America as "great foreign rival" is not necessary for Russia to balance its domestic problems and thus validate its great-power status. This need could reappear, however, if order at home is not restored and Putin's presidency is perceived by most Russians as another failure after the string of previous disappointments with Gorbachev and Yeltsin. The worst scenario for the United States and the world community would be the weak and rudderless Russia, the country that will not be able to get its act together. Unstable and neurotic, with anti-American outbursts, Russian politics will influence foreign policies of the weak Russian government in unpredictable ways. In this case, anti-Americanism will become not a passing phenomenon on the way of national maturity. It will affect—as a chronic disease—the growing generations of Russians and seriously complicate Russia's chances of integration into the international community.

Notes

Chapter 1

1. Those who are interested may review the works of classical, Soviet, and modern writers and thinkers, such as Radishev, Turgenev, Tolstoy, Mayakovsky, Blok, Nabokov, Ilf and Petrov, Solzhenitsyn, Avtorkhanov, Aksyonov, Sakharov, Pelevin, and many others.

2. Several Soviet periodicals published such anti-American and anti-Western caricatures with remarkable persistency. Check, for example, the third or fifth page of daily *Pravda* or the last page of the weekly, *Krokodil,* released in the 1960s or 1970s.

3. One of the authors, a school kid in the early 1970s, shared this veneration of American progress. As part of the school curriculum, he had to prepare a short lecture and then teach a class in front of his peers on the economic geography of the United States. Together with a friend, he put together a written presentation about America's economic and technological growth, citing various facts and examples from the journal *America* and other publications. Believing that their report lacked statistical information, the teenagers inadvertently did what Khrushchev's speechwriters had done with Soviet economic statistics back in 1959. They extrapolated the numbers of U.S.-produced cars, tractors, refrigerators, television sets, and homes and came up with some astronomical figures of the enormous potential of American wealth by 1990. Fortunately, it was the time of *détente* and no dire consequences or punishments resulted from this "anti-Soviet" presentation by two teenagers.

Chapter 2

1. This is still a very popular Russian expression that stands for the world's industrialized countries and is usually used to indicate Russia's uncivilized status.

2. The content of Gorbachev-Bush talks at Malta, December 2–3, 1989 and in Washington, July 1990, is known from Soviet transcripts and other documents at the Archive of the Gorbachev Foundation in Moscow. On the Bush administration avoiding "gloating," see the remarks of Brent

Scowcroft, former head of the NSC, at the conference "Intelligence and the End of the Cold War," November 19–20, 1999, The Bush Presidential Center, College Station, TX.

3. Among these individuals, were prominent Russian opinion leaders and activists: Gavriil Popov, Anatoly Sobchak, Galina Starovoitova, Sergei Shakhrai, Andrei Sakharov, Sergei Stankevich, Yuri Boldyrev, Grigory Yavlinsky, and Anatoly Chubais.

4. In the late 1980s, Soviet television and radio were not privatized and did not get substantial revenue from commercials. Our personal experience—and especially one of the author's work on St. Petersburg Television—suggests that most of the editors who, in fact, were handling the content of the social and politics-oriented programs were young, ambitious, and anti-Gorbachev oriented individuals, including such nationally recognized journalists as Bella Kurkova, Vadim Konovalov, and Tamara Maksimova.

5. Some of our colleagues pulled out of the assortment of books' most speculative assertions and displayed them as justifications of their pro-Americanism. Some recalled that Vladimir Lenin wrote in the early 1910s about the "American way" of a country's development as the fastest and the least painful one. Others, more informed, cited Alexis de Tocqueville who made, in the1830s, a prediction that the United States and Russia would be dominant powers in the twentieth century.

6. Only a few resisted this pro-American temptation. One of us recalls when he traveled in the United States with Leonid Smirnyagin, the economic geographer who taught then at the MGU and later became one of Yeltsin's advisers on the nationalities. Leonid was ecstatic about everything he saw in the United States. But back home, at a party, he suddenly declared that "this all is not for us. We, the Russians, by history are destined to other ways."

7. "Gorbachevites" were also maintaining good informal relationships with the cabinet members and many senior officers in the Bush administration (see Chernyaev, 1993 among others).

8. One event had special symbolic meaning at that time. In 1990, Susan Eisenhower—granddaughter of the U.S. president—and Roald Sagdeev—prominent physicist and deputy of the Soviet parliament got married. It was something improbable and even dangerous, to pursue: Some Russian officials still believed that Sagdeev, head of the strategically important Institute of Space Research, was close to treason marrying an American woman. However, in the new spirit of partnership with the United States, official Moscow did not interfere with the marriage. One of us was invited by Susan herself to a small restaurant to celebrate the event, behind the gray building of the "Hammer" Center of International Trade in Moscow. Nothing in that situation resembled the gloomy times of the Gorky Park movie. The wedding party was organized at the Spaso House. The entire Moscow *beau monde* was there. Foreign Minister Shevardnadze acknowledged that their marriage should signify "the survival

and prosperity of all humankind" and should pull out "the chains of disconnectedness and distrust." The letter ends with another globalistic statement: "From this very day, our countries will be united not only by the ties of interdependence, by the direct telecommunication line of Vladimir Pozner, but by the strong union of Roald and Susan. With such a union, we believe, all of us to be confident in the fate of civilization" (Eisenhower 1995, 231).

9. In early November 1999, during an international meeting in Turkey, Clinton reminded Yeltsin of these developments—only to earn from the enraged Russian president a "son-of-a-bitch" expletive reply (see Chapter 7).

10. A well-known cognitive mechanism of attitude-formation (see, for example, Heider 1959) may be illustrated on Russia's case. A nation (i.e., the United States) that resisted the enemy (i.e., the Communist regime) deserves nothing but sympathy and gratitude. The long Cold War confrontation was seemingly over and Russia was free at last to join the world of developed nations that most educated Russians at the time thought it belonged to by rights (Johnson's List, 21 October 1999).

11. In 1988, the market price for a basic Panasonic model was about 2,400–2,500 rubles—the equivalent of five monthly salaries of a university professor.

12. Most of the video materials, however, were sneaked in Russia from European countries, not from the United States. It was much easier to bring something from Finland or Germany than from across the ocean, plus the compatibility of Russian and European video systems made PAL-SECAM tapes more attractive than America's NTSC.

13. One of us (Eric) remembers an episode when he and a small company of friends were having an informal dinner in the apartment of Alexander Morozov, a well-known composer and founder of Forum, a trendy techno-pop band of the 1980s. The doorbell rang and standing in the doorway was Valery Leontyev, perhaps the most popular male pop star in the Soviet Union. The purpose of his brief visit was simple: He was in Leningrad on tour and wanted to borrow a tape or two for the evening "VCR watching" in his leased apartment near the Oktyabrsky concert hall in downtown. Leontiev picked up—as far as memory goes—The Godfather Part I.

14. Among many were Larisa Dolina, Laima Vaikule, Vladimir Gustov, and Vladimir Presniakov.

15. Vassily Aksyonov was one of the first writers who masterfully described in his "The Crimea Island" the astonishing reaction of an average Russian person who was suddenly exposed to the shelves of a Western supermarket. To illustrate, one may use as example the feelings of a child visiting Disneyland for the first time.

16. There were some Europeans among them, like a Swede, Anders Aslund, who later found refuge in American foundations.

17. During Boris Yeltsin's visit to the United States in 1992, an American reporter told the Russian president that she saw two kids dying in a Russian hospital because of a lack of drugs. "Why didn't you give us the drugs?" Yeltsin fought back with no hesitation in his voice (*Argumenty I Facty*, 1992, No. 22–23, 1,3).

18. We do not intend to dive in the murky waters of psychoanalysis and assume that psychological complexes have an unconscious neurotic nature that manifests itself in the daily behavior of the individual. The interpretation of psychological complexes is rather close to one's understanding of attitude.

19. This word may have some parallels with an American label "rednecks," or a Vietnamese-American expression "FOB," i.e., "fresh off the boat," referring to very recent immigrants from Vietnam, both derogatory stereotypes attached to those considered not to be "civilized" enough. In Russia, a war veteran, a truck driver, a factory worker, a Communist Party supporter is typically labeled a "sovok." Poorly dressed individuals, neatly dressed people speaking with a southern accent also, in the eyes of prissy city dwellers may belong to this category. For many, a sovok is a person who is blindly pro-Russian, pro-tradition, and pro-discipline oriented. He or she is seen as being naïve and stupid, regardless of the individual's educational level.

Chapter 3

1. One can approach the issue of the links between frustration and subsequent actions from a psychological standpoint. On the individual level, the effervescent personality is expected to have and enjoy a lot of friends. The chronically forlorn, starving, and perturbed person may easily become fastidious. Our accomplishments and the favorable circumstances that accompany our lives generally stimulate a feeling of broad-spectrum satisfaction. On the contrary, failures and threats to our well-being generate almost inevitable frustration: Naturally, human beings either fight or flight. If there is no way to flight, there is always a way to fight. To find an adversary, to identify an obstacle becomes only a matter of time. Frustration and aggression often coalesce.

2. Perhaps the government could not do it—with no money to pay, but also did not want to do it—for strategic reasons. There were only two choices: the American way or the Ukrainian pro-stabilization and anti-inflation model.

3. Anatoly Chubais, an obscure professor of economics from Leningrad, who miraculously landed in the highest Kremlin offices during the political metamorphoses of perestroika, has been typically associated with the ill-fated—and cursed by millions of Russian people—privatization program. Both brutal and corrupt, the program was supported by the government as the only way to build a civilized capitalist society and divide the state property in a fair way.

4. This type of a mockery is called in Russian *styob*. This is not only a grotesque outlook on life. Styob is a public attitude, cultural standard of communication, a way of thinking. The great Russian writer, Vassily Aksyonov, wrote with a sense of horror about Russia's "post-democratic cynicism" and "degrading *styob* [mockery]" of the media (Aksyonov 1995). There is nothing enduring, sacred, and serious in your life. Everybody could be a liar. Promises mean little. Great ideas are false. Such a normative mockery "doesn't recognize truth but rather teaches us how to live without the truth" (Vail and Genis, 1989; p. 151).

5. In 1994, only 4 percent of Russians surveyed in one poll fully supported the actions of the government, and 31 percent said they believed it should resign (*Ekonomicheskie I Sotsialnye Peremeny: Monitoring Obshchestvennogo Mneniya,* No. 6, 1994, 63). In another poll, about 65 percent of respondents said their attitude toward the existing government was worse than it had been in the former U.S.S.R. Only 6 percent said their attitude was better (Grunt *et al.,* 1996). A set of surveys conducted in 1995 and 1996 also seem to confirm popular feelings that the government was untrustworthy. According to those surveys, the number of people who believed the country was moving in the right direction fell eleven points during a two-year period, reaching a low level of 19 percent in 1996 (*Index to International Public Opinion 1995–96,* 567–85; *Index to International Public Opinion 1993–94,* 612–23). Another survey in 1995 found respondents put their greatest trust in the Church (which received only a 33 percent approval rating) and the Army (which got a 32 percent approval rating). Least trusted were heads of banks (6 percent), parties and movements (7 percent), and the upper chamber of the national legislature, the Council of the Federation (9 percent). President Yeltsin, the legislature as a whole, and the cabinet of ministers each received just a 12 percent approval rating (Williams, 1996). Lastly, a poll conducted in July 1995 by Boris Grushin's Vox Populi service, revealed that 60 percent of those surveyed favored a change of leaders on the grounds that they had exhausted their potential (*Izvestia,* 13 October 1995, 6).

6. A Statement to U.S. Banking and Financial Services Committee indicates that the overall capital flight from Russia can be estimated between 100 to 500 billion dollars for the same 6-year period (Krasnow 1999).

7. Who should be blamed? Mostly Russian businessmen, of course, who—looking for a quick profit—fell for cheap products.

8. Even the official data indicate that during the first half of 1992 industrial production dropped by 13 percent, retail trade by 42 percent, personal income by 32 percent, capital investment by almost 50 percent. The basic consumer prices in 1991–1992 went up 20 to 25 times.

9. Generally pro-American *Argumenty I Facty* in a report (1994, No. 2–3, 13) about the 1994 Clinton television discussion with a Russian audience suggested that the president was a very good speaker; unfortunately, he repeated one phrase too many times: "Russia has to. . . ."

10. According to Romir Gallup Media, Muscovites are twice as likely as urban Russians as a whole to have traveled abroad. Moscow also offers a greater variety and choice of products than the rest of the country. In the mid-1990s, for example, imported and better quality goods comprised almost 70 percent of Moscow's market. As a consequence, people from nearby provinces travel to Moscow to buy better products (*Argumenty I Facty,* No. 27, July 1996).

Chapter 4

1. One of such lists, for example, was initiated by the House of Representatives based legislation that requires the president to report to Congress every six months which countries have helped Iran develop nuclear, chemical, or biological weapons or the missiles to carry them (Wilson 1999).

2. Almost insignificant developments began to irritate reporters. For example, what is inappropriate in an idea to conduct small Russian-American military exercises at the Totskoye training ground? Apparently, everything. Some were really upset that the United States sent 250 servicemen and 30 pieces of equipment to Russian soil, called it a "foreign intervention" and cried about Russian soil being "trampled" by American GIs who represent a country that arrogated unto itself the powers of the world's dictator (Cherkovets 1994).

3. *Pravda,* for example, in the June 28-July 5 (1995) issue attempted to frustrate the ready-to-believe reader by the impressive numbers describing military budgets of the two countries. Thus, the newspaper reported that in 1994, the Unites States spent 43 billion on arms purchases, whereas the Russian government picked up only a 2 billion dollar bill. Russians spent only 1 billion dollars on military-related research. Their military opponents overseas were given a generous 37 billion dollar sum. If these examples were too abstract to psychologically relate to, the newspaper went further and published the cost of one enlisted person to both nations. Russians paid just 1,200 dollars per person per year, which was 20 times lower than the amount of money spent on an average GI in the United States. Moral? While Russia weakened its armed forces, the United States increased their military might and became an increasingly serious threat.

4. In 1997 Defense Minister, Igor Sergeev, and Foreign Minister, Yevgeny Primakov, who were hard to label as pro-American officials, still were unable to persuade the State Duma Deputies to ratify the agreement.

5. There were other opinions, however, about a possible source of the external danger. Grigory Yavlinsky, for example, considered the People's Republic of China as "a major threat" to Russia because of the high density and growth of its population and the rapidly modernizing military (Yavlinsky 6 June 1996). This worrisome opinion about China was also supported by other experts and commentators (see, for example, Vail and Genis 1989, 254). China was portrayed as surpassing Russia in terms of strength of

armed forces and size of gross domestic product. Russia and China can be partners for a few years but no one can guarantee that the same situation will last.

6. Among such organizations, there were mentioned, for example, the American Association for the Advancement of Slavic Studies, the Hoover Institution on War, Revolution, and Peace, the American Committee for East-West Accord, the Rand Corporation, the American Council of Learned Societies, the International Research and Exchange Board, the Soros Foundation, Harvard University's Russian and East European Center.

7. The Communists and the party of Vladimir Zhirinovsky became the first political forces in Russia to propagate the complex of Neo-Conservative ideas and use them in politics (See Chapter 5). Gennady Zyuganov, for example, openly talked and wrote that animosity toward Western countries is one of the positive and justified characteristics of the Russian character. A Russian, he once said, is hostile to the West because of the "West's extreme individualism, militant soulessness, religious indifference, and adherence to mass culture" (Zyuganov 15 June 1996).

8. On this particular point, former Yeltsin assistants could find almost no disagreement in the camps of their former bitter enemies. As early as 1995, Leonid Abalkin, a mainstream economist of the Gorbachev era, wrote: "A powerful state cannot exist without a uniting national idea and a political doctrine shared both by the ruling and the opposing powers. There should be no vacuum. A state deprived of such a basis and being unable to find a new one in its place is beginning to break down." He concluded with an appeal to the consolidation of society around this great nation-state idea. "Without it nobody could ever have been able to achieve an economic wonder" (Abalkin 1995, 42, 70). The Communist leader Gennady Zyuganov also supported this theme during the presidential elections of 1996: "Russia will not be able to revive without a national-state idea" (Zyuganov 23 April 1996).

9. In the last years of the Soviet Union there was a popular and self-mocking joke according to which the U.S.S.R. was nothing else than "Upper Volta with missiles." The obvious reference was made to a low level of international "importance" that such country as Upper Volta can have; what makes it great, however, is the country's military might. Since the late 1990s, Russians took such jokes with some defensiveness: Very few compare Russia to Upper Volta.

Chapter 5

1. As a matter of political survival, public officials try to anticipate public approval and objections. Assumptions about a positive public reaction to a proposed action or policy contribute to a permissive policy climate, whereas anticipation of criticism may contribute to a non-permissive climate. Political opposition would not challenge foreign policy decisions if

the public support of such actions were going to be overwhelming. On the contrary, the opposition would be more likely to challenge the government if the public reaction were negative, split, or just anticipated to be negative or split.

2. Indeed, the administration ultimately supported all key U.N. resolutions imposing sanctions, including the 1992 imposition of economic sanctions on Belgrade. As well, Russian officials voted for Resolution No. 770 in August 1992, which allowed U.N. countries to use force to provide humanitarian help to Sarajevo.

3. Russia's initial liberal policy in Bosnia did reap some rewards. At first, Russian officials were treated fairly and equally in terms of being included in top-level decision-making. Moscow also gleaned some international prestige from playing a positive role in the crisis, most visibly in February 1994 when Vitaly Churkin, special Russian envoy to the Balkans, secured Serb agreement to a cease-fire in Sarajevo. But the approach of essentially following U.N. policy drew increasingly sharp opposition from the legislature. Attacks in the legislature first became strong in the summer of 1992, when legislators accused Yeltsin and Kozyrev of maintaining an anti-Serb course. The Supreme Soviet passed a resolution on June 26, 1992 directing the government to work for at least an easing of sanctions against the Serbs if a moratorium in the region appeared out of reach.

4. This victory of the opposition was particularly pronounced in the State Duma, one of two houses of the Federal Assembly. The Duma was entrusted by the Constitution with more legislative power than the other house.

5. There are many examples of such anti-American rhetoric. For instance, in February 1994, the Foreign Minister stated that Russia has no intention of listening to lectures on the rules of good behavior from Western politicians (Abarinov 1994). President Yeltsin, during a press conference, vigorously criticized America for its foreign policy course and accused European countries for allowing themselves to be dictated to from the United States. He also complained that for such a long time, the Western countries ignored his international initiatives (Press Conference with Boris Yeltsin. Official Kremlin International News Broadcast, 8 September 1995). Yeltsin stated on several occasions that he was reluctant to send his troops under American command in Bosnia (see, for example, Yeltsin's interview on French television; see MacKenzie, 1995).

6. The attacks were made, according to the official U.S. version, in response to assassination attempts on former U.S. President George Bush's life; the actions had been planned by the Iraqi special services. Reportedly, there were civilian casualties as a result of the retaliatory attack against Baghdad and this caused a wave of criticism in the Russian media.

7. There have also been signs of interpersonal conflicts in the administration— like a rift between a top Yeltsin aid Ryurikov and Kozyrev—as a result of which certain aides have fallen from the boss' favor (Kononenko 1994).

8. In the fall of 1995, as internal political struggle mounted with the election campaigns and the last stage of the armed conflict in Bosnia was being played out, a further change occurred in Moscow's Bosnia policy, in that main responsibility for determining Russia's conduct in Bosnia was shifted to the military. The Russian Foreign Ministry was practically excluded from negotiations in Dayton after November 21, 1995. Kozyrev openly complained that Defense Minister, Pavel Grachev, was conducting negotiations in Brussels alone and without even informing top foreign policy officials (*Izvestia,* 5 December 1995, 3). A change in Russian foreign-policy course was signified by the fact that it was left up to the generals now to negotiate Russia's form of involvement in an international conflict, the mechanism underlying the political control of Russian troops, and the channels through which Russia would interact with NATO council (Umbach, 1996, 408).

9. Vladimir Lukin, former Ambassador to the United States and new Chairman of the Duma's Committee on Foreign policy, did not support Kozyrev (who, allegedly, took the post in the autumn of 1990 on the recommendation of the same Lukin, who, at the time, was Chairman of the "old" Russian parliament's Joint Committee on Foreign Policy). Lukin was known as an advocate of a significantly tougher and more independent foreign policy for the Russian state (Protsenko 1993).

10. Kozyrev landed safely: He became the president of his own Foundation. He continued to travel to the West and enjoyed there the benefits of being an American friend.

11. It was recalled that the Russian president called George Bush first to inform him of the dissolution of the Soviet Union in 1991. George Bush replied that these events would serve American interests (*Izvestia,* 25 December 1991).

12. The United States was portrayed as an aggressor (MacWilliam 1997; Volobuev and Tyagumenko 1992). "Remember, if they [the United States] destroy the Serbs today, they will move against us tomorrow," warned *Pravda* (*Pravda,* 21 January 1993, 5). America was accused of violating international laws in Bosnia (Fadeev 1994) and expansionism (Peresvet 1995). In 1992, *Pravda* compared the sanctions against Yugoslavia to the U.S. blockade of Cuba in the 1960s, calling both these policies "imperialistic" (20 November 1992; see also *Pravda,* 2 June 1992, 3; *Pravda,* 16 September 1992, 3; *Pravda,* 19 November 1992, 7). The American intent in Bosnia was described as one "to defeat Russia" (*Pravda,* 3 March 1994, 3). *Pravda,* in its issue of June 28–July 5, 1995, presented statistical figures supporting its view of an unexaggerated military threat coming from the United States.

13. A clear anti-Western and anti-American tone is easily detectable in interviews given in 1995 by several leaders of Russia's main political parties, including leading liberal parties, they expressed deep dissatisfaction with Russia's policy in Bosnia (*Mezhdunarodnaya Zhizn,* No. 4, 1995, 5–26). For

example, Vladimir Lukin, Head of the Committee for International Affairs of the State Duma and Deputy Chair of the influential liberal Yabloko party, outright called Russian pro-Western policy in Bosnia a "fiasco" (24). Alexei Mitrofanov, Deputy Head of the Duma's International Affairs Committee and representative of the LDPR Duma faction, called NATO's involvement an "armed aggression" (14–16). Aleksandr Shabanov and Eduard Kovalev, Deputy Head and Head of the CPRF press-center respectively, also launched sharp and emotional criticisms against Russia's foreign policy in the former Yugoslavia (9–12). Yuri Skokov, an ally of General Lebed and Chair of the National Council of the Congress of Russia's Communities, labeled the Balkan war and NATO expansion "major threats" to Russia (12–14). Only Sergei Belyaev, First Deputy Chairman of the pro-government party Our Home Russia (*Nash Dom Rossiya*), offered a few cautious and neutral remarks about the war in Bosnia (5–8).

Chapter 6

1. They are often called the "*expats.*" There is a small community of American citizens who—due to a variety of reasons—decided to settle in Russia for good. Some of them were driven out of America by their hatred of capitalism; some of them were and still are deeply affected by Russia and Russians; some of them married somebody in Russia and chose to stay there.

2. U.S. Secretary of State M. Albright played a great role in easing him out of office.

3. Among these events, were the war in Chechnya and Abkhazia, continuous bloody confrontations in Tajikistan, the dispute over the Crimea Peninsula, the victory of the radical Taliban movement in Afghanistan, and Indian and Pakistani nuclear tests.

4. One can find numerous publications on this subject in *Izvestia, Komsomolskaya Pravda, Moskovsky Komsomolets, Argumenty I Facty,* and other leading Russian periodicals.

5. There were dirty headlines in Russian tabloids that echoed this conviction. We recall two: "Monica, squeeze your teeth tighter!" and "Bill, why did Monica not teach you love, but war instead?"

6. This notion about power and legitimacy is not new in the theory of international relations. Machiavelli and Napoleon, Von Bismark and Mao Tse-tung wrote about the relationships between these elements. What was new was the re-emergence of this concept—and the frustrating realization that Russia had only little to do about it—in the writings of Russian experts and commentators.

7. Incidentally, Vladimir Lukin, member of the "Yabloko" faction in the Duma and the chairman of the Duma's committee on foreign relations had written his doctoral thesis on this subject.

Chapter 7

1. The "family" label commonly referred to a group of close associates and relatives of Yeltsin; among its members were the president's daughter, Tatiana Diachenko, Boris Berezovsky, Roman Abramovich, and Anatoly Chubais.

2. In September 1997 he organized, for example, with great fanfare, the celebration of Moscow's 850th anniversary. In June 1999, another grandiose and publicity-driven celebration was staged for the 200th anniversary of the father of Russian literature—Alexander Pushkin.

3. According to the ROMIR polling service, more than 64 percent of Russians in February of 2000 supported the continuation of military operations in Chechnya (*www.romir.ru*). Moreover, 62 percent of Russians believed, in 2000, that the Russian military is capable of providing security to the country; whereas only 35 percent agreed with that statement in 1999 (Poll by FOM; *Argumenty I Facty,* 2000, No.12, 8).

4. In one episode, a Russian correspondent of Radio Liberty, Andrei Babitsky, well-known for his sympathies with Chechens, was arrested by the Federal Security Service and then disappeared for weeks.

5. The validity of Putin's victory was contested by Communist observers at the polling stations and discussed in Russia. Zyuganov claimed that it was possible that Putin received less than 50 percent of the vote—sufficient for declaring him a victor.

References

Abalkin, Leonid. 1995. *Economic Reform: Zigzags of Fate and Lessons for the Future.* Moscow: Institute of Economics, RAS.

Abarinov, V. 1996a. "*Igor Rodionov Vayal na ne To Derevo*" (Igor Rodionov was Barking up the Wrong Tree. *Segodnya,* 27 December, p. 3.

Abarinov, V. 1996b. "*Vsia Presidentskaya Rat*" (All Presidents' Men). *Segodnya,* 7 December, p. 1.

Abarinov, V. 1996c. "*Krizis v Zalive*" (Crisis in the Gulf). *Segodnya,* 20 September, p. 9.

Abarinov, V. 1996d. "*Odnostoronnaya Igra: Rol Utechki Informatsii v Dvukhstoronnikh Otnosheniyakh*" (One-sided Game: The Role of Information Leaks in Bilateral Relations). *Segodnya,* 31 May, p. 9.

Abarinov, V. 1994. "*Bosnia: Moskva Ne Otritsaet Vozmozhost Ispolzovania Sily s Vozdukha*" (Moscow Doesn't Rule Out The Use of Airpower). *Segodnya,* 15 February, p. 1.

Adorno, T., E. Frenkel-Brunswik, D. Levinson, and R. Sanford. 1950. *The Authoritarian Personality.* New York: Harper and Row.

Afanasievsky, Nikolai. 1997. Interview. *Kommersant-Daily,* 23 May.

Aksyonov, Vassily. 1995. Interview. *Izvestia,* 21 November, p.3.

Aksyonov, Vassily. 1987. *In Search of Melancholy Baby.* New York: Random House.

Alexandrovich, Georgi. 1971. *Yastreby i Salamandry* (Hawks and Salamanders). Leningrad: Lenizdat.

Alexeyeva, Ludmilla and Paul Goldberg. 1990. *The Thaw Generation: Coming of Age in the Post-Stalin Era.* Pittsburgh, PA: University of Pittsburgh Press.

Ambartsumov, Y. 1994. "In the World: Echoes of the Bosnian Bombings." *Moskovskie Novosti,* 10–17 April, p. A5.

Ambartsumov, Y. 1992. Chairman of the Joint Committee on International Affairs and Foreign Economic Relations of the Russian Parliament. Interview in *Izvestia,* 29 June, p. 3.

Andrew, Christopher and Vasili Mitrokhin. 1999. *The Sword and the Shield: The Mitrokhin Archive and the Secret History of the KGB.* New York: Basic Books.

Arbatov, Alexei. 1998. "Natsionalnaia Ideia I Rossiiskaia Bezopasnost" (National Idea and Russia's Security), *Mirovaia Ekonomika I Mezhdunarodniie Otnosheniia* (MEIMO) (Moscow), No. 5, pp. 5–13 and No. 6, pp. 5–19.

Arbatov, G. 1992. "Rescue Russia, or Else!" *Newsday,* 25 October.

Arbatov, G. 1992. *The System: An Insider's Life in Soviet Politics.* New York: Times Books.

Argumenty I Facty, 2000. Poll by FOM (Public Opinion Fund). No. 12, March, p.8.

Argumenty I Facty, 1996. Economic Statistics. No. 27, July.

Argumenty I Facty, 1994. Report on Clinton Visit. No. 2–3, January, p.13.

Argumenty I Facty, 1992, Results of a Survey by Sluzhba VP. No. 18, May.

Aronson, E. 1995. *The Social Animal.* New York: W. H. Freeman and Co.

Baker, J. III and Thomas M. Defrank. 1995. *The Politics of Diplomacy: Revolution, War and Peace, 1989–1992.* New York: Putnam.

Barkashov, A. 1994. *Azbuka Russkogo Natsionalizma* (The ABC of Russian Nationalism). Moscow: Slovo.

Barner-Barry, Carol. 1999. "Nation Building and the Russian Federation." In *The Russian Transformation,* edited by B. Glad and E. Shiraev. New York: St. Martin's Press, pp. 95–108.

Baturin, A. and S. Gryzunov. 1994. "Tanets s Metloi v Ispolnennyi Zhirinovskogo" (Dance with a Broom, Performed by Zhirinovsky), *Izvestia,* 1 February, p. 4.

Berezovsky, Boris. 1999. Interview. *Nezavisimaya Gazeta,* 23 April.

Bernstein, M., and F. Crosby 1980. "An Empirical Examination of Relative Deprivation Theory," *Journal of Experimental Social Psychology,* No. 16, pp. 442–456.

Beschloss, Michael R. and Strobe Talbott. 1993. *At the Highest Levels: The Inside Story of the End of the Cold War.* Boston: Little, Brown.

Bivens, M. 1999. "Laundering Yeltsin: How U.S. Hypocrisy Feeds Russian Corruption," *The Nation,* 4 October.

Bogaturov, Alexei. 1998. "Russia-U.S.: Politics of Selective Resistance," *International Affairs* (Moscow) Vol. 44, No. 4, pp. 29–39.

Bolshakov, Vladimir. 1994. "In the Name of the 'New Order,'" *Pravda,* 2 March, p. 6.

Brown, A. 1996. *The Gorbachev Factor.* New York: Oxford University Press

Brusilovskaia, Lilia. 1998. "Moscow's 'Broadway,' 'Jazz on the Bones' and 'Fire in the Jungles' (On the American Cultural Influence over the Soviet Society in the 1960s)," *Rodina,* No. 8, pp. 79–83.

Brzezinski, Zbigniew. 1999. "Russia Would Gain by Losing Chechnya," *The New York Times,* 19 November.

Buida, Yuri. 1993. "Russki Chelovek Dorozhe Russkoi Idei" (Russian Man is More Valuable than the Russian Idea), *Nezavisimaya Gazeta,* 14 May, p. 2.

Burbulis, G. 1992. Interview. *Argumenty I Facty,* No. 31, p. 2

Burr, W. (Ed.). 1998. *The Kissinger Transcripts: The Top Secret Talks with Beijing and Moscow.* New York: The New Press.

Busuev, Vitaly. 1992. "The Gangsters and Racketeers." *Rossiyskaya Gazeta,* 28 May, p.7.

Carr, E. H. 1958. *Socialism in One Country.* Vol. 1. London: Macmillan and Co.

Carter, M. 1999. "West was 'too Simplistic,'" Interview by Michael Heath, *The Russia Journal,* 18–24 October.

Centre TV, Moscow. 18 April 1999, 7:15 P.M.

Cherkovets, Oleg. 1994. "Yankees at Totskoye Training Ground" *Sovetskaya Rossia,* 3 September, p. 1.

Chernyaev, A. 1997. *Dnevnik Pomoshnika Prezidenta SSSR* (The Diary of an Assistant to the President of the U.S.S.R.). Moscow: Terra.

Chernyaev, A. 1993. *Shest let s Gorbachevym* (Six Years with Gorbachev). Moscow: Progress-Kultura.

Chernyaev A. 9 November 1989. *Personal Diary.* The Archive of the Gorbachev Foundation, Moscow.

Chernyavsky, Stanislav. 1998. "Southern Caucasus in the Plans of NATO," *Mezhdunarodnaia Zhizn,* No. 9, pp. 102–108.

The Christian Science Monitor, 1995. Editorial: "The Eagle and the Bear," 27 September, p. 20.

Chubais, A. 1999. Quoted by Interfax, 11 December.

Chuprov, V. and J. Zubok. 1996. "Youth and Social Change." In *Russian Society in Transition,* edited by C. Williams, V.Chuprov, and V. Staroverov, pp. 127–143. Aldershot, England: Dartmouth.

Churkin, Vitaly. 1994. Quoted in *Chicago Tribune,* 11 February.

CISS Index to International Public Opinion, 1995–1996.

Clinton, W. 2000. Quoted in *Time,* 1 January.

Communications between Chairman of the Council of Ministers of the U.S.S.R. with U.S. Presidents and Prime Ministers of Great Britain. 1957. Moscow: Political Literature

Daniels, Robert. 1999. "Egvenii Primakov: Contender by Chance," *Problems of Post-Communism,* Vol. 46, No. 5, September/October, pp. 27–36.

Denisov, Youri. 1996. "Pochemy Rossiyane ne Priemlyut Zolotoi Serediny, ili ob Umerennosti v Politike" (Why Russians don't Accept the Happy Middle, or on Moderation in Politics), *Polis,* No. 1, pp. 177–180.

Devlin, Judith. 1999. *Slavophiles and Commissars: Enemies of Democracy in Modern Russia.* New York: St.Martin's Press.

Dobrynin, A. 1995. *In Confidence: Moscow's Ambassador to America's Six Cold War Presidents (1962–1986).* New York: Random House.

Dobson, R. 1996. *Russians Choose a President. Results of Focus Group Discussions.* Washington, DC: USIA.

Dollard, J., L. Doob, N. Miller, O. Mowrer, and R. Sears. 1939. *Frustration and Aggression.* New Haven, CT: Yale University Press.

Doran, Charles and Sewell, Patrick. 1988. "Anti-Americanism in Canada?" In *Anti-Americanism. The Annals of the American Academy of Political and Social Science,* Vol. 497, edited by T.Thornton, pp. 105–119. Newbury Park: Sage Publications.

Dugin, Alexander. 2000. "Evraziiskaia Platforma" (Eurasian Platform). Available from www.arctogaia.com

Dugin, Alexander. 1990. *Kontinent Rossiya* (Continent Russia). Moscow: Znaniie.

Dugin, Alexander. 1998. *Osnovi Geopolitiki* (Fundamentals of Geopolitics). Moscow: Arktogea.

Dugin, Alexander. 1994. *Konservativnaia Revoliutsiia* (The Conservative Revolution). Moscow: Arktogea.

Dunham, Vera. 1976. *In Stalin's Time: Middleclass Values in Soviet Fiction.* Cambridge: Cambridge University Press.

Ebenstein, W. 1963. *Two Ways of Life.* New York: Holt, Rinehart, and Winston.

Ekho Moskvy. 3 May 1999. Radio station available from www.echo.msk.ru

The Economist. 1994. "Pax Russiana?" 19 February, p. 57

Eggert, Konstantin. 1995. "A 'Great-Power' Foreign Policy Is Too Expensive," *Izvestia*, 16 December, p. 3.

Eisenhower, Susan. 1995. *Breaking Free: A Memoir of Love and Revolution*. New York: Farrar, Straus and Giroux.

Ekedahl, K. and M. Goodman. 1997. *The Wars of Eduard Shevardnadze*. University Park, PA: Penn State University Press.

Ekonomicheskie I Sotsialnye Peremeny: Monitoring Obshchestvennogo Mneniya (Economic and Social Changes: Monitoring of Public Opinion). 1994. Moscow, No. 6, p. 63.

English, H. and A.C. English. 1958. *A Comprehensive Dictionary of Psychological and Psychoanalytical Terms*. New York: Longmans, Green, and Co.

English, Robert. 2000. *Russia and the Idea of the West: Gorbachev, Intellectuals and the End of the Cold War*. University Park, PA: Penn State University Press.

Erikson, E. H. 1950. *Childhood and Society*. New York: Norton.

Everts, Philip. 1996. "The 'Body Bag Hypothesis' as an Alibi for Public Support for UN Military Operations in the Netherlands: The Case of Bosnia-Hercegovina." *Politics, Groups and the Individual*, Vol. 1, No. 6, pp. 75–84.

The Exile. 1999. "One-Hundred and One Reasons why NATO's War Sucks." Moscow, 8–21 April, p. 62

Fadeev, Yevgeny. 1994. "Bosnia: NATO Begins and . . ." *Pravda*, 3 March, p. 3.

FCS (Federal Counterintelligence Service). 1995. Report. *Nezavisimaya Gazeta*, 10 January, p. 3.

Fetisov, V. 1998. *Overtime*. Moscow: Vagrius.

Filimonov V.D. 1999. "Chairman of the Impeachment Procedural Committee. Speech During the Impeachment Hearings. Russia's State Duma," *Transcript of Sessions*, No. 259 (401), Part 1, 13 May, pp. 4–16.

Gaidar, Yegor. 1997. *Dni Porazhenii I Pobed* (The Days of Defeats and Victories). Moscow: Vagrius.

Geller, M. 1997. "Gorbachev: Pobeda Glasnosti I Porazhenie Perestroiki" (A Victory of Glasnost and a Defeat of Perestroika). In *Sovetskoe Obshestvo: Vozniknovenie, Razvitie, Istoricheskii Final* (Soviet Society: Beginning, Development, and Historic Final), edited by Y. Afanasiev. Moscow: Russian State Institute for Humanity.

Gerasimov, Vladimir. 1995. "Eastern Europe: Better Together." *Pravda*, 20 April, p.3.

Gevorkian, Natalia, Alexei, Kolesnikov, and Natalia Timakova. 2000. *Ot Pervogo Litsa: Razgovori s Vladimirom Putinym* (From the First Person: Conversations with Vladimir Putin). Moscow: Vagrius.

Glukhov, Y. 1993. "Kremlin's American Card." *Pravda*, 28 April, pp. 1, 3.

Goldgeier, James. 1999. *Not Whether but When: The U.S. Decision to Enlarge NATO*. Washington, DC: Brookings Institute.

Golik, Yuri and Valentin Karasev. 1999. "Pochemu Dazhe 'Demokraticheskaia' Rossiia ne Ustraivaet 'Svobodnii' Zapad?" (Why Even 'Democratic' Russia Does not Suit 'Free' West?) No. 3, pp. 150–161.

Gorbachev, Mikhail and Zdenek Mlynar. 1994. *Dialog o Perestroike, "Prazhskoi vesne" i o Sotsializme* (A Dialogue About Perestroika, the "Prague Spring" and Socialism), a manuscript.

Gorbachev, Mikhail. 1993. *Godi Trudnikh Reshenii: Izbrannoie 1985–1992* (The Years of Difficult Decisions: Selected Documents, 1985–1992). Moscow: Alfa-Print.

Gornostaev, D. 1999. Quoted in *Nezavisimaya Gazeta,* 12 April.

Gornostaev, D. 1997. "Confrontation: Moscow and Washington Face a New Crisis. The Interests of Russia and the U.S. Clash Constantly and Everywhere," *Nezavisimaya Gazeta,* 15 January, pp. 1,4

Gozman, Leonid and Alexander Edkind. 1992. *The Psychology of Post-Totalitarianism in Russia.* London: Centre for Research Into Communist Economies.

Gromyko, Anatoly. 1997. *Andrei Gromyko: V Labirintakh Kremlia* (Andrei Gromyko: In the Labyrinth of the Kremlin). Moscow: Avtor.

Grunt, V., G. Kertman, T. Pavlova, S. Patrushev and A. Khlopin. 1996. "Rossiyskaya Povsednevnost i Politicheskaya Kultura: Problemy Obnovleniya" (Ordinary Russian Life and Political Culture: Problems of Change), *Polis,* No. 4, pp. 56–61.

Grushin, Boris. 1994. "Is Peace at all Possible in Today's Russia?" *Mir Mnenii i Mnenia o Mire,* 8–12 December.

Grushin, Boris. 1994. "Does Fascist Dictatorship Threaten Russia?" *Mir Mnenii i Mnenia o Mire,* 8–11 October.

Grushin, Boris. 1994. "Has Russia Entered an Era of Democracy?" *Mir Mnenii i Mnenia o Mire,* 8–14 September.

Gryzunov, Sergei. 1995. "So Far, Nothing Threatens Fascism in Russia," *Izvestia,* 6 June, p. 5.

Gryzunov, S. and A. Baturin. 1994. "A Commentary," *Nezavisimaya Gazeta,* 4 February, p. 4.

Gurevich, V. 1987. "First Results of Economic Readjustment: 1986," *Soviet Life,* March, p. 26.

Hearings on Russian Money Laundering in the Bank of New York. U.S. Senate Foreign Relations Committee, September 1999.

Heider, F. 1959. *The Psychology of Interpersonal Relations.* New York: Wiley.

Herrmann, Richard and Richard Lebow. 1996. *The End of the Cold War.* A Concept Paper.

Hoffman, D. 2000. "Miscalculations Paved the Path to Chechen War," *The Washington Post,* 20 March, A1.

Holsti, Ole. 1992. "Public Opinion and Foreign Policy: Challenges to the Almond-Lippmann Consensus," *International Studies Quarterly,* No. 36, pp. 439–466.

Hosking, G. 1997. *Russia: People and Empire, 1952–1997.* Cambridge, MA: Harvard University Press.

Hough, J. 1999. "West Shares Blame for Scandal," *Los Angeles Times,* 23 September.

Ignatenko, Alexander. 1994. Interview in *Nezavisimaya Gazeta,* 10 March, p. 1.

Ilyin, Mikhail. 1996. "Khronologicheskoe Izmerenie: Za Predelami Povsednevnosti i Istorii" (Chronological Dimension: Beyond the Limits of Everyday Life and History), *Polis,* No. 1, pp. 55–77.

Ilyukhin, V.I. 1999. "Speech During the Impeachment Hearings," *Transcript of Sessions,* Russia's State Duma, No. 259 (401), Part 1, 13 May, pp. 17–30.

Index to International Public Opinion. 1995–1996, 1993–1994.

Interfax. 30 July 1999. Available from www.interfax.ru.

Interfax News agency, Moscow, In English, 1430 gmt, 21 September 1995.

Israelyan, Viktor. 1996. *Inside the Kremlin During the Yom Kippur War.* University Park, PA: Penn State University Press.

Ivanov, Igor. 2000. Quoted in *Nezavisimaia Gazeta,* 3 February, p. 11.

Ivanov, Igor. 1996. "And Once Again, as in the Past, It is Anti-Russian," *Nezavisimaya Gazeta,* 27 July, p. 2.

Ivanov, Y. 1995. "NATO Storm Clouds over Bosnia," *Sovetskaya Rossia,* 30 May, p. 3.

Johnson's List, 19 November 1999. Available from http://www.cdi.org/russia/johnson.

Johnson's List, 21 October 1999. Available from http://www.cdi.org/russia/johnson.

Izvestia, 5 December 1995, p. 3

Izvestia, 13 October 1995, Results of Vox Populi Opinion Poll, p. 6.

Izvestia, 16 January 1992, p. 1.

Izvestia, 25 December 1991, p. 1.

Judt, T. 1992. *Past Imperfect: French Intellectuals, 1944–1956.* Berkeley: University of California Press.

Kalashnikova, N. and V. Dymarsky. 1995. "Boris Yeltsin's Foreign Trip: Go-for-broke Diplomacy, But there is Nothing to Ante Up," *Kommersant-Dally,* 24 October, pp. 1, 3.

Kara-Murza, Alexei, Alexander Panarin, and Igor Pantin. 1995. "*Dukhovno-Ideologicheskaya Situatsiya v Sovremenoi Rossii: Perspektivy Razvitiya*" (Spiritual and Ideological Situation in Contemporary Russia: Prospects of Developments), *Polis,* No. 4, pp. 6–17.

Kara-Murza, Sergei. 5 May 1996. Interview. *Sovetskaya Rossia.*

Keen, S. 1986. *Faces of the Enemy.* New York: Harper & Row.

Kelley, Jack. 1994. "Clinton's Moscow Welcome Uncertain / Frustrated Russians Cool to the USA," *USA Today,* 12 January, 1A.

Kirsanova, Raisa. 1998. "*Stilyagi: Zapadnaia Moda v SSSR 40–50-kh Godov*" (Western Fashions in the USSR in the 1940s and 1950s), *Rodina,* No. 8, pp. 72–75.

Kissinger, Henry. 1994. *Diplomacy.* New York: Simon and Schuster.

Kliamkin, Igor and Lapkin, Vladimir. 1996. "*Socialno-politicheskaya Ritorika v Postsovetskom Obshestve*" (Social-Political Rhetoric in the Post-Soviet Society), *Polis,* No. 4, pp. 99–121.

Knight, Amy. 1996. *Spies Without Cloaks: The KGB's Successors.* Princeton, NJ: Princeton University Press.

Kondrashov, S. 1996. "The Departure of Faithful Andrei: Why and What Next?" *Izvestia,* 10 January, p. 3.

Kondrashov, S. 1994. "Who Was Forced to Do Something Against His Own Interests in Goradze, and How Did That Happen?" *Izvestia,* 20 April, p. 3.

Kondrashov, S. 1994. "Toward Partnership Without Illusions Through Bosnia and 'Ames Affair,'" *Izvestia,* 5 March, p. 3.

Koenigsberg, R. 1992. *Hitler's Ideology.* New York: Library of Social Science.

Kononenko, V. 1994. "Split in President's Team Increases Opposition's Chances," *Izvestia,* 27 September, p. 2.

Koopman C., E. Shiraev, J. Snyder, and R. McDermott. 1997. "Beliefs About International Security Among Russian and American National Security Elites," *Peace and Conflict: Journal of Peace Psychology,* pp. 35–57.

Kortunov, Sergei. 1998a. "Is the Cold War Really Over?" *International Affairs (Moscow),* Vol. 44, No. 5, pp. 141–154.

Kortunov, Sergei. 1998b. "Russia's Way: National Identity and Foreign Policy," *International Affairs (Moscow),* Vol. 44, No. 4, pp. 139–163.

Kostyrchenko, Gennadi. 1995. *Out of the Red Shadows: Anti-Semitism in Stalin's Russia.* Amherst, NY: Prometheus Books.

Kovalev, Sergei. 2000. "Putin's War," *The New York Review of Books,* Vol. 47, No. 2, 10 February, pp. 4–8.

Kozhokim, Y. 1999. Quoted in *Financial Times,* 12 April.

Kozlov, A. 1998. *Kozyol na Sakse* (Kozyol Playing Saxophone). Moscow: Vagrius.

Kozlova, Natalia. 1996. *Gorizonti Povsednevnosti Sovetskoi Epokhi: Golosa iz Khora* (The Horizons of Everyday Life of the Soviet Era: Voices from the Choir). Moscow: IFRAN.

Kozlova, Natalia. 1994. "Krestianskii Syn: Opis Issledovaniia Biografii" (Peasant's Son: A Biographic Case Study), *Socis,* No. 6, pp. 112–123.

Kozyrev, A. 1995. "The Russian Federation Minister of Foreign Affairs Answers Questions From a Segodnya Commentator," Interview by Vladimir Abarinov, *Segodnya,* 20 October, p. 9.

Kozyrev, A. 1992. "The Ministry of Foreign Affairs Proposes and Defends a Foreign Policy for Russia: In the Republic's National Interests," *Rossiiskiye Vesti,* 3 December, p. 2.

Kozyrev, A. 1992. Interview. *Izvestia,* 16 January, p. 3.

Krasnow, W. G. 1999. Statement During U.S. Banking and Financial Services Committee Hearings, 28 September. Washington, DC: House Committee on Banking and Financial Services, James A. Leach, Chairman.

Kremenyuk, V. 1997. Interview. *The Moscow Times,* 8 February.

Kremenyuk, V. 1994. "Deputy Director of the Russian Academy of Sciences' Institute of the U.S. and Canada Comments on President Bill Clinton's Visit to Moscow," *Novaya Yezhednevnaya Gazeta,* 15 January, p. 2.

Kurginian, Sergei. 1992. *Sedmoi Stsenarii* (Seventh Script), Parts 1–3. Moscow: Eksperementalty Tvorchesky Tsentr.

Laquer, W. 1994. *Black Hundred: The Rise of the Extreme Right in Russia.* New York: Harper Perennial.

Lebed, Alexander. 1996. Interview. Radio Russia, Moscow, 13 June.

Lebed, Alexander. 1996. Interview. Radio Russia, Moscow, 24 May.

Lebed, Alexander. 1996. Press Conference. Moscow, 13 May.

Levesque, J. 1997. *The Enigma of 1998: The U.S.S.R. and the Liberation of Eastern Europe.* Berkeley, CA: University of California Press.

Lieven, Anatol. 1999/2000. "The (Not So) Great Game," *The National Interest,* winter, pp. 69–80.

Levy, D. A. 1997. *Tools of Critical Thinking: Metathoughts for Psychology.* Boston, MA: Allyn & Bacon.

Ligachev, Y. 1999. A Transcript of an Interview with V. Zubok. Personal files.

Livshits, A. 1999. Comments and Quotations of an Interview Given to NTV. 6 October, AFP.

Lowenhardt, J. (1995). *The Reincarnation of Russia: Struggling with the Legacy of Communism,* 1990–1994. Durham, NC: Duke University Press.

Lukin, Vladimir. 1999. "A statement in the State Duma. Excerpts." *Yabloko Press Release.* 17 December. Available from www.yabloko.ru

MacWilliam, I. 1997. "Bread Impresses Russians More than NATO." *The Moscow Times, 8* February.

MacKenzie, Jean. 1995. "High-Profile President Looks Like a Candidate," *The Moscow Times,* 20 October, p. 1.

Malashenko, A. 1999. Interview. The Carnegie Endowment for International Peace. Reuters, 7 December.

Malashenko, I. 1997. Transcript of an Interview with E. Shiraev and V. Zubok, 1 December. Washington, DC. Personal files.

Malashenko, I. 1999. "Containment to Disengagement." *Newsweek International,* 4 October.

Malashenko, I. 1999. *Interview to Ekho Moskvy,* 17 November, Interfax.

Markowitz, Frank. 1999. "Not Nationalists: Russian Teenagers' Soulful A-politics," *Europe-Asia Studies,* Vol. 51, No. 7, pp. 1183–1198.

Marshall, Tyler. 1999. "Anti-NATO Axis Could Pose Threat, Experts Say," *Los Angeles Times,* 27 September.

Mezhdunarodnaya Zhizn. 1995. A Series of Interviews with Leading Russian Politicians. No. 4, pp. 5–26

Melville, Andrei. 1999. "Russia's Open-Ended Transition: Toward an Integrated Research Model." In *The Russian Transformation,* edited by B. Glad and E. Shiraev, pp. 239–252. New York: St. Martin's Press.

Merry, W. 1999. "Testimony Before the Committee on Banking and Financial Services, United States House of Representatives," *Hearing on Russian Money Laundering,* September 22.

Mezhuev, V.M. 1997. Transcript of presentation. Round Table: *Piat Let Posle Belovezhia* (Five Years after the Belovezh Agreement). Moscow: Aprel–85, pp. 65–69.

Mikhailov, Sergei. 1999. Quoted by Reuters, 7 December.

Mikheyev, V. 1994. "Nato Ultimatum s Ugrozami Vozdushych Udarov Protiv Serbov ne Pouchili Podderzhki v Moskve" (The NATO Ultimatum Threatening Bombing in Bosnia Gets No Support in Moscow), *Izvestia,* 1 February, p. 1.

Mikoyan, Anastas. 1999. *Tak Bylo: Razmishleniia o Minuvshem,* (So It Was: Thoughts about the Past). Moscow: Vagrius.

Mikulski, K.I. (Ed.) 1995. *Elita Rossii o Nastoyashen I Budushem Strany,* (Russian Elites about the present and Future of the Country). Moscow: Vekhi.

Mlechin, L. 1994. *"Moskva Sovershaet Oshibky Izbegaya Sovmestnykh s Zapadom Deistvii v Bosnii"* (Moscow is Making a Mistake by Shunning Joint Actions with the West in Bosnia), *Izvestia,* 23 April, pp. 1, 3.

MMMM. *Mir Mnenii i Mnenia o Mire* (The World of Opinions and Opinions about the World). January 1999 and December 1991. Edited by B. Grushin. A monthly bulletin publication of Sluzhba VP, Moscow.

Moscovici, S. and M. Zavalloni.1969. "The Group as a Polarizer of Attitudes," *Journal of Personality and Social Psychology,* No. 12, pp. 124–135.

The Moscow Times, 1999. "Kremlin Rattles Nuclear Sword," Editorial, 13 November.

Narodnaya Pravda, 3 January 1993.

Naumov, Vladimir. 1999. Paper presented at the conference "Stalin and the Cold War," Organized by the Cold War International History Project of Woodrow Wilson Center for International Scholars in Washington D.C., and Yale University, New Haven, CT, 16–17 September.

Neumann, Iver. 1996. *Russia and the Idea of Europe: A Study in Identity and International Relations.* New York: Routledge.

Negavisimaya Gazeta, 15 January 1997, p.1.

Negavisimaya Gazeta, 27 July 1996, p. 2.

Nezavisimaia Gazeta, 23 April 1999.

Newsline on the Web. 6 May 1997. "Opposition Continue Protests Against NATO Expansion." Available from http://www.rferl.org/newsline/

Nightline, 2000. ABC, 24 March.

Nikonov, Vadim. 1996. Transcript of presentation. Round Table: *Piat Let Posle Belovezhia* (Five Years after the Belovezh Agreement), Moscow: Aprel–85, pp. 49–51.

Nisbet, Robert. 1975. "Public Opinion versus Popular Opinion," *Public Interest,* No. 41, p. 67.

Odnokolenko, Oleg. 1999. Editorial Article. *Segonia,* 11 December.

Ogonyok, 1998. Letters to Editor, No. 12, March, p. 2.

Ogonyok, June 1995, No. 25, p. 73.

Olshanskaya, E. 1991. "Kiseleva, Kishmareva, Tyuricheva" (Publication of the Diaries of Evgeniia Grigorievna Kiseleva), *Noyi Mir,* No. 2, pp. 9–27.

Openkin, L. 1996. "I Reka Vremeni Vspiat ne Techet (And a River of Time Doesn't Flow Backwards)." *Rossyiskaya Gazeta,* 7 June, p. 3.

Ovchinnikov, Vsevolod. 1996. "American blunder. Seeking to Prevent a New Split into Opposing Blocs, Asia is Shaping a New Geopolitical Order," *Rossiiskaya Gazeta,* 20 August, p. 7.

Panin, Dimitri. 1998. *Misli o Raznom* (Various Thoughts). Moscow: Raduga, Vol. 1–2.

Parks, J. 1983. *Culture, Conflict and Coexistence: American-Soviet Cultural Relations, 1917–1958.* Jefferson, NC: McFarland & Company.

Patterson, Thomas. 1996. *The American Democracy.* New York: McGraw-Hill.

Pavlovsky, Gleb. 1996. "Kak Oni Unichtozbili SSSR" (How They Destroyed the U.S.S.R.), *Nezavisimaia Gazeta,* 14 November, p. 5.

Peresvet, A. 1992. Quoted by *Nezavisimaya Gazeta,* 14 July, p.3.

Pfleger, K. 1999. "Russians Get Lessons in Democracy," Associated Press, 2 September.

Pontuso, James. 1990. *Solzhenitsyn's Political Thought.* Charlottesville: University Press of Virginia.

Pravda, 1995. A Comparison between U.S. Russia Military Budgets, 28 June–5 July, p. 3.

Pravda, 3 March 1994, p. 3.

Pravda, 21 January 1993, p. 5.

Pravda, 19 November 1992, p. 7.

Pravda, 16 September 1992, p. 3.

Pravda, 2 June 1992, p. 3.

Protsenko, A. 1993. "Person of the Week: Grigory Yavlinsky has Come Out of the Prompter's Box and is Demanding a Leading Role." *Megapolis-Express,* No. 42, 27 October, p. 5.

Prussakov, V. 1997. "Who Does not Care for Primakov?" *Pravda,* 22 April, p. 3.

Pushkov, A. 1995. "Rossiyskaya Vneshnaya Politika" (Russia's Foreign Policy). *Nezavisimaya Gazeta,* 16 November, pp. 1, 5.

Pushkov, A. 1994. "Rossiya I Amerika: Konets Medovogo Mesatsa" (Russia and America: The Honeymoon is Over), Part 3, *The Moscow News,* 10 January.

Putin, V. 1999. "*Interview of Vladimir Putin, the Russian Prime Minister.*" By Richard Lambert and John Thornhill, *Financial Times* (UK), 11 December.

Putin, V. 1999. Transcript of a statement. Vremya, Informational Program, ORT, 9:10 P.M., 14 December.

Putnam, R. 1988. "Diplomacy and Domestic Politics: The Logic of Two-level Games," *International Organization,* Vol. 42, No. 3, pp. 427–460.

Rasputina, Masha. 1992. Interview. *Argumenty I Facty,* No. 5, p. 6.

Reuters from Moscow, 29 March 1999.

Reuters World Service. 16 January 1995. Available from *http://www.reuters.com*

Reuters. 23 November 1999. Available from *http://www.reuters.com*

Rivera, S. 1995. "Tendentsii Formirovania Sostava Postcommunisticheskoi Elity Rossii" (The Tendencies in Formation of the Structure of Post-Communist Elite in Russia), *Polis,* No. 6, pp. 61–66.

Rodin, I. 1994. "MIDu ne Nravitsia Proekt Podgotovlennyi Tremia Fraktsiami" (Foreign Ministry doesn't Like the Three Factions' Draft), *Nezavisimaya Gazeta,* 22 January, p.2.

Rodionov, Igor. 1996. Interview. *Moskovskiye Novosti,* No. 32, 11–18 August, p. 7.

Rogov, Sergei. 1998. *Mezhdunarodnaia Zhizn,* No. 10, p. 102.

Rossyiskaya Gazeta, 2 June 1995.

Rozov, V.S. 1997. A Transcript of a Comment. Round Table: *Piat Let Posle Belovezhia* (Five Years after the Belovezh Agreement). Moscow: Aprel–85, pp. 57–59.

Rubtsov, V. 1995. "Nakazanie Svobodoi" (Punishment by Freedom), *Polis,* No. 6.

Russia and Eastern Europe Archival Database, the National Security Archive at George Washington University, Washington D.C.

Russian State Duma. 1999. *Transcript of Sessions.* No. 259 (401), Part 1, 13 May, pp. 27–29.

Ryurikov, Dmitriy. 1999. *Russia Survives.* Washington DC: Nixon Center.

Sakharov, A. 1997. "O Prichinakh Samorazrusheniya SSSR" (On the Reasons of the U.S.S.R.'s self-destruction). In *Sovetskoe Obshestvo: Vozniknovenie, Razvitie, Istoricheskii Final* (Soviet Society: Beginning, Development, and Historic Final), edited by Y. Afanasiev. Moscow: Russian State Institute for Humanity.

Sakwa, R. 1993. *Russian Politics and Society*. Routledge, London & New York.

Scowcroft, Brent. 1999. Former head of the NSC, Presentation. Conference: "Intelligence and the End of the Cold War," 19–20 November, The Bush Presidential Center, College Station, TX.

Sears, D. 1996. "Presidential Address: Reflections on the Politics of Multiculturalism in American Society," *Political Psychology*, Vol. 17, No. 3, pp. 409–420.

Segodnia, 2 August 1995. Results of a public opinion poll.

Shakhnazarov, Georgi. 1996. Transcript of Presentation. Round table: *Piat Let Posle Belovezhia* (Five Years After the Belovezh Agreement), Moscow: Aprel–85, pp. 10–19.

Shakhrai, Sergei. 1994. Interview. *Rossiiskie Vesti*, 13 April, p.1.

Shatalov, Alexander. 1995. "Love, Sex and the Color of the Russian Soul," *The Moscow Times*, 12 April.

Shchedrov, Oleg. 1999. "Elections Seen Fuelling Russia-U.S. Row," Reuters from Moscow, 12 December.

Sherman, Peter (Ed.). 1995. *Russian Foreign Policy Since 1990*. Boulder: Westview.

Shiraev, E. and V. Zubok. 2000. "Against the West: Anti-Western Attitudes as a Mediating Factor in Russia's Opinion-Policy Links (1991–1999)." In *Decision-Making in the Glass House*, edited by R. Shapiro, B. Nacos, and P. Isernia, (forthcoming). Boulder: Rowman & Littlefield.

Shiraev, E. 1999a. "The New Nomenclature and Increasing Income Inequality." In *The Russian Transformation*, edited by B. Glad and E. Shiraev, pp. 109–118. New York: St. Martin's Press.

Shiraev, E. 1999b. "The Post-Soviet Orientations toward the United States and the West." In *The Russian Transformation*, edited by B. Glad and E. Shiraev, pp. 227–235. New York: St. Martin's Press.

Shiraev, E. and S. Tsytsarev. 1995. "Addictive Behavior in Addictive Societies," Paper delivered at the Annual Meeting of International Society of Political Psychology, Washington, D.C.

Shiraev, E. and A. Bastrykin. 1988. *Moda, Kumiry, I Sobstvennoye Ya* (Fashion, Idols, and the Self). Leningrad: Lenizdat.

Shlapentokh, Vladimir. 1999. "Soviet Inequality in Post-communist Russia: The Attitudes of the Political Elite and the Masses (1991–1998)," *Europe-Asia Studies*, Vol. 51, No. 7, pp. 1167–1181.

Shlapentokh, Vladimir. 1996. "Russia: Privatization and Illegalization of Social and Political Life," *The Washington Quarterly*, Vol. 19 (winter), pp. 65–85.

Shlapentokh, Vladimir. 1988. "The Changeable Soviet Image of America." In *Anti-Americanism. The Annals of the American Academy of Political and Social Science*, Vol. 497, edited by T. Thornton, pp. 157–171. Newbury Park: Sage Publications.

Shlapentokh, Vladimir. 1986. *Soviet Public Opinion and Ideology: Mythology and Pragmatism in Interaction*. New York: Praeger.

Sidorov, Sergei. 1994. "Rossiyskaya Positsia Yasna: Nyet Natovskim Vozdushnym Udaram Protiv Bosniyskih Serbov" (Russia's Position is Clear: No NATO Air Strikes Against the Bosnian Serbs), *Krasnaya Zvezda*, 19 February, p. 1.

Sigelman, Lee and Eric Shiraev. 2000. "The Rational Attacker in Russia?" (Paper under review).

Simes, D. and P. Saunders. 1999. "Testimony Before the Committee on Banking and Financial Services, United States House of Representatives," *Hearing on Russian Money Laundering*, 21 September.

Simes, Dimitri K. 1999. *After the Collapse: Russia Seeks Its Place as a Great Power.* New York: Simon and Schuster.

Simes, Dimitri. 1994. "The Imperial Consensus; From Czars to Reformers, Why Russia Keeps Returning to the Dream of Empire," *The Washington Post*, 25 December.

Smirnov, Andrei. 1997. "Paradoxes Of Post-Soviet Perceptions," *Segodnya*, 20 September, pp. 1, 4.

Smith, Raymond. 1989. *Negotiating With the Soviets.* Bloomington: Indiana University Press.

Smolyakov, L. 1997. A Transcript of a Comment. Round Table: *Piat Let Posle Belovezhia* (Five Years after the Belovezh Agreement). Moscow: Aprel–85, pp. 84–87.

Sobel Richard (1996), "U.S. and European Attitudes toward Intervention in the Former Yugoslavia: *Mourir pour la Bosnie.*" In *The World and Yugoslavia's Wars*, edited by R.H. Ullman, pp.145–181. New York: Council of Foreign Relations Books.

Sokov, Nikolai. 2000. "Foreign Policy Under Putin: Pro-Western Pragmatism Might Be a Greater Challenge to the West," *Memo No. 101*, Program on New Approaches to Russian Security (POHARS), Harvard University, January.

Solzhenitsyn, Alexander. 1999. "Nobel Laureate Solzhenitsyn Compares NATO with Hitler." The Reagan Information Interchange, 12 May. Available from http://reagan.com/Hottopics.main/HotMike/document.

Solzhenitzyn, Alexander. 1998. "Ugodilo Zyornishko Mezhdu Dvukh Zhernovov: Ocherki Izgnaniia" (Between a Rock and a Hard Place: Essays in Exile), *Novy Mir*, No. 9, September, pp. 47–125.

Solzhenitsyn, Alexander. 1998. *Russia in a Collapse* (Rossiya v Obvale), Moscow: Russki Put.

Solzhenitsyn, Alexander. 1996. "Excerpts from telephone conversations at the Komsomolskaya Pravda headquarters, April 15," *Komsomolskaya Pravda*, 23 April.

Solzhenitsyn, Alexander. 1978. *Commencement Address.* Harvard University. Available from http://www.hno.harvard.edu/hno.subpages/speeches/solzhenitsyn.html

Soros, George. 2000. "Who Lost Russia?" *The New York Review of Books*, 13 April, pp. 10–17.

Spiro, Herbert. 1988. "Anti-Americanism in Western Europe." In *Anti-Americanism. The Annals of the American Academy of Political and Social Science*, Vol. 497, edited by T.Thornton, pp. 120–132. Newbury Park: Sage Publications.

Sterligov, A. 1992. Interview. *Argumenty I Facty*, No. 36, pp. 1,2.

Stimson, James. 1991. *Public Opinion in America: Moods, Cycles, and Swings.* Boulder, CO: Westview.

Stites, R. 1992. *Russian Popular Culture.* New York: Cambridge University Press.

Sukhova, Svetlana. 1997. "Boris Yeltsin Will Push for a Greater Europe at Strasbourg Summit," *Segodnya*, 10 October, p. 3.

Surikov, A. 1997. "'Pruning' of Missiles in Exchange for Handouts," *Pravda,* 19 September, p. 4.

Tajfel, H. (Ed.). 1982. *Social Identity and Intergroup Relations.* Cambridge: Cambridge University Press.

Thornton, Thomas. 1988. "Preface." In *Anti-Americanism. The Annals of the American Academy of Political and Social Science,* Vol. 497, edited by T. Thornton, pp. 3–19. Newbury Park: Sage Publications.

Tretyakov, Vitalyi. 1999. Quoted in *Nezavisimaya Gazeta,* 23 April.

Tsipko, Alexander. 1996. Transcript of Presentation. Round Table: *Piat Let Posle Belovezhia* (Five Years After the Belovezh Agreement). Moscow: Aprel–85, pp. 43–45.

Umbach, F. 1996. "The Role and Influence of the Military Establishment in Russia's Foreign and Security Policies in the Yeltsin Era," *The Journal of Slavic Military Studies,* No. 3, pp. 467–500.

Urban, Joan. 8 March 1999. Personal Conversation. Research Archive of V. Zubok.

U.S. News and World Report, 5 April 1993.

Vail, P. and A. Genis. 1989. *The Sixties: The World of the Soviet Man.* Ann Arbor: Ardis.

Vasilchuk, Yevgeny. 1999. "Transatlanticheskie Lektsii ne Knoroshi Dlia Russkogo Zdorovia" (Transatlantic Lectures Are Good for Russia's Health), *Rossiyskaya Gazeta,* 29 October.

Vasiliev, N. 1955. *Amerika s Chernogo Khoda* (America from a Backdoor). Moscow: Molodaya Gvardia.

Velekhov, L. 1996. "Metamorphoses: High-ranking Russian Foreign Ministry Official Versus Jesse Helms: Moscow Changes Position on Cuban Question Yet Again," *Segodnya,* 24 February, p. 3

Volkan, V. 1988. *The Need to Have Enemies and allies.* New Jersey: Jason Aronson.

Volkogonov, Dmitry. Collection. Manuscript Division, Library of Congress, Washington, D.C.

Volkov, D. 1994. "Rossiyskie Otnoshenia s NATO Okhlazhdautsia" (Russia's Attitude toward NATO Cools), *Segodnya,* 26 February, p. 1.

Volobuev, Pavel and Lyudmila Tyagumenko. 1992. "It Makes a Difference to Russia," *Pravda,* 27 February, pp. 1, 3.

Volski, Dmitry. 1993. "Eastern Europe—Counterbalance to Russia?" *New Times,* No. 21, p. 22.

Wedel, J. 1998. "The Harvard Boys Do Russia," *Nation,* 1 June.

Williams, C. 1996. "Economic Reform and Political Change in Russia, 1991–96." In *Russian Society in Transition,* edited by C. Williams, V. Chuprov, and V. Staroverov. Aldershot, England: Dartmouth.

Wilson, C. 1999. "Congressional Leaders Blast Clinton's Russia policy," Reuters, 14 September.

Woolsey, J. 1999. "Testimony before the Committee on Banking and Financial Services. U.S. House of Representatives," *Hearing on Russian Money Laundering,* 21 September.

www.arctogeia.com (A website of Arctogeia Society.)

Wyman, M. 1997. *Public Opinion in Post-Communist Russia.* London: Macmillan Press.

Yabloko Press Release, 21 January 1999. Available from www.yabloko.ru.

Yavlinsky, G. 1999. Press-Conference. Excerpts. *Johnson's Russia List (Moscow)*, No. 3546, 6 October.

Yavlinsky, G. 1999. Interview with *Echo Moskvy* Radio Station, 24 March. Available from www.yabloko.ru.

Yavlinsky, G. 1996. Press Conference. Moscow, The International Press Center, 6 June.

Yeltsin, Boris. 1999. Footage and Transcript by *Vremya,* ORT Television Network, 9 December.

Yeltsin, Boris. 1998. President Yeltsin's Address to Russian Diplomats, Speech in the Ministry of Foreign Affairs of Russia on 12 May 1998," *International Affairs* (Moscow) Vol. 44, No. 3, pp. 1–6.

Yeltsin, Boris. 1996. Interview. Rossiya TV Channel, 6 April.

Yeltsin, Boris. 1995. Press-Conference. Official Kremlin International News Broadcast, 8 September.

Yeltsin, Boris. 1990. Speech in Ufa, 13 August. Personal file.

Yevtushenko, Yevgeny. 1993. Interview. *Argumenty I Facty,* No. 6, 1993.

Yuriev, Alexander. 1992. *Vvedenie v Politicheskuyu Psikhologiyu* (Introduction to Political Psychology). St. Petersburg: St. Petersburg University Press.

Yushin, Maxim. 1994. "Otnoshenia Mezhdu Rossiei I Amerikoi prokhodiat Cherez Samyi Trudnyi Kriziz za Poslednie Gody" (Relations Between Russia and the U.S. are Going through the Most Serious Crisis in Recent Years), *Izvestia,* 12 March, p. 3.

Zakharov, Alexander and Natalia Kozlova. 1993. "Letters from the Recent Past," *Svobodnaia Mysl,* No. 7.

Zakharov, Alexandr, and Natalia Kozlova. 1993. "Pisma iz Nedalekogo Proshlogo" (Letters from the Recent Past), *Svobodnaia Misl,* No. 7.

Zhirinovsky, Vladimir. 1996. Interview. Ostankino Radio Mayak, Moscow, 16 June.

Zhirinovsky, Vladimir. 1996. Interview. St. Petersburg TV channel 5, 14 June.

Zhirinovsky, Vladimir. 1996. Press Conference. Moscow. 13 June.

Zhirinovsky, Vladimir. 1996. Russian Public TV, Moscow, 10 June.

Zhirinovsky, Vladimir. 1996. Interview. Russian Public TV, Moscow, 22 May.

Zinoviev, Alexandr. 1999. *Russkaia Sudba, Ispoved Otschementsa* (Russian Fate, Confession of the Renegade). Moscow: Tsentrpoligraf.

Zoellick, R. 2000. Transcript of a talk at SAIS, 8 February.

Zolotov, Andrei. 2000. "Aven: Putin Should Follow Pinochet," *The Moscow Times,* 1 April.

Zubkova, Elena. 1993. *Obschestvo I Reformy, 1945–1964* (Society and Reforms). Moscow: Rossiia Molodaia.

Zubok, Vladislav. 1998. "Zato my delaem rakety (Well, We Make Rockets). The First American Exhibition in the USSR, Sokolniki, 1959," *Rodina,* No. 8, pp. 76–78.

Zubok, Vladislav and Constantine Pleshakov. 1996. *Inside the Kremlin's Cold War*. Cambridge: Harvard University Press.

Zubok, Vladislav M. 1994. "The Collapse of the Soviet Union: Leadership, Elites, and Legitimacy." In *The Fall of Great Powers: Peace, Stability and Legitimacy,* edited by Geir Lundestad, pp. 157–174, New York: Oxford University Press.

Zyuganov, G. 1995. *Rossiya I Sovremenny Mir* (Russia and Modern World). Moscow: Obozrevatel.

Zyuganov, G. 1996. In "Russian Exceptionalism," *The Economist,* 15–21 June, p. 19.

Zyuganov, G. 1996. Interview. Radio Vozrozhdenie. Transcript. Moscow, 13 June.

Zyuganov, G. 1996. Press Conference. Transcript. Moscow, 23 April.

Zyuganov, G. 1996. Press Conference. Transcript. Moscow, 23 February.

Index